EDUCATORS GUIDE TO FREE INTERNET RESOURCES
Elementary/Middle School Edition

*

Edited by
Kathleen Suttles Nehmer

*

SEVENTEENTH ANNUAL EDITION
2017-2018

EDUCATORS PROGRESS SERVICE, INC.
214 Center Street
Randolph, Wisconsin 53956

Published by

Educators Progress Service, Inc.

Randolph, Wisconsin 53956

Copyright EDUCATORS GUIDE TO FREE INTERNET RESOURCES
Elementary/Middle School Edition

2002, 2003, 2004, 2005, 2006, 2007, 2008, 2009, 2010, 2011, 2012, 2013, 2014, 2015, 2016, 2017

by Educators Progress Service, Inc.

All rights reserved.

Reproduction of this work, in whole or in part,
without written permission of the publisher is prohibited.

Printed and Bound in the United States of America

International Standard Book Number 978-0-87708-620-8

TABLE OF CONTENTS

FROM THE PUBLISHER'S DESK	V
HOW TO USE THE EDUCATORS GUIDE TO FREE INTERNET RESOURCES–Elementary/Middle School Edition	VI
ANALYSIS	VIII
ART, DRAMA AND MUSIC	1
COMPUTER EDUCATION	6
DICTIONARIES	10
EARLY LEARNING	12
FAMOUS PEOPLE	15
FOREIGN LANGUAGES	19
GENERAL EDUCATION	23
GEOGRAPHY	26
GOVERNMENT	33
GUIDANCE	36
HEALTH AND PHYSICAL EDUCATION	40
HISTORY	44
HOLIDAYS	49
LANGUAGE ARTS	51
MATHEMATICS	58
SAFETY	64
SCIENCE	66

SPECIAL EDUCATION	78
TEACHER REFERENCE	136
TITLE INDEX	93

    Know the title of the material you want? These pages will help you find it.

SUBJECT INDEX	109

    If you are interested in a certain subject, the "yellow pages" will lead you to appropriate materials.

SOURCE INDEX	141

    Here are the names of the 806 sponsoring sources listed in this edition, with page references.

FROM THE PUBLISHER'S DESK

It is impossible to ignore the magnitude and impact of the Internet on the field of education. Students as young as grade two are being taught how to connect to the Internet and type in a web address for sites that offer fun and games. (Of course, children even younger are using the computer with a little help from Mom and Dad). Older students know that they need to type only a few keywords into a search engine to find information that fills in gaping holes in reports that are dangerously close to being overdue. Teachers know that they can find lesson plans, teaching materials, articles, activities, and even books on the Internet. But if you don't know exactly where these teaching aids are, precious hours (even days) can be lost trying to find just the right material.

That's where the 2017-2018 EDUCATORS GUIDE TO FREE INTERNET RESOURCES–Elementary/Middle School Edition comes in. 992 educational materials–some for teacher use, some for student use–are pinpointed for you. You don't have to burn the midnight oil to find the perfect material for teaching the Cherokee or Urdu language, or the most up-to-date map of Russia, or important information on stopping the terrifying spread of school violence. These are just a few of 992 teaching materials pinpointed for you through the pages of this GUIDE.

The proliferation of these excellent sites is amazing. No single title can hope to list all the educational sites that exist and still be a book that could be carried about. That's why we introduced a second guide a few short years ago that is devoted to Internet resources for the elementary and middle school level. Together, these two titles list nearly three thousand web sites of educational value!

As you might imagine, the process of revising the annual editions of the EDUCATORS GUIDES is a time consuming process (there are now sixteen titles in the series). In our efforts to find new materials every year, we write thousands of letters to companies inquiring about materials they are willing to offer free to educators and others. Each and every year these letters are written. If no response is received, no materials from that source are included. In the case of Web sites, each and every site is visited to make sure it still exists as well as checked for content.

It's a lot of work but it is very rewarding. It really is a pleasure to be able to point educators to teaching aids that not only **save tight school budgets** but **add to the educational environment**. We like to find materials that "help teachers teach," not only to make their jobs easier but to help students learn more. This is "double" fun when it comes to free computer materials, for computers really are the tool of the future.

We hope you share this excitement for the world of computers with us. Let me know your opinions–they are invaluable to us.

Kathy Nehmer

P. S. **Be sure to use only the 2017-2018 GUIDE for the current school year**, as hundreds of titles available last year are no longer available!

HOW TO USE THE EDUCATORS GUIDE TO FREE INTERNET RESOURCES

The 2017-2018 EDUCATORS GUIDE TO FREE INTERNET RESOURCES–Elementary/Middle School Edition takes the work out of web surfing for you. Easy to find information tells you just what you may expect to find at each web site you visit.

The **BODY** of the GUIDE (white pages) gives you full information on each of the 992 titles, **ALL of which are new in this edition**. These 992 new titles dramatically illustrate one reason that it is so important to use only the most current edition of the GUIDE.

The **TITLE INDEX** (blue pages) is an alphabetical listing of all items appearing in the body of the GUIDE, with page references. This enables readers to locate any item whose title is known. The TITLE INDEX guides you directly to any specific item in the GUIDE, where you can read the description of the material and find all ordering information.

In the **SUBJECT INDEX** (yellow pages) all materials relating to topics of a more specific nature than the general subject headings in the body of the GUIDE are categorized. These "yellow pages" work like the familiar "yellow pages" of a telephone directory.

The **SOURCE INDEX** (green pages) provides an alphabetical list of the 806 names of producers of these excellent materials. Also included in each entry are page numbers which indicate where the materials from that particular source appear in the body of the GUIDE.

ANALYSIS OF EDUCATORS GUIDE TO FREE INTERNET RESOURCES–Elementary/Middle School Edition 2017

	TOTAL ITEMS
Art, Drama, and Music	53
Computer Education	43
Dictionaries	22
Early Learning	38
Famous People	40
Foreign Languages	43
General Education	28
Geography	75
Government	28
Guidance	46
Health and Physical Education	44
History	58
Holidays and Ceremonies	21
Language Arts	75
Mathematics	63
Safety	21
Science	141
Special Education	17
Teacher Reference	<u>136</u>
TOTALS	**992**

ART, DRAMA, AND MUSIC

Artist Research Poster Lesson
Create a poster about a well-known contemporary artist.
Suggested Grade: 5-12
Format: Online Lesson Plan
Source: Dorothy Morris
World Wide Web URL: http://www.princetonol.com/groups/iad/lessons/high/Dorothy-poster.htm

ArtMagick
A gallery of paintings and poetry from the 19th and 20th centuries.
Suggested Grade: 6-Adult
Format: Web Site
Source: Frances Rawnsley
World Wide Web URL: http://www.artmagick.com/default.aspx

Australian Folk Songs
Words, music, and information about many Australian folk songs.
Suggested Grade: All ages
Format: Web Site
Source: Mark Gregory
World Wide Web URL: http://folkstream.com/

Bird Cross Stitch Patterns
For those who love to do cross stitch, here are a number of free charts for creating your own works of art.
Suggested Grade: 4-Adult
Format: Free Patterns
Source: Jenny Rasmussen
World Wide Web URL: http://www.birdcrossstitch.com/

Brush with Wildlife, A
Introduce yourself to the animated principles of art, then create your own composition.
Suggested Grade: 7-Adult
Format: Online Art Lessons
Source: Carl Rungius
World Wide Web URL: http://www.wildlifeart.org/Rungius/

Colomusic
Color plus music. Explains how we can feel music "through our eyes."
Suggested Grade: 4-12
Format: Web Site
Special Notes: This URL will lead you to a subject page. Then click on the appropriate subject heading.
Source: ThinkQuest
World Wide Web URL: http://www.thinkquest.org/pls/html/think.library

Craftplace
Here are the instructions for making a number of craft projects.
Suggested Grade: All ages
Format: Web Site
Source: Craft & Hobby Association
World Wide Web URL: http://www.craftplace.org/

Create-a-Composition
Students will compose their own musical piece.
Suggested Grade: 2-6
Format: Online Lesson Plan
Source: Cheryl Nelson
World Wide Web URL: http://youth.net/cec/cecmisc/cecmisc.30.txt

Creating Music
A place to explore musical composition for young children.
Suggested Grade: K-8
Format: Web Site
Source: Morton Subotnick
World Wide Web URL: http://www.creatingmusic.com/

Dramatic Education, A
Lesson plans include auditioning, costuming, dialects, masks, pantomime, and much more.
Suggested Grade: 6-12
Format: Online Lesson Plans
Source: Peter Marston Sullivan
World Wide Web URL: http://www.angelfire.com/nm/marston6/

Draw and Color with Uncle Fred
Children will learn how to draw a series of cartoon characters.
Suggested Grade: 1-5
Format: Web Site
Source: Fred Lasswell, Inc.
World Wide Web URL: http://www.unclefred.com

Early American Weaving
Experience the Native American and Colonial American art of weaving with this activity.
Suggested Grade: 2-12
Format: Online Lesson Plan
Source: TeachersFirst
World Wide Web URL: http://www.teachersfirst.com/summer/weaving.htm

Early Childhood Art Lessons
Here are links to several art lessons, submitted by others, that are perfect for early learners.
Suggested Grade: preK-2
Format: Online Lesson Plans
Source: Ken Rohrer
World Wide Web URL: http://www.princetonol.com/groups/iad/lessons/early/early.html

Elementary Art Lesson Plans
Lots of art lessons from a very experienced art teacher.
Suggested Grade: preK-8
Format: Online Lesson Plans

All materials listed in this 2017-2018 edition are BRAND NEW!

ART, DRAMA, AND MUSIC

Source: Sandy Meadors
World Wide Web URL:
http://syrylynrainbowdragon.tripod.com/home.html

Ethnic Art: African, Mexican and Caribbean Perspectives
Designed to help students become familiar with artistic aspects of their culture and compare these cultures through art.
Suggested Grade: 6-12
Format: Online Lesson Plan
Source: Val-Jean Belton
World Wide Web URL: http://www.cis.yale.edu/ynhti/curriculum/units/1995/4/95.04.05.x.html

FastMIDI Player
Automatically plays MIDI files in a user-selected directory.
Suggested Grade: All ages
Format: Downloadable FULL PROGRAM
Source: DynoTech Software
World Wide Web URL: http://www.dynotech.com/other.htm

Grand Pantheon, The
A play that teaches history through literature.
Suggested Grade: 6
Format: Downloadable Play Script
Special Notes: This is a PDF file which will open automatically on your computer.
Source: Michele Delattre
World Wide Web URL: http://orias.berkeley.edu/GrandPantheon.pdf

Harmonica Lessons
Information and lesson plans on how to play this musical instrument.
Suggested Grade: All ages
Format: Web Site
Special Notes: While this is a subscription site, there is a lot of free information to be found here as well.
Source: Harmonica Lessons.com
World Wide Web URL: http://www.harmonicalessons.com/

HymnSite.Com
This site presents a large number of MIDI music for downloading--all songs are religious.
Suggested Grade: 4-12
Format: Downloadable MIDI music
Source: HymnSite
World Wide Web URL: http://hymnsite.com/

Jack's Harmonica Page
Here are ten lessons for learning how to play the harmonica.
Suggested Grade: All ages
Format: Online Tutorial
Source: Jack Mearl
World Wide Web URL: http://www.volcano.net/~jackmearl/

JazClass
Online music courses in basic theory, jazz, and more.
Suggested Grade: 4-12
Format: Online Tutorial
Source: Michael Furstner
World Wide Web URL: http://www.jazclass.aust.com/

Lesson 29: Textured Pottery Using Self-Hardening Clay and Multicultural Designs
Learn how to create clay vessels that pay tribute to other cultures.
Suggested Grade: Teacher Reference
Format: Online Lesson Plan
Source: American Art Clay Co., Inc.
World Wide Web URL: http://www.amaco.com/amaco-lesson-plans/

Lesson Plans
Here are a number of lesson plans, for all ages, covering all sorts of art lessons.
Suggested Grade: All ages
Format: Online Lesson Plans
Source: Dick Blick Art Materials
World Wide Web URL: http://www.dickblick.com/lessonplans/

Lift Every Voice and Sing
The popular title for this work is "The Negro National Anthem." Here you can listen to the song.
Suggested Grade: All ages
Format: Online Music
Source: James Weldon Johnson
World Wide Web URL: http://www.cyberhymnal.org/htm/l/i/liftevry.htm

Make a Papier Mache Bowl
Students learn about the history of pottery created by Native Americans, they are challenged to create their own similar bowl using papier mache.
Suggested Grade: All ages
Format: Online Lesson Plan
Source: Marilyn J. Brackney
World Wide Web URL: http://www.kid-at-art.com/htdoc/lesson37.html

Make a Splash with Color
Students will learn more about color and how our eyes view it.
Suggested Grade: 4-12
Format: Web Site
Source: Adobe Systems
World Wide Web URL: http://www.thetech.org/exhibits/online/color/intro/

Making a Pinata
Here are directions for making a pinata--a common element in the celebration for the feast day of Our Lady of

All materials listed in this 2017-2018 edition are **BRAND NEW!**

ART, DRAMA, AND MUSIC

Guadalupe.
Suggested Grade: All ages
Format: Online Lesson Plan
Source: Catherine Fournier
World Wide Web URL: http://www.domestic-church.com/CONTENT.DCC/19981101/FRIDGE/pinata.htm

Mix 'n Match
Students will put together many melody patterns.
Suggested Grade: 2-4
Format: Online Lesson Plan
Source: Jimmy Lazenby
World Wide Web URL: http://youth.net/cec/ceclang/ceclang.38.txt

Museum of Musical Instruments, The
A virtual museum which focuses on the music and musical instruments of the 19th and 20th century, with an emphasis on guitars.
Suggested Grade: All ages
Format: Web Site
Source: MoMi.org
World Wide Web URL: http://www.themomi.org/museum/index.html

Music from Across America
In this unit, students listen to a variety of popular, traditional and ethnic American music.
Suggested Grade: 3-5
Format: Online Lesson Plan
Source: EDSITEment
World Wide Web URL: http://edsitement.neh.gov/view_lesson_plan.asp?id=252

Music of Yesterday and Today
History of music.
Suggested Grade: 4-12
Format: Web Site
Special Notes: This URL will lead you to a subject page. Then click on the appropriate subject heading.
Source: ThinkQuest
World Wide Web URL: http://www.thinkquest.org/pls/html/think.library

Native American Technology and Art
Presents articles on the many types of art crafted by Native Americans.
Suggested Grade: 4-Adult
Format: Web Site
Source: Tara Prindle
World Wide Web URL: http://www.nativetech.org/

Origami Fun
Directions for folding several origami figures.
Suggested Grade: All ages
Format: Web Site
Source: Origami-Fun
World Wide Web URL: http://www.origami-fun.com/

Performing Medieval Narrative Today: A Video Showcase
A database of video clips of contemporary performances of medieval narrative.
Suggested Grade: 6-12
Format: Online Video Performances
Source: Evelyn Birge Vitz, Nancy Freeman Regalado, and Marilyn Lawrence
World Wide Web URL: http://www.nyu.edu/projects/mednar/

Pics4Learning
Lots of images that are copyright free that can be used in a classroom setting.
Suggested Grade: All ages
Format: Web Site
Source: Tech4Learning
World Wide Web URL: http://www.pics4learning.com/

San Francisco Symphony Site for Kids
Learn all about music from this site--and listen to some as well.
Suggested Grade: K-8
Format: Web Site
Source: San Francisco Symphony
World Wide Web URL: http://www.sfskids.org/templates/home.asp?pageid=1

Sociology Through Five Plays
Students learn more about sociology by studying five classic plays.
Suggested Grade: 6-12
Format: Curriculum Unit
Source: Lula M. White
World Wide Web URL: http://www.yale.edu/ynhti/curriculum/units/1986/1/86.01.08.x.html

Songs4Teachers
More than 120 free theme-related songs and poems, all ready to print.
Suggested Grade: All ages
Format: Web Site
Source: O'Flynn Consulting
World Wide Web URL: http://www.songs4teachers.com/

Songs for Teaching
Helpful information and activities for using music in the elementary classroom.
Suggested Grade: Teacher Reference
Format: Web Site
Source: S. Ruth Harris
World Wide Web URL: http://www.songsforteaching.com/index.htm

All materials listed in this 2017-2018 edition are BRAND NEW!

ART, DRAMA, AND MUSIC

SoundJunction
Learn all about music.
Suggested Grade: All ages
Format: Web Site
Source: Associated Board of the Royal Schools of Music
World Wide Web URL: http://www.soundjunction.org/default.aspa

Stage Line/Time Line: A Musical Adventure
An interdisciplinary approach to learning, combining literature, history, music, and dance.
Suggested Grade: 5-8
Format: Online Lesson Plan
Source: Richard Canalori and Joyce Listro
World Wide Web URL: http://www.yale.edu/ynhti/curriculum/units/1985/2/85.02.07.x.html

Stepping Into the World of the American Musical Theatre: Dance Sets the Pace
This curriculum unit has been designed to explore the wondrous magic that exists in the Broadway musical.
Suggested Grade: 6-Adult
Format: Online Lesson Plan
Source: Donna Lombardi
World Wide Web URL: http://www.yale.edu/ynhti/curriculum/units/1985/2/85.02.04.x.html

Stories Behind the Songs
An interdisciplinary reference that examines the origins and inspirations for contemporary song lyrics.
Suggested Grade: All ages
Format: Online Reference Guide
Source: Musicians United for Songs in the Classroom, Inc.
World Wide Web URL: http://www.learningfromlyrics.org/Introduction.html

Swiss Anthem
Here are the lyrics and music for the national anthem of Switzerland.
Suggested Grade: All ages
Format: Online Music Lyrics
Source: TRAMsoft GmbH
World Wide Web URL: http://www.about.ch/culture/anthem.html

Teaching Resources Using Comics
Exercises, lesson plans, study guides, and more for using comics to teach art skills.
Suggested Grade: 6-12
Format: Web Site
Source: National Association of Comics Art Educators
World Wide Web URL: http://www.teachingcomics.org/

Un-Birthday Present, The
Thoroughly research a famous artist and then create an art project in that person's style.
Suggested Grade: 5-12
Format: Online Lesson Plan
Source: Sara Gant
World Wide Web URL: http://www.princetonol.com/groups/iad/lessons/high/SaraUnbirthday.htm

Using Drama and Theatre to Promote Literacy Development: Some Basic Classroom Applications
Explores some readily applicable strategies for classroom application.
Suggested Grade: Teacher Reference
Format: Online Article
Source: Ping-Yun Sun
World Wide Web URL: http://www.ericdigests.org/2004-1/drama.htm

Using Drama as a Resource for Giving Language More Meaning
Uses pictures, mime, and acting to help students appreciate spoken language.
Suggested Grade: 5-8
Format: Online Lesson Plan
Source: Sam Smith
World Wide Web URL: http://www.developingteachers.com/articles_tchtraining/dramalp1_sam.htm

Virtual Museum of Music Inventions, The
Teaching tips and a virtual display of musical instruments.
Suggested Grade: 4-6
Format: Web Site
Source: Elizabeth Rexford
World Wide Web URL: http://www.musicinventions.org/

Welcome to the Renaissance Art World
Michelangelo, Leonardo da Vinci, and Raphael, are featured with biographical info and examples of their work. Brueghel and Holbein are also considered.
Suggested Grade: 6-12
Format: Web Site
Special Notes: This URL will lead you to a subject page. Then click on the appropriate subject heading.
Source: ThinkQuest
World Wide Web URL: http://www.thinkquest.org/pls/html/think.library

Woodwind Fingering Guide, The
Fingering charts for virtually every woodwind instrument.
Suggested Grade: 4-12
Format: Web Site
Source: Tim Reichard
World Wide Web URL: http://www.wfg.woodwind.org/index.html

Yarn Painting (Ofrendas)
The Huichol Indians of Mexico are known for their yarn paintings--here is how students can make their own.
Suggested Grade: 4-8
Format: Online Lesson Plan

All materials listed in this 2017-2018 edition are **BRAND NEW!**

ART, DRAMA, AND MUSIC

Source: KinderArt
World Wide Web URL:
http://www.kinderart.com/multic/yarn.shtml

Young Composers
Presents music composed by young people and offers information on how to submit your own.
Suggested Grade: 6-Adult
Format: Web Site
Source: Able Minds, Inc.
World Wide Web URL: http://www.youngcomposers.com/

*All materials listed in this 2017-2018 edition are **BRAND NEW!***

COMPUTER EDUCATION

Ainsworth Computer Seminar
Students will learn more about all aspects of computers with this self-paced program.
Suggested Grade: All ages
Format: Downloadable FULL PROGRAM
Source: Dick Ainsworth
World Wide Web URL: http://www.qwerty.com/startacs.htm

Banner Generator, The
A free service that lets you create graphical banners for your web pages.
Suggested Grade: 6-Adult
Format: Online FULL PROGRAM
Source: Prescient Code Solutions
World Wide Web URL: http://coder.com/creations/banner

Becoming Webwise
Learn at your own pace about the Internet.
Suggested Grade: All ages
Format: Online Course
Source: BBC Learning
World Wide Web URL: http://www.bbc.co.uk/webwise/0/

bNetS@vvy
Designed to give adults tools to connect with kids and help them stay safer online.
Suggested Grade: Adults
Format: Online newsletter; bimonthly
Source: National Education Association Health Information Network
World Wide Web URL: http://bnetsavvy.org/wp/

Building a School Web Site
Designed to accompany the book of the same name, this site presents useful information to potential web site builders, even without the book.
Suggested Grade: 4-Adult
Production Date: 2003
Format: Web Site
Source: Jeanne Marie
World Wide Web URL: http://www.wigglebits.com/

CGI Made Really Easy
A tutorial that will tell you how to write CGI scripts to process HTML forms on the World Wide Web.
Suggested Grade: 6-Adult
Format: Online Tutorial
Source: James Marshall
World Wide Web URL: http://www.jmarshall.com/easy/cgi/

CGI Resource Index, The
A lists of numerous links to resources on programming in CGI.
Suggested Grade: 6-Adult
Format: Web Site
Source: Matt's Script Archive, Inc.
World Wide Web URL: http://cgi.resourceindex.com/

C-Language Course
Contains a complete course for you to learn this programming language.
Suggested Grade: 6-12
Format: Downloadable Tutorial
Source: Christopher Sawtell
World Wide Web URL: http://www.fi.uib.no/Fysisk/Teori/KURS/OTHER/newzealand.html

Classroom Learning 2.0
A site for teachers to learn more about the Internet.
Suggested Grade: Teacher Reference
Format: Online Tutorial
Source: California School Library Association
World Wide Web URL: http://classroomlearning2.blogspot.com/

Computer Almanac
Presents all sorts of interesting and useful numbers regarding computer use.
Suggested Grade: 4-12
Format: Web Site
Source: Brad A. Myers
World Wide Web URL: http://www-2.cs.cmu.edu/afs/cs.cmu.edu/user/bam/www/numbers.html

Computer and Internet Use by Children and Adolescents in 2001: Statistical Analysis Report
Describes computer and Internet use by children and teens ages five to seventeen.
Suggested Grade: Teacher Reference
Production Date: 2004
Format: Downloadable Booklet
Source: ED Pubs
World Wide Web URL: http://www.edpubs.org

Computers and How They Work
Explains how computers utilize information.
Suggested Grade: 7
Format: Online Article
Source: Crews Middle School
World Wide Web URL: http://www.crews.org/curriculum/ex/compsci/articles/howcomput.htm

Computers: History and Development
Provides detailed information on the history of computing.
Suggested Grade: 4-12
Format: Web Site
Source: Christopher LaMorte and John Lilly
World Wide Web URL: http://www.dia.eui.upm.es/asignatu/sis_op1/comp_hd/comp_hd.htm

All materials listed in this 2017-2018 edition are **BRAND NEW!**

COMPUTER EDUCATION

Creating a Blog: A Workshop for Teens
A complete curriculum for downloading that will teach teens how to create and maintain their own blogs.
Suggested Grade: 7-Adult
Format: Downloadable Curriculum
Special Notes: This is a PDF file which will open automatically on your computer.
Source: Children's Partnership, The
World Wide Web URL: http://www.childrenspartnership.org/storage/documents/Publications/TCP_blogging_workshop.pdf

Few Scanning Tips, A
Here are some scanning tips and hints, fundamentals, and other general information to help beginners get off to a quick start with their flatbed scanners.
Suggested Grade: 4-Adult
Format: Web Site
Source: Wayne Fulton
World Wide Web URL: http://www.scantips.com

FILExt
A very useful site. Explains what programs create the file extensions you see at the end of a file name.
Suggested Grade: 4-Adult
Format: Web Site
Source: Computer Knowledge
World Wide Web URL: http://filext.com/

Find Lost Files and Folders
A "techtorial" that will help you to learn how to find files you saved on your hard drive.
Suggested Grade: 6-Adult
Format: Online Article
Special Notes: This is a PDF file which will open automatically on your computer.
Source: Lorrie Jackson
World Wide Web URL: http://www.educationworld.com/a_tech/techtorial/techtorial050.pdf

First Guide to PostScript, A
Here is a simple introduction to programming in the PostScript page description language.
Suggested Grade: 6-Adult
Format: Online Tutorial
Source: Peter Weingartner
World Wide Web URL: http://www.cs.indiana.edu/docproject/programming/postscript/postscript.html

Free Animated GIFs
Graphics that are animated for use on your web or intranet site.
Suggested Grade: 6-Adult
Format: Downloadable FULL PROGRAM
Source: Lawrence Goetz
World Wide Web URL: http://www.lawrencegoetz.com/programs/free.html

GetNetWise
Information about safe Internet usage for parents and teachers alike.
Suggested Grade: Adult
Format: Web Site
Source: Internet Education Foundation
World Wide Web URL: http://www.getnetwise.org/

Goetz's Programming Kit
Allows children and adults alike to easily write programs for their computer.
Suggested Grade: 6-Adult
Format: Downloadable FULL PROGRAM
Source: Lawrence Goetz
World Wide Web URL: http://www.lawrencegoetz.com/programs/free.html

HJ-Install 2.9
Add a simple automatic installation procedure to your products with this program. Includes a compression utility as well.
Suggested Grade: 6-Adult
Format: Downloadable FULL PROGRAM
Source: Henk Hagedoorn
World Wide Web URL: http://www.freebyte.com/freeware/

How Do They Do That with HTML?
How to understand HTML--HyperText Markup Language--so that you can build your own web page.
Suggested Grade: 6-Adult
Format: Online Tutorial
Source: Carl Tashian
World Wide Web URL: http://www.tashian.com/htmlguide/

How the Internet Came to Be
Details the history of this medium of communication.
Suggested Grade: 4-12
Format: Online Article
Source: Vinton Cerf
World Wide Web URL: http://www.netvalley.com/archives/mirrors/cerf-how-inet.txt

HTML Goodies
This site hosts seven primers for learning about HTML in addition to over 100 different tutorials.
Suggested Grade: 6-Adult
Format: Web Site
Source: Joe Burns
World Wide Web URL: http://www.htmlgoodies.com/

HTML Imager Version 1.2a
Produces web pages showing all GIF and/or JPG pictures from the directory you select.
Suggested Grade: 6-Adult
Format: Downloadable FULL PROGRAM
Source: Eric G. V. Fookes
World Wide Web URL: http://www.fookes.com/software/html-img.htm

All materials listed in this 2017-2018 edition are BRAND NEW!

COMPUTER EDUCATION

Jan's Illustrated Computer Literacy 101
Lessons written to help all users understand computers.
Suggested Grade: All ages
Format: Online Lessons
Special Notes: Also available on CD for $15.00.
Source: Jan Smith
World Wide Web URL:
http://www.jegsworks.com/Lessons/index.html

Karbosguide.com
A detailed online-magazine with more than 500 illustrated articles to help you learn all about computers.
Suggested Grade: 6-Adult
Format: Online Magazine
Source: Michael Karbo
World Wide Web URL: http://www.karbosguide.com/

Learn 2 Type
Interactive exercises to help you improve your typing.
Suggested Grade: All ages
Format: Web Site
Source: RJ Networks
World Wide Web URL: http://www.learn2type.com/

Lissa Explains It All
A very helpful primer about Web page construction put together by a 12-year-old girl.
Suggested Grade: 6-Adult
Format: Web Site
Source: Lissa
World Wide Web URL: http://www.lissaexplains.com/

Making the Connection: How to Go Online
Explains how to get online and choose the best Internet service provider.
Suggested Grade: 4-Adult
Production Date: 2001
Format: Online Article; 9 pages
Special Notes: Use the on-site search engine to easily find this title. You may request a printed copy mailed to you for a fee.
Source: Federal Citizen Information Center
World Wide Web URL:
http://publications.usa.gov/USAPubs.php

Menuz
A collection of cool javascript menu sets that you can download and use on your own personal/non-profit websites.
Suggested Grade: 6-Adult
Format: Downloadable MENU SETS
Source: Alison & Charlie
World Wide Web URL: http://www.groan-zone.net/menuz

Philip and Alex's Guide to Web Publishing
A complete book that tells how to set up a really great website.
Suggested Grade: 6-Adult
Format: Online Book
Source: Philip Greenspun
World Wide Web URL:
http://www.philip.greenspun.com/panda/

Primer on Digital Literacy, A
Discusses the concept of "digital literacy"--directed at the field of education.
Suggested Grade: Teacher Reference
Format: Online Primer
Source: Paul Gilster
World Wide Web URL:
http://horizon.unc.edu/projects/resources/digital_literacy.asp

Privacy Pirates
Introduces children to the concept of online privacy and teaches them to distinguish between information that is appropriate to give out and information better kept private.
Suggested Grade: 2-5
Format: Online game
Source: MediaSmarts
World Wide Web URL: http://mediasmarts.ca/game/privacy-pirates-interactive-unit-online-privacy-ages-7-9

Programming in C
A tutorial for learning how to program in this language.
Suggested Grade: 6-Adult
Format: Online Tutorial
Source: Dave Marshall
World Wide Web URL:
http://www.cs.cf.ac.uk/Dave/C/CE.html

SkillsDEN
Sheds new light on information technology.
Suggested Grade: 4-Adult
Format: Online Course
Source: Act360 Media Ltd.
World Wide Web URL: http://www.actden.com/

Teach Me HTML
Learn how to create web basics--in only 1 hour.
Suggested Grade: 6-Adult
Format: Downloadable FULL PROGRAM
Source: Pinsoft Software
World Wide Web URL:
http://www.pinsoft.com.au/teachhtml.htm

Technology Tips for Classroom Teachers
Lots of tips for using technology, including tips for specific software programs as well.
Suggested Grade: Teacher Reference
Format: Web Site
Source: Marilyn Western
World Wide Web URL: http://www.edzone.net/~mwestern/

*All materials listed in this 2017-2018 edition are **BRAND NEW!***

COMPUTER EDUCATION

Tutorial on Using Perl and CGI to Enhance a Homepage, A
Advanced computer students learn Perl and CGI, extensions of HTML.

Suggested Grade:	6-Adult
Format:	Web Site
Special Notes:	This URL will lead you to a subject page. Then click on the appropriate subject heading.

Source: ThinkQuest
World Wide Web URL:
http://www.thinkquest.org/pls/html/think.library

Typing Bingo
After students have learned how to use the tab key, they produce a bingo card.

Suggested Grade:	4-5
Format:	Online Lesson Plan

Source: Jodi Cochran
World Wide Web URL: http://www.lessonplanspage.com/CITypingBingoTabKey45.htm

Web Pages for Absolute Beginners
Here is information on how to make your own web pages using HTML code, using Windows 95 and Microsoft Internet Explorer.

Suggested Grade:	6-Adult
Format:	Online Tutorial
Special Notes:	This is a PDF file which will open automatically on your computer.

Source: Ruth Livingstone
World Wide Web URL:
http://www.nuceng.ca/teach/web4beginners.pdf

You've Got Spam: How to "Can" Unwanted E-Mail
Find out how marketers get your email address, how to reduce the amount of spam you receive, and more.

Suggested Grade:	6-Adult
Format:	Online Article
Special Notes:	Use the on-site search engine to easily find this title. You may request a printed copy mailed to you for a fee.

Source: Federal Citizen Information Center
World Wide Web URL:
http://publications.usa.gov/USAPubs.php

*All materials listed in this 2017-2018 edition are **BRAND NEW!***

DICTIONARIES

ABC's of Legal Terms
A glossary of legal terms aimed at kids.
Suggested Grade: 4-8
Format: Online Dictionary
Source: U. S. Department of Justice
World Wide Web URL: http://www.justice.gov/usao/eousa/kidspage/glossary.html

Acronym Finder
A searchable database containing acronyms and abbreviations about all subjects--over 69,000 acronyms defined.
Suggested Grade: 4-Adult
Format: Online Glossary
Source: Mountain Data Systems
World Wide Web URL: http://www.AcronymFinder.com/

Alan Cooper's Homonym List
A listing of homonyms and their definitions.
Suggested Grade: 2-12
Format: Online Glossary
Source: Alan Cooper
World Wide Web URL: http://www.cooper.com/alan/homonym_list.html

AllWords.com
Type in the word you wish to have translated into Dutch, French, German, Italian, or Spanish and it will give you the proper word. Also includes links to other dictionaries.
Suggested Grade: All ages
Format: Online Glossary
Source: AllWords.com
World Wide Web URL: http://www.allwords.com/

Baroque Reference, The
Tells about this era of music and provides an extensive glossary.
Suggested Grade: 4-12
Format: Web Site
Special Notes: This URL will lead you to a subject page. Then click on the appropriate subject heading.
Source: ThinkQuest
World Wide Web URL: http://www.thinkquest.org/pls/html/think.library

Biographical Dictionary
Covers more than 19,000 notable men and women who have shaped our world from ancient times to the present day.
Suggested Grade: 4-12
Format: Online Glossary
Source: S9.com
World Wide Web URL: http://www.s9.com/biography/

Dictionary.com
A multi-source dictionary search service.
Suggested Grade: 6-Adult
Format: Online Glossary
Source: Dictionary.com
World Wide Web URL: http://dictionary.reference.com/

Encyclopedia.com
Presents more than 14,000 articles from The Concise Columbia Electronic Encyclopedia, Third Edition.
Suggested Grade: 4-Adult
Format: Online Encyclopedia
Source: HighBeam Research, Inc.
World Wide Web URL: http://www.encyclopedia.com/

Fact Monster
A searchable dictionary, encyclopedia, and homework help site.
Suggested Grade: All ages
Format: Web Site
Source: Pearson Education
World Wide Web URL: http://www.factmonster.com/

Familiar Quotations--Passages, Phrases and Proverbs Traced to Their Sources
Find out who said what.
Suggested Grade: 4-12
Format: Online Glossary
Source: Project Bartleby
World Wide Web URL: http://www.bartleby.com/100/

GardenWeb Glossary
Currently contains 4,400 terms relating to botany, gardening, horticulture, and landscape architecture.
Suggested Grade: 4-Adult
Format: Online Glossary
Source: GardenWeb
World Wide Web URL: http://glossary.gardenweb.com/glossary/

Glossary of Internet & Web Terms
Defines many of the words unique to the World Wide Web.
Suggested Grade: 4-Adult
Format: Online Glossary
Source: Scholastic--Teaching with Technology
World Wide Web URL: http://www2.scholastic.com/browse/article.jsp?id=4394

Internet Acronym Server
A list of acronyms spelled out so that you know what they stand for.
Suggested Grade: 4-12
Format: Online Glossary
Source: Peter Flynn
World Wide Web URL: http://acronyms.silmaril.ie/cgi-bin/uncgi/acronyms

Internet Glossary of Soil Science Terms
Defines the many terms relating to soil science.
Suggested Grade: 6-Adult
Format: Online Glossary
Special Notes: Print copies are available for $5 each.

*All materials listed in this 2017-2018 edition are **BRAND NEW!***

DICTIONARIES

Source: Soil Science Society of America
World Wide Web URL:
https://www.soils.org/publications/soils-glossary

LOGOS Multilingual Portal
A freely accessible database that currently has 7,580,560 entries for all languages.
Suggested Grade: 4-Adult
Format: Online Glossary
Source: Logos Group
World Wide Web URL: http://www.logos.it/

OneLook Dictionaries
Allows you to search a number of online dictionaries at the same time.
Suggested Grade: 4-Adult
Format: Web Site
Source: Study Technologies
World Wide Web URL: http://www.onelook.com

RhymeZone Rhyming Dictionary, The
Type in the word for which you want to find a rhyme and it will pop up.
Suggested Grade: All ages
Format: Online Glossary
Source: Doug Beeferman
World Wide Web URL: http://www.rhymezone.com/

Surnames: What's in a Name?
Our last names tell a lot about our family history. Here's a place to see if your name is listed and what history it has.
Suggested Grade: 4-Adult
Format: Online Glossary
Source: Larry Hoefling
World Wide Web URL:
http://www.mohrministries.org/singarch/whatsiname.htm

TechEncyclopedia
Find more than 13,000 definitions of computer terms and concepts.
Suggested Grade: All ages
Format: Online Glossary
Source: CMPnet
World Wide Web URL:
http://www.techweb.com/encyclopedia/

Urban Conservation Glossary, The
Defines terms relating to the environment.
Suggested Grade: All ages
Format: Online Glossary
Source: Neil Grieve
World Wide Web URL:
http://www.trp.dundee.ac.uk/research/glossary/glossary.html

Weather Glossary
Defines more than 800 weather-related terms.
Suggested Grade: All ages
Format: Online Glossary
Source: Weather Channel, The
World Wide Web URL:
http://www.theweatherchannelkids.com/weather-ed/glossary/

Word Central
Look up words, build your own dictionary, or stump your friends with today's daily buzzword.
Suggested Grade: All ages
Format: Web Site
Source: Merriam-Webster, Incorporated
World Wide Web URL: http://www.wordcentral.com/

*All materials listed in this 2017-2018 edition are **BRAND NEW!***

EARLY LEARNING

ABC's of Snacking, The
Snacks, recipes, and ideas that you can use to go with most of the letters of the alphabet.
Suggested Grade: preK-2
Format: Web Site
Source: Barbara Pratt
World Wide Web URL: http://www.fastq.com/~jbpratt/education/theme/alphabet/abcsnacking.html

ALFY: The Web Portal for Kids
Presents activities that develop literacy and numerical and reasoning skills.
Suggested Grade: preK-3
Format: Web Site
Source: Alfy.com
World Wide Web URL: http://www.alfy.com/

Alphabet Soup
Units, games, activities, and more for young children are found here.
Suggested Grade: preK-2
Format: Web Site
Source: Alphabet Soup
World Wide Web URL: http://www.alphabet-soup.net/

Chubbie Cubbie's Activity Ideas
A multitude of preschool activity ideas.
Suggested Grade: preK
Format: Online Activity Plans
Source: Chubbie Cubbie's Preschool & Curriculum
World Wide Web URL: http://chubbiecubbie.com/prekacts.htm

Color Code Writing
Intended for students having difficulty forming letters--manuscript or cursive.
Suggested Grade: K-3
Format: Online Lesson Plan
Source: Priscilla Mestas
World Wide Web URL: http://youth.net/cec/ceclang/ceclang.18.txt

Drawing for Children
A drawing program for small children.
Suggested Grade: preK
Format: Downloadable FULL PROGRAM
Source: Mark Overmars
World Wide Web URL: http://www.cs.uu.nl/~markov/kids/index.html

Enchanted Learning Web Site
Lots of online activities for children are found on this vendor's web site.
Suggested Grade: preK-2
Format: Web Site
Special Notes: Joining the site for a fee is an option, but not necessary.
Source: Enchanted Learning Software
World Wide Web URL: http://www.EnchantedLearning.com/

Everything Preschool
A nifty site with all sorts of themes and activities for preschool teachers and parents. Songs, recipes, articles, project ideas, and much more.
Suggested Grade: preK
Format: Web Site
Source: Everything Preschool.com
World Wide Web URL: http://www.everythingpreschool.com/

First-School
Activities and printable worksheets for the early learner.
Suggested Grade: preK-1
Format: Web Site
Source: First-School.ws
World Wide Web URL: http://www.first-school.ws/

4Kids2Play
Flash-animated games for learning.
Suggested Grade: K-3
Format: Web Site
Source: 4Kids2Play
World Wide Web URL: http://www.4kids2play.nl/eng/

Funbrain.com
Presents math, spelling, and creative writing games that double as interactive lessons--kids won't even know they are learning something!
Suggested Grade: All ages
Format: Web Site
Source: Funbrain.com
World Wide Web URL: http://www.funbrain.com/

Funschool.com
Educational, yet fun activities open to anyone who wants to have fun learning.
Suggested Grade: preK-2
Format: Web Site
Source: Kaboose Network, The
World Wide Web URL: http://www.funschool.com/

Game Goo
Education games to help students develop early reading and language skills.
Suggested Grade: preK-2
Format: Web Site
Source: Earobics
World Wide Web URL: http://www.earobics.com/gamegoo/index.html

Green Bean's Treehouse
A site to help youngsters learn the alphabet and a little bit of math.

*All materials listed in this 2017-2018 edition are **BRAND NEW!***

EARLY LEARNING

Suggested Grade: preK-1
Format: Web Site
Special Notes: This URL will lead you to a subject page. Then click on the appropriate subject heading.
Source: ThinkQuest
World Wide Web URL:
http://www.thinkquest.org/pls/html/think.library

ICT Games
Lots of educational online games and activities.
Suggested Grade: preK-K
Format: Web Site
Source: James Barrett
World Wide Web URL:
http://www.ictgames.com/resources.html

Idea Box
Provides users access to craft, recipe, and activity ideas for teachers, parents and students.
Suggested Grade: preK-2
Format: Web Site
Source: Idea Box
World Wide Web URL: http://www.theideabox.com/

Ivy's Coloring Page Search Engine
A great site for youngsters who want to find coloring pages on the web. A search engine to help them find just the picture they wish to color.
Suggested Grade: preK-2
Format: Web Site
Source: IvyJoy.com
World Wide Web URL:
http://ivyjoy.com/coloring/search.html

Kids Farm
Here is information and resources about farms and farm animals, wild animals, kids' rodeos, and more.
Suggested Grade: K-3
Format: Web Site
Special Notes: A CD of this site and program is available for a fee.
Source: Kids Farm
World Wide Web URL: http://www.kidsfarm.com/

Kids Heart, A
Lots of activities for kids.
Suggested Grade: preK-2
Format: Web Site
Source: Roxie Carroll
World Wide Web URL: http://www.akidsheart.com/

KidsPsych
Features interactive games and activities that are designed to help young children master specific developmental skills.
Suggested Grade: preK-2
Format: Web Site
Source: KidsPsych
World Wide Web URL:
http://www.kidspsych.org/index1.html

KinderArt Littles
Activities and crafts for young children.
Suggested Grade: preK-2
Format: Web Site
Source: KinderArt
World Wide Web URL:
http://www.kinderart.com/littles/index.html

Larry's Animals-n-Things
Shows animals and objects for a child to click on, using the mouse, and the images will then make appropriate sounds or more.
Suggested Grade: preK-2
Format: Downloadable FULL PROGRAM
Source: Lawrence Goetz
World Wide Web URL:
http://www.lawrencegoetz.com/programs/free.html

Larry's Count
An applet to teach counting.
Suggested Grade: preK-2
Format: Downloadable FULL PROGRAM
Source: Lawrence Goetz
World Wide Web URL:
http://www.lawrencegoetz.com/programs/free.html

Larry's Songs
Plays 10 different songs while various figures march around the screen--almost like a digital music box.
Suggested Grade: preK-2
Format: Downloadable FULL PROGRAM
Source: Lawrence Goetz
World Wide Web URL:
http://www.lawrencegoetz.com/programs/free.html

Learn Letters
Teaches children to know and make the 26 letters of the alphabet.
Suggested Grade: preK-1
Format: Downloadable FULL PROGRAM
Source: Owl & Mouse Educational Software
World Wide Web URL:
http://www.yourchildlearns.com/owlmouse.htm

Letter Sounds
Preschoolers learn letter sound relationships while playing an alphabet game.
Suggested Grade: preK-1
Format: Downloadable FULL PROGRAM
Source: Owl & Mouse Educational Software
World Wide Web URL:
http://www.yourchildlearns.com/owlmouse.htm

Literacy Center
Provides opportunities for young children to practice literacy skills.
Suggested Grade: preK-K
Format: Web Site

*All materials listed in this 2017-2018 edition are **BRAND NEW!***

EARLY LEARNING

Source: Early Childhood Education Network
World Wide Web URL:
http://www.literacycenter.net/lessonview_en.htm

Little Red House, The
Written to help children develop auditory, visual, language, gross motor, and fine motor activities using this story.
Suggested Grade: preK
Format: Online Lesson Plan
Source: Kathleen Beveridge
World Wide Web URL:
http://youth.net/cec/ceclang/ceclang.22.txt

Mouse Club, The
Activities to introduce youngsters to using the Internet and their computer.
Suggested Grade: preK-2
Format: Web Site
Source: Digital by Design, Ltd.
World Wide Web URL: http://www.themouseclub.co.uk/

Mystery Pictures
An activity to help children learn to follow verbal instructions.
Suggested Grade: preK-2
Format: Online Lesson Plan
Source: Miriam Furst
World Wide Web URL:
http://youth.net/cec/ceclang/ceclang.46.txt

Poison Prevention Game
An online game designed to help youngsters learn what is poisonous.
Suggested Grade: preK-2
Format: Online Game
Source: University of Michigan Poison Prevention Project
World Wide Web URL: http://www-personal.umich.edu/~gweiss/poison/TILEGAME/TileGame.html

Preschool Coloring Book
A number of themed pages you can print on your computer that youngsters will enjoy coloring.
Suggested Grade: preK-2
Format: Downloadable Coloring Sheets
Source: Preschool Education/Preschool Coloring Book
World Wide Web URL:
http://www.preschoolcoloringbook.com/

Rainbow Raccoons, The
Four brightly colored raccoons invite kids to learn about health, science, history, and more.
Suggested Grade: preK-4
Format: Web Site
Source: Rainbow Raccoons
World Wide Web URL: http://www.rainbowraccoons.com/

Reinforcing Alphabet Names/Sounds
A reinforcement activity for learning the alphabet.
Suggested Grade: K-1
Format: Online Lesson Plan
Source: Julie Van Osdol
World Wide Web URL:
http://youth.net/cec/ceclang/ceclang.34.txt

Room 108
An educational activity center for kids.
Suggested Grade: preK-8
Format: Web Site
Source: John Rickey
World Wide Web URL:
http://www.netrover.com/~kingskid/108.html

StoryPlace: The Children's Digital Library
Online stories and activities for young children.
Suggested Grade: preK-2
Format: Web Site
Source: Charlotte Mecklenburg Library
World Wide Web URL: http://www.storyplace.org/

SupperTime
Practice setting the table--good practice for using a mouse.
Suggested Grade: preK-2
Format: Downloadable FULL PROGRAM
Source: Bry-Back Manor
World Wide Web URL:
http://www.bry-backmanor.org/funstuff.html

Teaching Ideas and Resources
A helpful site for teachers.
Suggested Grade: preK-6
Format: Web Site
Source: RM
World Wide Web URL: http://www.teachingideas.co.uk/

All materials listed in this 2017-2018 edition are BRAND NEW!

FAMOUS PEOPLE

Abraham Lincoln Online
A clearinghouse of information about this famous man.
Suggested Grade: 4-12
Format: Web Site
Source: Abraham Lincoln Online
World Wide Web URL:
http://www.showcase.netins.net/web/creative/lincoln.html

Anne Frank in the World Teacher Workbook
Students will learn more about Anne Frank and the discrimination that prevailed in that time.
Suggested Grade: 3-12
Format: Downloadable Teacher's Guide
Source: Utah State Office of Education
World Wide Web URL:
http://www.uen.org/annefrank/information.shtml

Artists of the Renaissance
In-depth look at twelve artists of the Renaissance, with biographies and copies of their art.
Suggested Grade: 6-12
Format: Web Site
Special Notes: This URL will lead you to a subject page. Then click on the appropriate subject heading.
Source: ThinkQuest
World Wide Web URL:
http://www.thinkquest.org/pls/html/think.library

Artists: The Good, the Bad, and the Ugly
Young students study artists.
Suggested Grade: 6-12
Format: Web Site
Special Notes: This URL will lead you to a subject page. Then click on the appropriate subject heading.
Source: ThinkQuest
World Wide Web URL:
http://www.thinkquest.org/pls/html/think.library

Astronaut Biographies
Here is biographical information on the members of the space flight crews and candidates for future missions as well.
Suggested Grade: 6-12
Format: Online Biographies
Source: NASA Johnson Space Center
World Wide Web URL: http://www.jsc.nasa.gov/Bios/

Baseball Hall of Fame and Museum
Learn about the greatest players of all time, test your knowledge of this sport, and more.
Suggested Grade: 4-12
Format: Web Site
Source: National Baseball Hall of Fame and Museum, The
World Wide Web URL: http://www.baseballhalloffame.org/

Biographies of Explorers and Associated People
Here you will find biographies of famous explorers and their contributions to "expanding the world."
Suggested Grade: 4-12
Format: Online Biographies
Source: Mariner's Museum, The
World Wide Web URL: http://76.12.123.11/education/biographies-explorers-and-associated-people

Biography-Center
At this writing, there are 25,495 biographies found here--10,890 in English.
Suggested Grade: 4-12
Format: Online Biographies
Source: EuropeanServers SARL
World Wide Web URL: http://www.biography-center.com/

Biography.com
A searchable database of over 20,000 of the greatest lives, past and present.
Suggested Grade: All ages
Format: Web Site
Source: A&E Television Networks
World Wide Web URL: http://www.biography.com

Colonial Hall
Presents over 100 biographies of people who played a major role in the founding of the United States.
Suggested Grade: 3-12
Format: Web Site
Source: John Vinci
World Wide Web URL:
http://colonialhall.com/index_t1.php

Confucius--His Life and Times
Find a comprehensive guide to information about this philosopher.
Suggested Grade: 6-12
Format: Web Site
Special Notes: This URL will lead you to a subject page. Then click on the appropriate subject heading.
Source: ThinkQuest
World Wide Web URL:
http://www.thinkquest.org/pls/html/think.library

Contemporary Art Experience, The
Students encounter living contemporary women artists and interact with them and their work.
Suggested Grade: 6-12
Format: Web Site
Special Notes: This URL will lead you to a subject page. Then click on the appropriate subject heading.
Source: ThinkQuest
World Wide Web URL:
http://www.thinkquest.org/pls/html/think.library

Do You Know Van Gogh?
Information about Van Gogh.
Suggested Grade: 6-12
Format: Web Site

All materials listed in this 2017-2018 edition are BRAND NEW!

FAMOUS PEOPLE

Special Notes: This URL will lead you to a subject page. Then click on the appropriate subject heading.
Source: ThinkQuest
World Wide Web URL: http://www.thinkquest.org/pls/html/think.library

Dr. Martin Luther King, Jr.
Includes a timeline and activities for studying about Dr. King.
Suggested Grade: 4-8
Format: Online Lesson Plan
Source: Mrs. Taverna
World Wide Web URL: http://www2.lhric.org/pocantico/taverna/98/king.htm

Einstein: Man in Spacetime
Provides an extensive time line covering the life, works, and legacy of Albert Einstein.
Suggested Grade: 6-12
Format: Web Site
Special Notes: This URL will lead you to a subject page. Then click on the appropriate subject heading.
Source: ThinkQuest
World Wide Web URL: http://www.thinkquest.org/pls/html/think.library

Elizabeth Cady Stanton & Susan B. Anthony Papers Project Online, The
An ambitious effort to locate and make available all manuscripts and printed texts from this 52-year friendship based on a mutual commitment to establish "perfect political equality among all classes of citizens."
Suggested Grade: 4-Adult
Format: Web Site
Source: Papers of Elizabeth Cady Stanton and Susan B. Anthony Project, The
World Wide Web URL: http://ecssba.rutgers.edu/

Famous Canadians
This WebQuest will introduce you to famous people from this country.
Suggested Grade: 5-6
Format: WebQuest
Source: Gerald Robillard and Bob Colvil
World Wide Web URL: http://www.swlauriersb.qc.ca/english/edservices/pedresources/webquest/famous_canadians/index.html

Famous Hispanics in the World and History
Alphabetical listings of names linked to brief biographical information on famous Hispanics.
Suggested Grade: 6-12
Format: Web Site
Source: Coloquio.com
World Wide Web URL: http://coloquio.com/famosos/alpha.html

Famous People with Perfect Pitch
Okay there isn't enough information here to create a paper on anyone, but it's kind of a fun site to visit.
Suggested Grade: 4-12
Format: Web Site
Source: Pablo Stafforini
World Wide Web URL: http://www.perfectpitchpeople.com/

Famous Person--Who Am I?
A review activity about historical personalities.
Suggested Grade: 4-9
Format: Online Lesson Plan
Source: Steve Silcox
World Wide Web URL: http://youth.net/cec/cecsst/cecsst.39.txt

4000 Years of Women in Science
Information on more than 125 women who have contributed to science.
Suggested Grade: 4-12
Format: Online Articles
Source: University of Alabama
World Wide Web URL: http://www.astr.ua.edu/4000WS/

Gallery of Achievers
Presents the stories of individuals who have shaped the twentieth century by their accomplishments.
Suggested Grade: 4-12
Format: Web Site
Source: Academy of Achievement
World Wide Web URL: http://www.achievement.org/

Great Thinkers: A Study in Philosophy
Enjoyment and modern application of mankind's greatest philosophers.
Suggested Grade: 6-12
Format: Web Site
Special Notes: This URL will lead you to a subject page. Then click on the appropriate subject heading.
Source: ThinkQuest
World Wide Web URL: http://www.thinkquest.org/pls/html/think.library

Helen Keller Biography
Presents a complete biography of Helen Keller.
Suggested Grade: 4-12
Format: Online Biography
Source: American Foundation for the Blind
World Wide Web URL: http://www.afb.org/info_document_view.asp?documentid=1351

Heroism in Action
Not only provides the biographies of many "heroes," but explains what constitutes a hero and how you can demonstrate "heroism in action."
Suggested Grade: 6-12
Format: Web Site

All materials listed in this 2017-2018 edition are BRAND NEW!

FAMOUS PEOPLE

Special Notes: This URL will lead you to a subject page. Then click on the appropriate subject heading.
Source: ThinkQuest
World Wide Web URL:
http://www.thinkquest.org/pls/html/think.library

Hitler & Stalin
Biographies of two of the most powerful dictators of the twentieth century.
Suggested Grade: 6-12
Format: Web Site
Special Notes: This URL will lead you to a subject page. Then click on the appropriate subject heading.
Source: ThinkQuest
World Wide Web URL:
http://www.thinkquest.org/pls/html/think.library

Indexes of Biographies
Biographies of famous mathematicians--from a to z--and from -500 AD to today.
Suggested Grade: 4-Adult
Format: Web Site
Source: John J. O'Connor and Edmund F. Robertson
World Wide Web URL:
http://www-groups.dcs.st-and.ac.uk/~history/BiogIndex.html

Invention Dimension
Features a different inventor every week. Also includes "The Inventor's Handbook."
Suggested Grade: 6-12
Format: Web Site
Source: MIT
World Wide Web URL:
http://web.mit.edu/invent/invent-main.html

Laura Ingalls Wilder
Provides biographical information about this famous woman.
Suggested Grade: All ages
Format: Web Site
Special Notes: This URL will lead you to a subject page. Then click on the appropriate subject heading.
Source: ThinkQuest
World Wide Web URL:
http://www.thinkquest.org/pls/html/think.library

Leonardo Da Vinci: A Man of Both Worlds
Da Vinci was a painter, sculptor, architect, musician, engineer, inventor and scientist.
Suggested Grade: 6-12
Format: Web Site
Special Notes: This URL will lead you to a subject page. Then click on the appropriate subject heading.
Source: ThinkQuest
World Wide Web URL:
http://www.thinkquest.org/pls/html/think.library

Life of Abraham Lincoln, The: An Illustrated Timeline for Young Readers
Written by young children, for young children, this site tells about the life and times of the 16th President of the United States.
Suggested Grade: K-5
Format: Web Site
Source: Berwick Academy First Grade Students
World Wide Web URL:
http://www.berwickacademy.org/lincoln/lincoln.htm

Meet Amazing Americans
Discover the inventors, politicians, performers, activists and other everyday people who made this country what it is today.
Suggested Grade: All ages
Format: Web Site
Source: Library of Congress
World Wide Web URL:
http://www.americaslibrary.org/cgi-bin/page.cgi/aa

Mop Top the Hip Hop Scientist
Highlights the lives and work of more than a dozen African-Americans in the sciences. Includes interactive activities as well.
Suggested Grade: K-5
Format: Web Site
Source: Jackie Johnson
World Wide Web URL: http://www.moptopshop.com/

National Women's Hall of Fame
Read biographies of the great women who have contributed to our history.
Suggested Grade: 6-12
Format: Web Site
Source: National Women's Hall of Fame
World Wide Web URL: http://www.greatwomen.org/

Philosopher's Lighthouse, The--Shedding Light on Philosophy
Thoughts of Plato, Descartes, Kant, Aristotle, and Augustine.
Suggested Grade: 6-12
Format: Web Site
Special Notes: This URL will lead you to a subject page. Then click on the appropriate subject heading.
Source: ThinkQuest
World Wide Web URL:
http://www.thinkquest.org/pls/html/think.library

Picasso
Learn about the artist, Picasso.
Suggested Grade: 6-12
Format: Web Site
Special Notes: This URL will lead you to a subject page. Then click on the appropriate subject heading.

All materials listed in this 2017-2018 edition are BRAND NEW!

FAMOUS PEOPLE

Source: ThinkQuest
World Wide Web URL:
http://www.thinkquest.org/pls/html/think.library

Shakespeare--His Life and Times
Learn all about this famous playwright.
Suggested Grade: 5-12
Format: Web Site
Special Notes: This URL will lead you to a subject page. Then click on the appropriate subject heading.
Source: ThinkQuest
World Wide Web URL:
http://www.thinkquest.org/pls/html/think.library

"Smart Art"
Teaches all about art through biographies of artists.
Suggested Grade: All ages
Format: Web Site
Special Notes: This URL will lead you to a subject page. Then click on the appropriate subject heading.
Source: ThinkQuest
World Wide Web URL:
http://www.thinkquest.org/pls/html/think.library

Stamps on Black History
Presents complete biographies of the many black Americans who have been honored on a U. S. postage stamp.
Suggested Grade: 4-12
Format: Web Site
Special Notes: This URL will lead you to a subject page. Then click on the appropriate subject heading.
Source: ThinkQuest
World Wide Web URL:
http://www.thinkquest.org/pls/html/think.library

Will the Real Ben Franklin Please Stand Up?
Students will research and debate Benjamin Franklin's most significant role and contribution to the history of the United States.
Suggested Grade: 7-12
Format: Online Lesson Plan
Source: Anna Chan Rekate
World Wide Web URL: http://www.thirteen.org/edonline/lessons/ben_franklin/index.html

*All materials listed in this 2017-2018 edition are **BRAND NEW!***

FOREIGN LANGUAGES

Aboriginal English
Explains the "features" of Aboriginal English--the name given to the various kinds of English spoken by Aboriginal people throughout Australia.
Suggested Grade: 6-12
Format: Online Article
Source: Diana Eades
World Wide Web URL: http://www.hawaii.edu/satocenter/langnet/definitions/aboriginal.html

African Languages at the K-12 Level
Explores the use of dialects and languages of African origin.
Suggested Grade: Teacher Reference
Production Date: 1996
Format: Online Article
Source: Patricia Kuntz
World Wide Web URL: http://www.cal.org/resources/digest/kuntz001.html

Alien Language
The aliens are on a mission to collect creatures from around the galaxy. Blast off and learn the parts of the body with them in four languages.
Suggested Grade: 5-8
Format: Web Site
Source: Alienlanguage.co.uk
World Wide Web URL: http://www.alienlanguage.co.uk/alienlanguage/index.htm

American Sign Language as a Foreign Language
Explores how sign language can be taught as a foreign language.
Suggested Grade: Teacher Reference
Production Date: 1999
Format: Online Article
Source: Sherman Wilcox
World Wide Web URL: http://www.cal.org/resources/digest/ASL.html

Appreciating African Languages
There are over 1,000 languages spoken in Africa! Here is a student lesson plan to help students learn more about the many languages spoken in this country.
Suggested Grade: 2
Format: Online Lesson Plan
Source: Lisa Marchant
World Wide Web URL: http://teacherlink.ed.usu.edu/tlresources/units/byrnes-africa/lismar/index.html

Brain Research: Implications for Second Language Learning
Discusses the value of learning a second language.
Suggested Grade: Teacher Reference
Production Date: 2000
Format: Online Article
Source: Fred Genesee
World Wide Web URL: http://www.ericdigests.org/2001-3/brain.htm

Civilisation Francaise
Online teaching modules for teaching French.
Suggested Grade: 6-12
Format: Web Site
Source: Marie Ponterio
World Wide Web URL: http://www.cortland.edu/flteach/civ/

Coptic Language, The
Presents a history and some lessons on this ancient Egyptian language.
Suggested Grade: 6-12
Format: Web Site
Source: Hany N. Takla
World Wide Web URL: http://www.stshenouda.com/coptlang.htm

Deutsch Plus
A dynamic introduction to German taking you through the basics of the language.
Suggested Grade: 7-12
Format: Online Course
Source: BBC Learning
World Wide Web URL: http://www.bbc.co.uk/languages/german/dplus/

EspanOle!
Information designed to help you find all the information you need to appreciate the Spanish language, its literature, art, people, and much more.
Suggested Grade: 4-12
Format: Web Site
Source: Susan Seraphine-Kimel
World Wide Web URL: http://www.espanole.org/

Free Online Pronunciation Guide
Online pronunciation guides to 7 varieties of the English language and 9 other languages.
Suggested Grade: All ages
Format: Web Site
Source: Fonetiks.org
World Wide Web URL: http://www.fonetiks.org/

French Language Course
Written to help you understand written French and to write a letter to a French friend or correspondent.
Suggested Grade: 4-Adult
Format: Online Language Tutorial
Source: Jacques Leon
World Wide Web URL: http://www.jump-gate.com/languages/french/

All materials listed in this 2017-2018 edition are BRAND NEW!

FOREIGN LANGUAGES

French Online Grammar Quiz
Lots of quizzes to test your knowledge of French grammar.
Suggested Grade: 6-12
Format: Online quizzes
Source: Carol Reitan
World Wide Web URL:
http://fog.ccsf.cc.ca.us/~creitan/grammar.htm

German American Contributions to Mainstream Culture
Explores the many words that are German in origin that have become a part of the American language and way of life.
Suggested Grade: 6-12
Format: Online Lesson Plan
Source: Dolores J. Hoyt
World Wide Web URL:
http://maxkade.iupui.edu/nameword/nameword.html

German for Music Lovers
A web-based multi-media course for learning, reviewing, and improving language skills in German.
Suggested Grade: 4-12
Format: Web Site
Source: A. Campitelli
World Wide Web URL: http://www.acampitelli.com/

Guidelines for Starting an Elementary School Foreign Language Program
How to set up a program to teach young students foreign languages is presented.
Suggested Grade: Teacher Reference
Production Date: 1995
Format: Online Article
Source: Marcia Rosenbusch
World Wide Web URL:
http://www.ericdigests.org/1996-1/starting.htm

Hausa Online Grammar
Provides basic information about the structure of the Hausa language.
Suggested Grade: 6-12
Format: Online Language Lessons
Source: Russell Schuh
World Wide Web URL:
http://aflang.humnet.ucla.edu/Hausa/
Hausa_online_grammar/grammar_frame.html

Integrating Language and Content: Lessons from Immersion
Discusses the language immersion program.
Suggested Grade: Teacher Reference
Production Date: 1995
Format: Online Article
Source: National Center for Research on Cultural Diversity and Second Language Learning
World Wide Web URL:
http://www.cal.org/resources/digest/ncrcds05.html

Interactive On-Line Reference Grammar, An
Lessons on the Russian language.
Suggested Grade: 6-Adult
Format: Online Language Lessons
Source: Robert Beard
World Wide Web URL:
http://www.alphadictionary.com/rusgrammar/index.html

Irish Lessons
Lessons in Irish or English to help you learn "Gaeilge."
Suggested Grade: 4-Adult
Format: Web Site
Source: Mat Brandy
World Wide Web URL: http://www.klammeraffe.org/
~brandy/gaelic/Kurs/index.html

Italian Electronic Classroom, The
Written to provide free on-line, useful information on difficult aspects of the Italian language to students, teachers, translators, and writers.
Suggested Grade: 6-12
Format: Online Language Lessons
Source: Centro Studi Italiani
World Wide Web URL:
http://www.locuta.com/classroom.html

Jambo Means Hello: An Introduction to Swahili
A brief introductory lesson to this language which is one of the most common in Africa.
Suggested Grade: 2-4
Format: Online Lesson Plan
Source: Jane Jurinak-Harris
World Wide Web URL:
http://teacherlink.ed.usu.edu/tlresources/units/
byrnes-africa/janjur/index.html

Kamusi Project, The
A collaborative work by people all over the world, here is a 56,000 entry lexicon for this language.
Suggested Grade: Teacher Reference
Format: Web Site
Source: Kamusi Project
World Wide Web URL: http://www.kamusiproject.org/

Kanienkehaka Language Homepage
Presents the language of the Iroquois.
Suggested Grade: 4-12
Format: Web Site
Source: Kahon:wes
World Wide Web URL:
http://www.kahonwes.com/language/kanienkehaka.html

Languages Across the Curriculum
Learn how to adapt foreign language teaching throughout the curriculum.

All materials listed in this 2017-2018 edition are BRAND NEW!

FOREIGN LANGUAGES

Suggested Grade: Teacher Reference
Production Date: 1998
Format: Online Article
Source: H. Stephen Straight
World Wide Web URL:
http://www.cal.org/resources/digest/lacdigest.html

Learn to Read Bengali
Here are lessons on how to read this language.
Suggested Grade: 4-12
Format: Web Site
Source: UK India
World Wide Web URL:
http://www.ukindia.com/zip/zben01.htm

Learn to Read Punjabi
Lessons on reading this Indian language.
Suggested Grade: 4-12
Format: Web Site
Source: UK India
World Wide Web URL:
http://www.ukindia.com/zpun01.htm

Learn to Read Sanskrit
Here are lessons on how to read this ancient language.
Suggested Grade: 4-12
Format: Web Site
Source: UK India
World Wide Web URL:
http://www.ukindia.com/zip/zsan01.htm

Learn to Read Spanish
Tips on learning to read Spanish.
Suggested Grade: 4-12
Format: Web Site
Source: UK India
World Wide Web URL:
http://www.ukindia.com/zspan1.htm

Learn to Read Tamil
Lessons on reading this language.
Suggested Grade: 4-12
Format: Web Site
Source: UK India
World Wide Web URL:
http://www.ukindia.com/zip/ztm1.htm

Learn to Read Urdu
Here are lessons on how to read this language.
Suggested Grade: 4-12
Format: Web Site
Source: UK India
World Wide Web URL:
http://www.ukindia.com/zurdu1.htm

Little Czech Primer in Pictures
Learn the language of Czechoslovakia pictorially.
Suggested Grade: 4-12
Format: Web Site
Source: Owen Leonard
World Wide Web URL: http://www.czechprimer.org/

Middle Schools and Foreign Languages: A View for the Future
Discusses this issue.
Suggested Grade: Teacher Reference
Production Date: 1996
Format: Online Article
Source: Myriam Met
World Wide Web URL:
http://www.cal.org/resources/digest/met00002.html

On Line Te Reo Course
An online course to help you study the Maori language.
Suggested Grade: 4-12
Format: Online Language Lessons
Source: Maori.org.nz
World Wide Web URL: http://www.maori.org.nz/kotereo/

Planning for Success: Common Pitfalls in the Planning of Early Foreign Language Programs
Discusses these pitfalls.
Suggested Grade: Teacher Reference
Production Date: 2000
Format: Online Article
Source: Helena Curtain
World Wide Web URL:
http://www.ericdigests.org/2001-3/common.htm

Primer on Speaking and Writing Luganda, A
Learn the language of Buganda.
Suggested Grade: 4-12
Format: Web Site
Source: Empandiika y'Oluganda
World Wide Web URL:
http://www.buganda.com/luganda.htm

Quick and Dirty Guide to Japanese, The
Lots of information about this language.
Suggested Grade: 6-12
Format: Online Language Lessons
Source: Tad Perry
World Wide Web URL:
http://users.tmok.com/~tumble/qadgtj.html

Role of Metacognition in Second Language Teaching and Learning, The
Examines the role of "thinking about thinking" in second language teaching and learning.
Suggested Grade: Teacher Reference
Production Date: 2002
Format: Online Article
Source: Neil J. Anderson
World Wide Web URL:
http://www.ericdigests.org/2003-1/role.htm

All materials listed in this 2017-2018 edition are BRAND NEW!

FOREIGN LANGUAGES

Say Hello to the World
If you wanted to say hello to everybody in the world you would have to greet 5,720,000,000 people. If you wanted to say it in their own language, you would have to learn 2,796 languages. Here is a site that will tell you how to say "hello" in each of those languages.
Suggested Grade: 4-12
Format: Web Site
Source: Lorri Mon
World Wide Web URL: http://www.ipl.org/div/hello/

Swedish Language Course, A
Lessons to help you learn "Svenska."
Suggested Grade: 4-Adult
Format: Web Site
Source: Aaron Rubin
World Wide Web URL:
http://www.personal.psu.edu/faculty/a/d/adr10/swedish.html

Verb Conjugation on line
An on-line verb conjugator--117 languages are represented.
Suggested Grade: 6-12
Format: Online Program
Source: Verbix
World Wide Web URL:
http://www.verbix.com/webverbix/index.asp

We Can Talk: Cooperative Learning in the Elementary ESL Classroom
Examines the critical variables for language teaching.
Suggested Grade: Teacher Reference
Production Date: 1995
Format: Online Article
Source: Spencer Kagan
World Wide Web URL:
http://www.cal.org/resources/digest/kagan001.html

Your Voyage to Break the Language Barrier
Learn Spanish, French, German, Italian, or Portuguese.
Suggested Grade: 4-Adult
Format: Web Site
Source: Helen Smith and Will Dechent
World Wide Web URL: http://Deutsch98.tripod.com/Four/

*All materials listed in this 2017-2018 edition are **BRAND NEW!***

GENERAL EDUCATION

ABCteach
A collection of resources on a large number of topics.
Suggested Grade: K-6
Format: Web Site
Source: Sandy Kemsley
World Wide Web URL: http://abcteach.com/

Baltimore Curriculum Project Lesson Plans
Lots of lesson plans.
Suggested Grade: K-5
Format: Online Lesson Plans
Source: Baltimore Curriculum Project
World Wide Web URL: http://www.cstone.net/~bcp/BCPIntro2.htm

Brain Food
Hundreds of word games, logic puzzles, riddles, and more.
Suggested Grade: 4-Adult
Format: Web Site
Source: Samuel Stoddard
World Wide Web URL: http://www.rinkworks.com/brainfood/

EducatingJane.com
Designed specifically for girls and their parents and teachers.
Suggested Grade: 6-Adult
Format: Web Site
Source: EducatingJane.com
World Wide Web URL: http://www.educatingjane.com/

Football Review
A game where students can review and reinforce material they have learned.
Suggested Grade: All ages
Format: Online Lesson Plan
Source: Kelly J. Glodt
World Wide Web URL: http://youth.net/cec/cecmisc/cecmisc.25.txt

Free Education on the Internet
More than 120 different vocational and academic courses.
Suggested Grade: 6-Adult
Format: Online Courses
Source: Free-Ed, Ltd.
World Wide Web URL: http://www.free-ed.net

Fun Facts, Amazing Animal Facts, World Facts and More!
People facts, animal facts, weather facts, and more as well as puzzles and games.
Suggested Grade: All ages
Format: Web Site
Source: GotFacts.com
World Wide Web URL: http://www.gotfacts.com/

Girlstart
Girlstart is a nonprofit organization that promotes, mathematics, science, and technology related skills for girls. This site provides games, activities, and information to this audience.
Suggested Grade: 5-8
Format: Web Site
Source: Girlstart
World Wide Web URL: http://www.girlstart.org/

Hoagies' Gifted Education Page
A resources site with articles, research, and more for parents and educators of gifted children.
Suggested Grade: Teacher Reference
Format: Web Site
Source: Carolyn K.
World Wide Web URL: http://www.hoagiesgifted.org/

How to Earn Commendable Marks in Fourth Grade
A great welcoming device for your fourth grade students at the beginning of the school year.
Suggested Grade: 4
Format: Online Lesson Plan
Source: Randy Bartholomew
World Wide Web URL: http://youth.net/cec/cecmisc/cecmisc.40.txt

Involving Community Members, Parents, and Community Agencies in Student Learning.
Student performance improves when teachers, administrators, parents, and community are involved in education. Here are ideas for exercises.
Suggested Grade: 3-6
Format: Online Lesson Plan
Source: Michelle C. Massion
World Wide Web URL: http://youth.net/cec/cecmisc/cecmisc.17.txt

KidsKonnect
Created by educators to maintain child safety on the Internet, this site is a great homework helper site.
Suggested Grade: K-8
Format: Web Site
Source: KidsKonnect.com
World Wide Web URL: http://www.kidskonnect.com

Knowledge Master
A new question of the day, everyday.
Suggested Grade: All ages
Format: Web Site
Source: Academic Hallmarks
World Wide Web URL: http://www.greatauk.com

Multiage-Educators Home Page, The
Advice and good information on how to set up and maintain a solid multiage program.

All materials listed in this 2017-2018 edition are BRAND NEW!

23

GENERAL EDUCATION

Suggested Grade: K-8
Format: Web Site
Source: Russell Cates
World Wide Web URL: http://www.multiage-education.com

NewsDEN
Presents current events in exciting new ways.
Suggested Grade: All ages
Format: Online Course
Source: Act360 Media Ltd.
World Wide Web URL: http://www.actden.com/

NFBkids
A portal for fun, safe, entertaining, and educational activities. From science adventures, to games with a huggable teddy bear, to making online animation all sorts of activities are here.
Suggested Grade: preK-8
Format: Web Site
Source: National Film Board
World Wide Web URL: http://nfbkids.ca/

Noodle Tools
Complete a short questionnaire and this site selects the best search strategy to achieve them. After the research is done, another program creates a bibliography for you.
Suggested Grade: 6-College
Format: Web Site
Source: Abilock Productions
World Wide Web URL: http://www.noodletools.com/

Process of Sequencing--A Picture Card Game Activity
A game which will allow students to practice the thinking process involved in the sequence of events.
Suggested Grade: K-12
Format: Online Lesson Plan
Source: Sue Worthen
World Wide Web URL: http://youth.net/cec/cecmisc/cecmisc.32.txt

Prongo.com
Games, screensavers, clip art, braintests, and more for children.
Suggested Grade: K-5
Format: Web Site
Source: Prongo.com
World Wide Web URL: http://www.prongo.com

Questioning Techniques
Learn to sharpen your questioning skills.
Suggested Grade: 5-Adult
Format: WebQuest
Source: Syque
World Wide Web URL: http://changingminds.org/techniques/questioning/questioning.htm

Quiz Hub
Age-appropriate learning activities are found here that cover music, science, social studies, math, and more.
Suggested Grade: 3-8
Format: Web Site
Source: Dyann Schmidel and Wanda Wojcik
World Wide Web URL: http://quizhub.com/quiz/quizhub.cfm

Student News Net
Provides current event news, world news, sports information, and much more.
Suggested Grade: 3-8
Format: Web Site
Source: StudentNewsNet
World Wide Web URL: http://www.studentnewsnet.com/

StudyStack.com
An interactive site with virtual flash cars in geography, mathematics, science, history, medicine, and languages.
Suggested Grade: 3-12
Format: Web Site
Source: John Weidner
World Wide Web URL: http://www.studystack.com/java-studysta/frames.jsp

Test Anxiety
Overcome this dreadful hurdle to passing tests.
Suggested Grade: 6-Adult
Format: Online Article
Source: Counseling Center
World Wide Web URL: http://ub-counseling.buffalo.edu/anxiety.shtml

Test of Applied Creativity, Logic, and Reasoning
While this "test" might at first seem to be a joke, it will help students to think logically and with common sense. Sample question: There are 12 one-cent stamps in a dozen. How many two-cent stamps are in a dozen?
Suggested Grade: All ages
Format: Online Lesson Plan
Source: Paul T. Williams
World Wide Web URL: http://youth.net/cec/cecmisc/cecmisc.53.txt

Turn on Inventiveness--Potato Possibilities
The purpose of this lesson is to promote creative right hemispheric thinking by incorporating visual thinking, inventive thinking, and humor in learning.
Suggested Grade: 4-6
Format: Online Lesson Plan
Source: Debbie Holm
World Wide Web URL: http://youth.net/cec/ceclang/ceclang.16.txt

*All materials listed in this 2017-2018 edition are **BRAND NEW!***

GENERAL EDUCATION

UpToTen
Offers over 600 age appropriate learning games and activities.
Suggested Grade: preK-5
Format: Web Site
Special Notes: To gain full access, you must register, however registration is free.
Source: UpToTen
World Wide Web URL: http://www.uptoten.com/

Where Oh Where
This lesson plan can be adjusted from current events to studies of the way of life of people long ago, or various ethnic group projects.
Suggested Grade: 4-12
Format: Online Lesson Plan
Source: Lanette Westerland
World Wide Web URL:
http://youth.net/cec/cecsst/cecsst.62.txt

*All materials listed in this 2017-2018 edition are **BRAND NEW!***

GEOGRAPHY

Achievements and Challenges of Peru, The
Lots of lessons on some of the aspects of Peruvian life and history that are of great significance to understanding the people of Peru today and their situation.
Suggested Grade: 6-12
Format: Online Lesson Plans
Source: Odyssey, The
World Wide Web URL:
http://www.worldtrek.org/odyssey/teachers/perulessons.html

Across the USA
Learn about the landmarks in the United States.
Suggested Grade: 4-9
Format: WebQuest
Source: Linda Starr
World Wide Web URL:
http://www.educationworld.com/a_tech/webquest_orig/webquest_orig004.shtml

Afghanistan: The Harrison Forman Collection
Presents photographs taken in 1969 of this country, before the Russian invasion. The site documents the life and culture of the area during the 1960s.
Suggested Grade: 6-12
Format: Web Site
Source: Harrison Forman
World Wide Web URL:
http://www4.uwm.edu/libraries/digilib/afghan/

Africa: Eating Senegal Style
Students will demonstrate how to eat as people do in Senegal and present information to the class about an individual eating tradition in their own family.
Suggested Grade: 2-4
Format: Online Lesson Plan
Source: Carin Dewey
World Wide Web URL:
http://teacherlink.ed.usu.edu/tlresources/units/byrnes-africa/cardew/index.html

AfriCam
Sit at your computer and watch live pictures of Africa's greatest wilderness areas.
Suggested Grade: All ages
Format: Web Site
Source: AfriCam
World Wide Web URL:
http://www.africam.com/wildlife/index.php

African Art and Culture
Shows students how traditional African art is closely related to African culture, daily life, and religion, and to get students to think about whether their own culture has similar items that could be considered art.
Suggested Grade: 5-10
Format: Online Lesson Plan
Source: Social Studies School Service
World Wide Web URL:
http://www.socialstudies.com/c/%40FDn.LN.XlZjDM/Pages/article.html?article@africanart

African Flags Archive
Click on each image to view the flag of each African country.
Suggested Grade: All ages
Format: Web Site
Source: University of Pennsylvania, African Studies Center
World Wide Web URL:
http://www.sas.upenn.edu/African_Studies/Flags_GIFS/menu_Flag.html

African Folk Tales
Here are several African folk tales to be enjoyed by elementary students.
Suggested Grade: 2-8
Format: Online Folk Tales
Source: Loreen McDonald
World Wide Web URL:
http://www.canteach.ca/elementary/africa.html

Africa--South of the Sahara
You can search by country or region or specific topics to find selected information about Africa.
Suggested Grade: 6-12
Format: Web Site
Source: Karen Fung
World Wide Web URL:
http://www-sul.stanford.edu/depts/ssrg/africa/guide.html

AgMag
Produced and distributed three times each school year and is geared for students in grades 4-6. It's a great resource for your Minnesota studies (geography, history, environmental ed.) and science.
Suggested Grade: 4-6
Format: Downloadable Activity Books
Source: Minnesota Department of Agriculture
World Wide Web URL:
http://www.mda.state.mn.us/kids/agmags.aspx

Another Face--Masks Around the World
Emphasizes the faces of culture and the art of expression using masks from around the world.
Suggested Grade: All ages
Format: Web Site
Source: Yi-Ching Chen
World Wide Web URL: http://gallery.sjsu.edu/masks/

Appomattox Court House Teacher's Packet
A teacher's packet of information for teaching about this historical park in Virginia.
Suggested Grade: All ages
Format: Downloadable Packet of Materials

All materials listed in this 2017-2018 edition are BRAND NEW!

GEOGRAPHY

Source: Appomattox Court House National Historical Park
World Wide Web URL:
http://www.nps.gov/apco/forteachers/index.htm

Buen Viaje a Espana!
Design a brochure that will make others want to visit Madrid, Spain.
Suggested Grade: 5-8
Format: WebQuest
Source: R. De Vall
World Wide Web URL:
http://dupagechildrens.org/resources/learn-online/

Building an African Compound
Students will learn more about the different forms of shelter found in Africa as they construct a model of a compound that might be found in a rural African village.
Suggested Grade: 2-4
Format: Online Lesson Plan
Source: Rebecca Caldwell
World Wide Web URL:
http://teacherlink.ed.usu.edu/tlresources/units/byrnes-africa/REBCAL/REBCAL%7E1.HTM

Canada on Postcards
Students will learn about Canada while creating postcards to share with others.
Suggested Grade: 3-4
Format: Online Lesson Plan
Source: Sara J. Archambault
World Wide Web URL:
http://lessonopoly.org/teacherlessons?q=node/7641

Child's Daily Life in South Africa, A
Students will learn about the daily life of a child in South Africa and compare with the life of a child in America.
Suggested Grade: 2-4
Format: Online Lesson Plan
Source: Alison Batt
World Wide Web URL:
http://teacherlink.ed.usu.edu/tlresources/units/byrnes-africa/AliBat/index.html

Chinese Dragon
Learn how to make this "critter".
Suggested Grade: K-2
Format: Online Lesson Plan
Source: Ilona Lelli
World Wide Web URL:
http://www.kinderart.com/multic/chinesedragon.shtml

Common African Food, A: Fou-Fou
Learn how Africans make, and eat, this common dish.
Suggested Grade: 2-4
Format: Online Lesson Plan
Source: Trecia Olson
World Wide Web URL: http://teacherlink.ed.usu.edu/tlresources/units/byrnes-africa/treols/index.html

Communicating Values and History Through Masks
Students will create an African style mask that depicts a value or character that is important in their community.
Suggested Grade: 2-4
Format: Online Lesson Plan
Source: Tricia McGregor
World Wide Web URL:
http://teacherlink.ed.usu.edu/tlresources/units/byrnes-africa/trimcg/index.htm

Country Reports on Human Rights Practices
Here are copies of reports submitted by the Bureau of Democracy, Human Rights, and Labor on human rights practices in virtually all countries.
Suggested Grade: 6-Adult
Format: Web Site
Source: U. S. Department of State
World Wide Web URL: http://www.state.gov/g/drl/hr/

Cuisine and Etiquette in Sierra Leone, Uganda, and Zambia
Upon completion of this unit, students will make inferences about cultural norms from customs related to eating in three African countries.
Suggested Grade: 3-5
Format: Online Lesson Plan
Source: Peace Corps
World Wide Web URL:
http://www.peacecorps.gov/wws/publications/looking/index.cfm

Cultural Spaces
Many students assume only their cultural and traditional practices are accepted and practiced--this unit will show them differently.
Suggested Grade: 7-12
Format: Online Lesson Plan
Source: Ray McCarter
World Wide Web URL:
http://www.questconnect.org/Africa_Lesson_Plans/Columbia_Education_Center/Cultural_Spaces.htm

Culture of the Frisians
Presents the culture of this province in the Netherlands.
Suggested Grade: 4-Adult
Format: Web Site
Source: Syts and Ade Van der Mal
World Wide Web URL:
http://www.fehmarn-genealogy.com/culture_of_the_frisians.htm

Cultures of the Andes
Provides basic lessons in quechua, literature in English and quechuan, and more to help students learn the cultures of the Andes.

All materials listed in this 2017-2018 edition are BRAND NEW!

GEOGRAPHY

Suggested Grade: 4-Adult
Format: Web Site
Source: Ada and Russ Gibbons
World Wide Web URL: http://www.andes.org/

Edible State Map
Students will make an edible map that shows the major cities in that state.
Suggested Grade: 4
Format: Online Lesson Plan
Source: Mandy Wallace
World Wide Web URL: http://www.atozteacherstuff.com/pages/295.shtml

Electronic Mapping
Here is an interdisciplinary activity which not only helps students locate places on a map but introduces students to the concepts of scale, electricity, and group interaction.
Suggested Grade: 7-12
Format: Online Lesson Plan
Source: Gary E. Meredith
World Wide Web URL: http://ofcn.org/cyber.serv/academy/ace/soc/cecsst/cecsst124.html

ePALS Classroom Exchange
Gives K-12 students and teachers a sense of what everyday life is like in a foreign country--by communicating with others from that country.
Suggested Grade: K-12
Format: Web Site
Source: ePALS
World Wide Web URL: www.epals.comhttp://www.epals.com

Everyday Life in Africa
Students will compare the life of a boy in Africa with their own as well as act out stories they have written in a group.
Suggested Grade: 2-3
Format: Online Lesson Plan
Source: Tara Berge
World Wide Web URL: http://teacherlink.ed.usu.edu/tlresources/units/byrnes-africa/tarber/index.html

Everyone Has a Culture--Everyone Is Different
Invites students to identify aspects of culture that influence our own behavior and sometimes make it difficult to understand the behavior of others.
Suggested Grade: All ages
Format: Online Lesson Plan
Source: Peace Corps
World Wide Web URL: http://www.peacecorps.gov/wws/publications/looking/index.cfm

Expanding Fifth Grade Ethnic Awareness (Latino and Native American) Through Literature
Examines the life of a Latina teenage girl with that of a Native American girl of the same age.
Suggested Grade: 5
Format: Online Lesson Plan
Source: Jean E. Sutherland
World Wide Web URL: http://www.cis.yale.edu/ynhti/curriculum/units/1995/4/95.04.08.x.html

Exploring African Music
Students will come to appreciate African Music and the rich culture it represents.
Suggested Grade: 2-4
Format: Online Lesson Plan
Source: Christine M. Brady
World Wide Web URL: http://teacherlink.ed.usu.edu/tlresources/units/byrnes-africa/chrbra%20folder/index.html

Exploring Caves
Covers geology, cartography, and hydrology in a lighthearted story about Bat, who finds two lost children in a cave and teaches them various lessons as he guides them to safety.
Suggested Grade: K-3
Format: Online Teaching Packet
Source: USGS Information Services
World Wide Web URL: http://egsc.usgs.gov/isb/pubs/teachers-packets/exploringcaves/

Games and Toys Reflect Resources
Students will demonstrate their understanding that different games reflect local resources by creating a type of ball.
Suggested Grade: 2-4
Format: Online Lesson Plan
Source: Ruth Ann Bingham
World Wide Web URL: http://teacherlink.ed.usu.edu/tlresources/units/byrnes-africa/rutbin/index.html

Geographia
Lots of information on a number of countries and places.
Suggested Grade: All ages
Format: Web Site
Source: interKnowledge
World Wide Web URL: http://www.geographia.com

Global Online Adventure Learning Site
Students can log on and follow the adventure of real explorers as they travel.
Suggested Grade: 2-5
Format: Web Site
Source: GOALS, Inc.
World Wide Web URL: http://www.goals.com/index.htm

GEOGRAPHY

Guide to British Life, Culture and Customs
Lots of information about the life, culture, and customs of England.
Suggested Grade: 2-12
Format: Web Site
Source: Woodlands Junior School
World Wide Web URL: http://projectbritain.com/

H-AfrTeach
A discussion list whose mission is to provide a stimulating forum for considering the possibilities and problems involved in teaching about Africa.
Suggested Grade: Teacher Reference
Format: Online Discussion List
Source: H-Net, Humanities & Social Sciences OnLine
World Wide Web URL: http://www2.h-net.msu.edu/~afrteach/

Handbook of Texas Online
A multidisciplinary encyclopedia of Texas history, geography, and culture. Completely searchable.
Suggested Grade: 4-Adult
Format: Online Encyclopedia
Source: General Libraries at the University of Texas at Austin and the Texas State Historical Association
World Wide Web URL: http://www.tshaonline.org/handbook-texas-online-home-page/home/133

Helping Your Child Learn Geography
Teach children geography in ways that are challenging and fun.
Suggested Grade: K-4
Format: Online Article; 36 pages
Special Notes: Use the on-site search engine to easily find this title. You may request a printed copy mailed to you for a fee.
Source: Federal Citizen Information Center
World Wide Web URL: http://publications.usa.gov/USAPubs.php

Homes Around the World
Find out what types of homes other first grade students live in.
Suggested Grade: 1
Format: WebQuest
Source: Stephanie Ashley
World Wide Web URL: http://www.catawba.k12.nc.us/webquest/ashley/

Honoring the Animal Spirits
Explains the importance of animals in the Native American tradition.
Suggested Grade: All ages
Format: Web Site
Source: Powersource Art & Education Center
World Wide Web URL: http://www.powersource.com/gallery/objects/default.html

Hoover Dam Learning Packet
Information about this National landmark.
Suggested Grade: All ages
Format: Downloadable Information Packet
Source: Hoover Dam
World Wide Web URL: http://www.usbr.gov/lc/hooverdam/educate/index.html

Ideas for Exploring Our City and State
Students will explore the world outside their homes and neighborhoods as they study facts about the city and state in which they live.
Suggested Grade: 1-2
Format: Online Lesson Plan
Source: Tracey Roudez
World Wide Web URL: http://teacher.scholastic.com/lessonplans/unit_citiesandstates.htm

Japanese Education in Grades K-12
Discusses the educational system in Japan.
Suggested Grade: Teacher Reference
Production Date: 2001
Format: Online Article
Source: Lucien Ellington
World Wide Web URL: http://www.ericdigests.org/2002-2/japanese.htm

Kameshi Ne Mpuku: An African Game
As students learn the rules of this African game, they will learn more about how games reflect the environment of those who play them.
Suggested Grade: 2-4
Format: Online Lesson Plan
Source: Angie Bird
World Wide Web URL: http://teacherlink.ed.usu.edu/tlresources/units/byrnes-africa/angbir/index.htm

Learning the Compass
Teaches students how to read and follow the points on a compass.
Suggested Grade: 5
Format: Online Tutorial
Source: Three Dads Courseware
World Wide Web URL: http://www.angelfire.com/fl/compless/index.html

Let Me Tell You About My State!
The purpose of this activity is to develop an awareness of the concept of the "United" States and to "learn to learn."
Suggested Grade: 5
Format: Online Lesson Plan
Source: Melinda Swain
World Wide Web URL: http://youth.net/cec/ceclang/ceclang.60.txt

Living Gulf, The: A Place to Treasure
Identifies the many treasures of the Gulf of Mexico.

All materials listed in this 2017-2018 edition are BRAND NEW!

GEOGRAPHY

Suggested Grade: 4-12
Format: Downloadable Booklet
Special Notes: Also available on CD.
Source: Offshore Operators Committee
World Wide Web URL:
http://www.offshoreoperators.com/brochure.shtml

Make a Village
Set up streets, buildings, and more to learn about math, architecture, or even just for fun.
Suggested Grade: 2-8
Format: Downloadable FULL PROGRAM
Source: Owl & Mouse Educational Software
World Wide Web URL:
http://www.yourchildlearns.com/owlmouse.htm

Making an Illustrated Dictionary with Geographic Terms
As a result of this activity, students will be able to apply geographic terms in describing and understanding the specific places of study in the world.
Suggested Grade: 5-8
Format: Online Lesson Plan
Source: Anita M. Scanga
World Wide Web URL: http://ofcn.org/cyber.serv/academy/ace/soc/cecsst/cecsst120.html

Masai and I: A Cultural Comparison
Students will orally share similarities and differences between their culture and the Masai culture.
Suggested Grade: 2-4
Format: Online Lesson Plan
Source: Amy McMillan
World Wide Web URL:
http://teacherlink.ed.usu.edu/tlresources/units/byrnes-africa/amymcm/index.html.htm

Mathematics of Cartography
A tutorial on map making.
Suggested Grade: 4-12
Format: Online Tutorial
Source: Cynthia Lanius
World Wide Web URL:
http://math.rice.edu/~lanius/pres/map/

MegaMaps--Walk Through the Continents
Print U. S. and world maps ranging from a single page to 8 pages.
Suggested Grade: All ages
Format: Downloadable FULL PROGRAM
Special Notes: Also available in an online version.
Source: Owl & Mouse Educational Software
World Wide Web URL:
http://www.yourchildlearns.com/owlmouse.htm

Mexican WebQuest
Students will use the Internet to research a topic related to Mexico's culture, history, or geography.
Suggested Grade: 5-8
Format: WebQuest
Source: Kim Whittaker
World Wide Web URL: http://www.ga.k12.pa.us/academics/US/ModLang/mexico/mexico98.htm

Mini-Unit Topic: Native Americans
An introductory unit to Native Americans and discusses what is important to Native Americans.
Suggested Grade: 2
Format: Online Lesson Plan
Source: Diana Altenhoff
World Wide Web URL: http://www.ed.uiuc.edu/YLP/Units/Mini_Units/94-95/Altenhoff.Native-American/index.html

Minnesota State Highway Map
A downloadable map of this state which features a city index, regional maps, state, parks, and more.
Suggested Grade: All ages
Format: Downloadable Map
Source: Minnesota Department of Transportation
World Wide Web URL:
http://www.dot.state.mn.us/statemap/

Mr. Dowling's Electronic Passport
A journey through time and space with information (and links to information) about periods of time as well as a multitude of countries.
Suggested Grade: 5-8
Format: Web Site
Special Notes: Also includes downloadable lesson plans.
Source: Mr. Dowling
World Wide Web URL: http://www.mrdowling.com

National Geographic GeoBee Challenge
Related to the National Geographic Society's annual Geographic Bee, here are interactive geography quizzes.
Suggested Grade: 3-8
Format: Web Site
Source: National Geographic Society
World Wide Web URL:
http://www.nationalgeographic.com/geobee

Nile Adventure
A virtual tour down the world's longest river.
Suggested Grade: All ages
Format: Web Site
Source: Tour Egypt
World Wide Web URL:
http://touregypt.net/wildegypt/nile1.htm

Not "Indians," Many Tribes: Native American Diversity
In this lesson, students will heighten their awareness of Native American diversity as they learn about three vastly different Native groups in a game-like activity.
Suggested Grade: 3-5
Format: Online Lesson Plan

All materials listed in this 2017-2018 edition are **BRAND NEW!**

GEOGRAPHY

Source: EDSITEment
World Wide Web URL:
http://edsitement.neh.gov/view_lesson_plan.asp?id=324

Passion for Change: Investigating the Evolution of Cultural Traditions
Students reflect upon traditional, cultural, or ritualized events and research the evolution of such events.
Suggested Grade: 6-12
Format: Online Lesson Plan
Source: Elyse Fischer and Javaid Khan
World Wide Web URL:
http://nytimes.com/learning/teachers/lessons/20030418friday.html

Pictures of Places.com
Offers links to websites offering pictures of geographical places and sights world-wide.
Suggested Grade: All ages
Format: Web Site
Source: MindTravellers Inc.
World Wide Web URL: http://www.picturesofplaces.com/

Quiero Viajar a Espana!
For Spanish level 3 learners and above, this WebQuest will help students learn more about Spain.
Suggested Grade: 7-Adult
Format: WebQuest
Source: Megan Simon and Asha Bandal
World Wide Web URL:
http://www.churchofsaintann.info/smith/IWantToTravelToSpainProject.htm

Search Hawaii! Cultural and Educational Pages
Lots of information about this beautiful state.
Suggested Grade: 4-12
Format: Web Site
Source: Search Hawaii
World Wide Web URL:
http://www.search-hawaii.com:8765/vacation/culture.html?cat=5

Sioux Indians, The
Students will learn about this tribe of Indians and make tortilla teepees.
Suggested Grade: 3
Format: Online Lesson Plan
Source: Kerri Byrd
World Wide Web URL:
http://www.lessonplanspage.com/SSTheSiouxIndiansAndTortillaTeepees3.htm

States Mania
An educational game covering all fifty states.
Suggested Grade: All ages
Format: Downloadable FULL PROGRAM

Source: Sheppard Software
World Wide Web URL:
http://www.sheppardsoftware.com/teachers.htm

Teaching About Africa
Provides a lot of suggestions for teaching about this country.
Suggested Grade: Teacher Reference
Format: Online Article
Source: Susan E. Hume
World Wide Web URL:
http://www.ericdigests.org/1996-4/africa.htm

This Dynamic Planet
A world map showing volcanoes, earthquakes, and plate tectonics.
Suggested Grade: 4-12
Format: Downloadable Map
Special Notes: Available for $7.00 by mail.
Source: USGS Information Services
World Wide Web URL:
http://pubs.usgs.gov/pdf/planet.html

United States Climate Page
A clickable map that allows you to locate a specific state and learn more about its weather and climate.
Suggested Grade: All ages
Format: Online Map
Source: National Oceanic and Atmospheric Administration
World Wide Web URL:
http://www.cdc.noaa.gov/USclimate/states.fast.html

U. S. States & Capitals Concentration Game
Match the state to its capital city.
Suggested Grade: 3-6
Format: Downloadable FULL PROGRAM
Source: School Express
World Wide Web URL:
http://www.schoolexpress.com/compsoft/software01.php

Vietnam: A Children's Guide
An easy-to-navigate site created for children, by children, to help them learn about this country.
Suggested Grade: K-5
Format: Web Site
Source: Mrs. Taverna
World Wide Web URL:
http://www.pocanticohills.org/vietnam/vietnam.htm

Virginia State Transportation Map
Print all 10 of the 8 1/2 x 11 inch pieces you can download here and you will have a complete map of Virginia.
Suggested Grade: All ages
Format: Downloadable Maps
Source: Virginia Department of Transportation
World Wide Web URL:
http://www.virginiadot.org/programs/prog-byways-map-printable.asp

All materials listed in this 2017-2018 edition are BRAND NEW!

GEOGRAPHY

World Factbook
Information on countries around the world.
Suggested Grade: All ages
Format: Online Book
Source: Central Intelligence Agency
World Wide Web URL:
https://www.cia.gov/library/publications/the-world-factbook/index.html

World on a String, The
A total group lesson using the themes of geography to illustrate the interdependence of countries.
Suggested Grade: 4-8
Format: Online Lesson Plan
Source: Shirley Lomax
World Wide Web URL: http://ofcn.org/cyber.serv/academy/ace/soc/cecsst/cecsst041.html

Yak's Corner
A weekly online magazine.
Suggested Grade: 3-8
Format: Online Magazine
Source: Detroit Free Press
World Wide Web URL: http://www.yakscorner.com/

*All materials listed in this 2017-2018 edition are **BRAND NEW**!*

GOVERNMENT

Annenberg Classroom
Includes lesson plans, curricular materials and other teaching aids for students and teachers of civics and government.
Suggested Grade: 6-12
Format: Web Site
Source: Annenberg Public Policy Center
World Wide Web URL:
http://www.annenbergclassroom.org/

Ask the Presidents
Penny shows her lack of understanding of and knowledge about the presidency when she e-mails to her teacher a joke about the president. Her teacher's reaction spurs Penny to go online to learn more about what a president does.
Suggested Grade: 3-6
Format: Downloadable Theater Script
Source: Cara Bafile
World Wide Web URL:
http://www.educationworld.com/a_curr/reading/ReadersTheater/ReadersTheater007.shtml

Ben's Guide to U. S. Government for Kids
Information for all ages, including games and activities, about how the U. S. Government works.
Suggested Grade: All ages
Format: Web Site
Source: U. S. Government Printing Office
World Wide Web URL: http://bensguide.gpo.gov/

Citizenship and the Constitution
This lesson helps students be informed citizens on a local, state, and national level.
Suggested Grade: 7-12
Format: Online Lesson Plan
Source: Tana Carney Preciado
World Wide Web URL:
http://youth.net/cec/cecsst/cecsst.92.txt

Constitution of the United States and the Declaration of Independence
Learn more about the foundations of our country's freedom with the full text of both historic documents.
Suggested Grade: 4-Adult
Production Date: 2003
Format: Online Article; 48 pages
Special Notes: Use the on-site search engine to easily find this title. You may request a printed copy mailed to you for a fee.
Source: Federal Citizen Information Center
World Wide Web URL:
http://publications.usa.gov/USAPubs.php

Constitution, The: Our Plan for Government
A lesson on the Constitution of the United States.
Suggested Grade: 8-9
Format: Online Lesson Plan
Source: Willie Jefferson
World Wide Web URL:
http://ofcn.org/cyber.serv/academy/ace/soc/cecsst/cecsst172.html

Declare the Causes: The Declaration of Independence
Explore the development of the Declaration of Independence.
Suggested Grade: 3-5
Format: Online Lesson Plan
Source: EDSITEment
World Wide Web URL:
http://edsitement.neh.gov/view_lesson_plan.asp?id=282

How a Bill Becomes a Law
Understand how our government introduces and passes laws, and makes policy decisions, and also develop an increased awareness of issues affecting their lives.
Suggested Grade: 7-8
Format: Online Lesson Plan
Source: David A. Rojo
World Wide Web URL:
http://youth.net/cec/cecsst/cecsst.29.txt

How Our Laws Are Made
Presented by the Parliamentarian to the United States House of Representatives, this web site presents the rules and regulations concerning how laws are made and passed in the United States.
Suggested Grade: 6-Adult
Format: Web Site
Source: John V. Sullivan
World Wide Web URL:
http://thomas.loc.gov/home/lawsmade.toc.html

Interactive Constitution
Search the Constitution, discover how it relates to more than 300 indexed topics, and search the Constitution by Supreme Court decisions.
Suggested Grade: 6-Adult
Format: Searchable Online Constitution
Source: National Constitution Center
World Wide Web URL:
http://www.constitutioncenter.org/constitution/

Issue-Centered Civic Education in Middle Schools
Discusses this topic.
Suggested Grade: Teacher Reference
Production Date: 1999
Format: Online Article
Source: Thomas S. Vontz and William A. Nixon
World Wide Web URL:
http://www.ericdigests.org/1999-4/civic.htm

All materials listed in this 2017-2018 edition are BRAND NEW!

GOVERNMENT

Justice
Students experience brainstorming and open-ended questioning strategies and research to develop a better understanding of the Justice System.
Suggested Grade: 7-12
Format: Online Lesson Plan
Source: Melanie McCool
World Wide Web URL:
http://youth.net/cec/cecsst/cecsst.104.txt

Justice for Kids and Youth
Information about the FBI, criminology, and the court system. There is something for all ages here.
Suggested Grade: K-12
Format: Web Site
Source: U. S. Department of Justice
World Wide Web URL:
http://www.usdoj.gov/usao/eousa/kidspage/

Kids Next Door
Designed to help students explore the principles of being a good citizen.
Suggested Grade: K-5
Format: Web Site
Source: U. S. Department of Housing and Urban Development
World Wide Web URL:
http://www.hud.gov/kids/index.html

Know Your Local Government
The purpose of this activity is to introduce students to the local government structure and the people in the various power positions.
Suggested Grade: 3-12
Format: Online Lesson Plan
Source: Peg Stout
World Wide Web URL:
http://inside.augsburg.edu/publicachievement/files/2012/12/KnowYourLocalGovernment.pdf

Laws--Who Needs Them?
Illustrates why laws and rules are needed.
Suggested Grade: 7-9
Format: Online Lesson Plan
Source: Deb Gehrman
World Wide Web URL:
http://ofcn.org/cyber.serv/academy/ace/soc/cecsst/cecsst016.html

Our Flag
Details the history and customs of the United States flag.
Suggested Grade: All ages
Production Date: 2003
Format: Downloadable Booklet; 52 pages
Special Notes: Use the on-site search engine to easily find this title. You may request a printed copy mailed to you for a fee.
Source: Federal Citizen Information Center
World Wide Web URL:
http://publications.usa.gov/USAPubs.php

Oyez Baseball
This game compares Supreme Court justices from the United States with baseball players--learn more about our highest court and the people who have served on it.
Suggested Grade: 7-Adult
Format: Online Game
Source: Jerry Goldman and Paul Manna
World Wide Web URL: http://baseball.oyez.org/

Politics & Political Campaigns
Info about U. S. elections and political parties, as well as biographies.
Suggested Grade: 6-12
Format: Web Site
Special Notes: This URL will lead you to a subject page. Then click on the appropriate subject heading.
Source: ThinkQuest
World Wide Web URL:
http://www.thinkquest.org/pls/html/think.library

Presidential Interview: A Panel of Presidents
A structured forum of the last five Presidents of the United States recapping their foreign and domestic policies, through interviews.
Suggested Grade: 8
Format: Online Lesson Plan
Source: Susie A. Scott
World Wide Web URL:
http://youth.net/cec/cecsst/cecsst.46.txt

Private See Dispute
This lesson is an eye-opener on reasonable expectations of privacy with regard to camera cellphones and digital cameras.
Suggested Grade: 6-12
Format: Online Lesson Plan
Source: Elyse Fischer and Javaid Khan
World Wide Web URL:
http://nytimes.com/learning/teachers/lessons/20031013monday.html

Reorganizing the Bill of Rights
Asks students to look critically at the 26 amendments.
Suggested Grade: 8
Format: Online Lesson Plan
Source: Scott Wallace
World Wide Web URL:
http://youth.net/cec/cecsst/cecsst.89.txt

Star Politics
Students are asked to examine their opinions about celebrities in politics and then do some research about the effectiveness of celebrities in government positions.

All materials listed in this 2017-2018 edition are BRAND NEW!

GOVERNMENT

Suggested Grade: 6-12
Format: Online Lesson Plan
Source: Michelle Sale and Bridget Anderson
World Wide Web URL:
http://nytimes.com/learning/teachers/lessons/20031009thursday.html

Teaching America's Founding Documents

Identifies four founding documents and the great ideas in them and discusses how to teach about these documents.
Suggested Grade: Teacher Reference
Production Date: 2002
Format: Online Article
Source: John J. Patrick
World Wide Web URL:
http://www.ericdigests.org/2003-3/documents.htm

Teaching Democracy

Discusses the status of democracy in the world and more.
Suggested Grade: Teacher Reference
Format: Online Article
Source: John J. Patrick
World Wide Web URL:
http://www.ericdigests.org/2004-2/democracy.html

ThisNation.com

A repository of basic information, resources and historical documents related to American government and politics.
Suggested Grade: 6-Adult
Format: Web Site
Source: Jonathan Mott
World Wide Web URL: http://www.thisnation.com/

Voting Simulation

Students will become aware of the rights and responsibilities of voting.
Suggested Grade: 4-12
Format: Online Lesson Plan
Source: Kathy L. Peck
World Wide Web URL:
http://youth.net/cec/cecsst/cecsst.90.txt

Your Own Classroom Court

Students will learn more about how the court system works while they set up their own classroom court.
Suggested Grade: 5-12
Format: Online Lesson Plan
Source: Rita Irene Esparza
World Wide Web URL:
http://ofcn.org/cyber.serv/academy/ace/soc/cecsst/cecsst006.html

*All materials listed in this 2017-2018 edition are **BRAND NEW!***

GUIDANCE

America's Career InfoNet
A comprehensive source of occupational and economic information to help you make informed career decisions.
Suggested Grade: 6-Adult
Format: Web Site
Source: America's Career InfoNet
World Wide Web URL: http://www.acinet.org/acinet/

Box of Crayons, A
A lesson to teach youngsters that people of all colors can get along.
Suggested Grade: K-2
Format: Online Lesson Plan
Source: Eileen Urbanski
World Wide Web URL: http://www.kinderart.com/multic/mlkjr_crayons.shtml

Career Development for All Students
Provides a model for career development education with activities for students of all ages.
Suggested Grade: 2-12
Format: Online Article
Source: Susan Schoket
World Wide Web URL: http://www.teachnet.com/lesson/real/career4all/index.html

Career Guide for the Atmospheric Sciences, A
Detailed information about the many careers available within this field.
Suggested Grade: 6-Adult
Format: Online Article
Source: American Meteorological Society
World Wide Web URL: http://www.ametsoc.org/atmoscareers/index.html

Careers and Industries Overview
Information about careers in various industries--many of which are new.
Suggested Grade: 6-Adult
Format: Web Site
Source: WetFeet, Inc.
World Wide Web URL: https://www.wetfeet.com/articles/careers-and-industries-overview

Careers in Accounting
Articles about a career in accounting.
Suggested Grade: 6-12
Format: Web Site
Source: Careers-in-accounting.com
World Wide Web URL: http://www.careers-in-accounting.com/

Careers in Aging
Explains the many opportunities for a career in this field and discusses the rewards of such a career.
Suggested Grade: 6-12
Format: Online Article
Special Notes: This is a PDF file which will open automatically on your computer.
Source: Association for Gerontology in Higher Education, The
World Wide Web URL: http://www.aghe.org/clientimages/40634/careersinaging_brochure.pdf

Careers in Psychology
Answers questions about what working in psychology is like and what educational requirements are needed.
Suggested Grade: 7-12
Format: Downloadable Brochure
Source: American Psychological Association
World Wide Web URL: http://www.apa.org/careers/resources/guides/careers.aspx

Careers in the Genetics Field
Provides descriptions of a variety of training and career opportunities through profiles of professionals who make unique contributions to the field of genetics.
Suggested Grade: 6-Adult
Format: Online Brochure
Source: Federation of American Societies for Experimental Biology
World Wide Web URL: http://genetics.faseb.org/genetics/gsa/careers/bro-menu.htm

Career WebQuest
Students must make a pamphlet about a career designed to help others consider that profession.
Suggested Grade: 4-8
Format: WebQuest
Source: Ms. L. MacDonald
World Wide Web URL: http://hrsbstaff.ednet.ns.ca/macdonlm1/webquest.htm

Challenges of Our Changing Atmosphere: Careers in Atmospheric Research and Applied Meteorology
Information on what to study to be a meteorologist. Also provides information on the duties and benefits of a career in this field.
Suggested Grade: 6-Adult
Format: Online Article
Source: American Meteorological Society
World Wide Web URL: http://www.ametsoc.org/pubs/careers.html

Changing Attitudes in America
Written to facilitate and foster greater interracial understanding, friendship, and cooperation among residents of the United States.
Suggested Grade: 5-6
Format: Online Lesson Plan
Source: Carolyn Kinder
World Wide Web URL: http://www.yale.edu/ynhti/curriculum/units/1994/4/94.04.04.x.html

*All materials listed in this 2017-2018 edition are **BRAND NEW!***

GUIDANCE

Communication Strategies for Employment Interviews
Here is preparation for individuals who are job seeking--suggests some resources to consult to help improve basic communication skills needed for the interview process.
Suggested Grade: Teacher Reference
Production Date: 1992
Format: Online Article
Source: Nola Kortner Aiex
World Wide Web URL: http://www.ericdigests.org/1992-4/interviews.htm

Coping with Death and Dying
Helpful information on coping with losing a loved one.
Suggested Grade: All ages
Format: Online Article
Source: Counseling Center
World Wide Web URL: http://ub-counseling.buffalo.edu/deathgrief.shtml

Cultural Plunge, A
Here is a well-written article, written by an adult, that attempts to picture the feelings of a new, non-English speaking, second grader on their first day of school in the United States.
Suggested Grade: Teacher Reference
Format: Online Article
Source: Gary Fortune
World Wide Web URL: http://www.edchange.org/multicultural/papers/garyfortune.html

Entertainment Careers
Tells about the many careers available in the entertainment industry--movies, television shows, and commercials.
Suggested Grade: 6-Adult
Format: Web Site
Source: EntertainmentCareers.Net
World Wide Web URL: http://www.entertainmentcareers.cc/

Exploring Occupations: Getting You Started on Your Career Path!
Lots of links to descriptions of various occupations.
Suggested Grade: 6-12
Format: Web Site
Source: University of Manitoba Counseling Service
World Wide Web URL: http://www.umanitoba.ca/counselling/careers.html

50 Careers in Trees
From accountant to writer, and 48 more in between, here is information about careers that involve trees.
Suggested Grade: 6-Adult
Format: Web Site
Source: Tree Foundation of Kern
World Wide Web URL: http://www.urbanforest.org/index.cfm/fuseaction/Pages.Page/id/430

Gender Stereotypes and Advertisements
Shows students how to focus on the subtle messages, and not so subtle ones, that contain stereotypes and bias toward either females and/or males in magazine ads.
Suggested Grade: 4-6
Format: Online Lesson Plan
Source: Christopher Colson
World Wide Web URL: http://www.ricw.state.ri.us/lessons/86.htm

Handouts and Information Guides
Here are a number of articles covering a range of preK-12 educational, career planning, and decision-making topics and issues.
Suggested Grade: All ages
Format: Web Site
Source: State of Queensland, The
World Wide Web URL: http://education.qld.gov.au/students/service/career/handouts.html

In My Other Life
Designed to challenge stereotypes about cultures unfamiliar to us and to expand awareness of the range of factors that help constitute a cultural identity.
Suggested Grade: 6-8
Format: Online Lesson Plan
Source: EDSITEment
World Wide Web URL: http://edsitement.neh.gov/view_lesson_plan.asp?id=272

Job Genie
Provides descriptions for 12,741 different jobs. (Available on CD for $99--website is absolutely free.)
Suggested Grade: 6-Adult
Format: Web Site
Special Notes: Available to purchase on CD for $99.
Source: Stephen Fournier
World Wide Web URL: http://www.stepfour.com/jobs/

Language in Classroom Texts
The overall objective of this lesson is to teach children to be more aware of the kind of bias, stereotyping, and discrimination that is present in school materials.
Suggested Grade: 4-6
Format: Online Lesson Plan
Source: Catharine A. Fisher
World Wide Web URL: http://www.ricw.state.ri.us/lessons/93.htm

Let's Get Along
A book by Eve Bunting teaches valuable lessons about getting along with people we do not know.
Suggested Grade: 3-8
Production Date: 2007
Format: Online Lesson Plan
Source: Kristina Davenport
World Wide Web URL: http://www.educationworld.com/a_tsl/archives/07-1/lesson014.shtml

All materials listed in this 2017-2018 edition are BRAND NEW!

GUIDANCE

LifeWorks
An interactive career web site on which users can browse for information on more than 100 medical science and health careers.
Suggested Grade: 6-12
Format: Web Site
    Source: National Institutes of Health, Office of Science Education
    World Wide Web URL: http://science.education.nih.gov/LifeWorks.nsf/feature/indexhtm

Marinecareers
Information on a wide range of marine career fields.
Suggested Grade: 6-12
Format: Web Site
    Source: WHOI Sea Grant Program
    World Wide Web URL: http://www.marinecareers.net/

Matching Yourself with the World of Work
Find out what jobs are available in the fields you enjoy.
Suggested Grade: 6-Adult
Format: Downloadable Booklet; 19 pages
Special Notes: Use the on-site search engine to easily find this title. You may request a printed copy mailed to you for a fee.
    Source: Federal Citizen Information Center
    World Wide Web URL: http://publications.usa.gov/USAPubs.php

Military Careers
Provides information about each of the 4,100 careers available in the armed services.
Suggested Grade: 6-Adult
Format: Web Site
    Source: Today's Military
    World Wide Web URL: http://www.todaysmilitary.com/careers

Occupational Outlook Handbook
The standard source for career information is online.
Suggested Grade: 6-Adult
Format: Online Book
    Source: Bureau of Labor Statistics
    World Wide Web URL: http://www.bls.gov/oco/

Out on a Limb--A Guide to Getting Along
Online exercises dealing with conflict resolution as well as a teacher's guide with lessons and activities.
Suggested Grade: 3
Format: Web Site
    Source: University of Illinois Extension Urban Programs Resource Network
    World Wide Web URL: http://urbanext.illinois.edu/conflict/index.html

Practical Do-Ables for Unlearning Racism
Tells how we can work to eliminate racism.
Suggested Grade: Teacher Reference
Format: Online Article
Special Notes: Originally published in the September/October 1998 issue of Message.
    Source: Caleb Rosado
    World Wide Web URL: http://edchange.org/multicultural/papers/caleb/Race_Message.txt

Quick Facts
Presents information about a career as a physician assistant.
Suggested Grade: 6-Adult
Format: Online Article
    Source: American Academy of Physician Assistants
    World Wide Web URL: http://www.ericdigests.org/1996-1/violence.htm

Random Acts of Kindness Activities
Hundreds of kindness activity ideas for schools, the community and the workplace.
Suggested Grade: All ages
Format: Downloadable Activity Guide
    Source: Random Acts of Kindness Foundation
    World Wide Web URL: http://www.randomactsofkindness.org/school-activity-ideas

Random Acts of Kindness Lesson Plans
Includes lessons for all ages.
Suggested Grade: All ages
Format: Online Lesson Plans
    Source: Random Acts of Kindness Foundation
    World Wide Web URL: http://www.randomactsofkindness.org/lesson-plans-pilot-program

Resolving Conflicts and Making Peace: Basic Skills for Young Children
It makes sense to initiate peacemaking behaviors and the skills to resolve conflicts in very young children. This article discusses how to do this.
Suggested Grade: K-5
Format: Online Article
Special Notes: This is a PDF file which will open automatically on your computer.
    Source: Ellen M. Ilfeld
    World Wide Web URL: http://www.ecdgroup.com/download/cc119bri.pdf

Right to Equal Opportunity
Designed to help students be able to recognize gender bias, stereotyping and discrimination in school materials and list strategies to cover such biases.
Suggested Grade: K-4
Format: Online Lesson Plan
    Source: Grethe Cobb
    World Wide Web URL: http://www.ricw.state.ri.us/lessons/29.htm

*All materials listed in this 2017-2018 edition are **BRAND NEW!***

GUIDANCE

Risk Behavior
Impacts upon students the extent their behavior has to do with the possible contraction of HIV and how they can control their lives.
Suggested Grade: 7-12
Format: Online Lesson Plan
Source: Shirley Kapitzke
World Wide Web URL:
http://youth.net/cec/cecmisc/cecmisc.70.txt

Roll of Thunder: Hear My Cry Web Quest
A WebQuest that discusses segregation and its effects.
Suggested Grade: 8
Format: WebQuest
Source: Jennifer Wronkovich
World Wide Web URL:
http://www.bgsu.edu/colleges/library/crc/webquest/rollofthunder/index.html

Self-Esteem Activity
This introduces the positive/negative ratio by asking "How positive are you feeling today?". Listening skills and good feelings come from this positive attention.
Suggested Grade: 4-7
Format: Online Lesson Plan
Source: Myrna Caron
World Wide Web URL:
http://youth.net/cec/cecmisc/cecmisc.09.txt

Talking to Your Child About Bias and Prejudice
Explains how to talk to your children about hatred and violence.
Suggested Grade: Adult
Format: Online Article
Source: Caryl M. Stern-LaRosa
World Wide Web URL: http://www.adl.org/issue_education/hateprejudice/Prejudice1.asp

Teen Central.Net
Allows teens to share their own stories, read stories by others, and get feedback from trained professionals who can help them.
Suggested Grade: 6-12
Format: Web Site
Source: KidsPeace
World Wide Web URL: http://www.teencentral.net/

Thinking of a Careers i Applied Mathematics
This brochure demonstrates that a career in applied mathematics isn't just about crunching numbers.
Suggested Grade: 7-12
Format: Downloadable Brochure
Source: Society for Industrial and Applied Mathematics
World Wide Web URL:
http://www.siam.org/careers/thinking.php

Use of "Substitution" As a Creative Thinking Tool, The
A creative thinking lesson--part of a six week unit.
Suggested Grade: 1-6
Format: Online Lesson Plan
Source: Miriam Furst
World Wide Web URL:
http://youth.net/cec/cecmisc/cecmisc.28.txt

What If?
A WebQuest about making decisions--based on what if people from history had performed different actions than they actually did.
Suggested Grade: 4
Format: WebQuest
Source: Amye J. Cooley
World Wide Web URL: http://www.my-ecoach.com/online/uploads/project4635stepdef103/WebQuest.htm

Who's in the Bag?
Often negative social attitudes and low self-esteem hinder interaction. This introduces teacher and students to each other.
Suggested Grade: 4-6
Format: Online Lesson Plan
Source: Lorna Hockett
World Wide Web URL:
http://youth.net/cec/cecmisc/cecmisc.05.txt

Women in Oceanography
This site focuses on women who have dedicated their professional lives to academic research in the field of oceanography.
Suggested Grade: 6-Adult
Format: Web Site
Source: Scripps Institution of Oceanography
World Wide Web URL:
http://web.archive.org/web/20010802232238/http://www.siommg.ucsd.edu/wio/

*All materials listed in this 2017-2018 edition are **BRAND NEW!***

39

HEALTH AND PHYSICAL EDUCATION

Adolescent & School Health
Visitors to this site will find the latest research on student health as well as information on school health strategies. Designed to improve the physical fitness of young people.
Suggested Grade: All ages
Format: Web Site
Source: Adolescent and School Health
World Wide Web URL:
http://www.cdc.gov/nccdphp/dash/index.htm

Ah Choo!
Students use the Internet to find and compare illnesses that they have had or that they have heard about in the media.
Suggested Grade: 5-8
Format: Online Lesson Plan
Source: Jerry Citron
World Wide Web URL:
http://www.thirteen.org/edonline/lessons/achoo/index.html

Alcohol, Peer Pressure and Underage Drinking Info for Young Teens
Offers valuable information about underage drinking, alcohol addiction, and more.
Suggested Grade: 5-8
Format: Web Site
Source: National Institute on Alcohol Abuse and Alcoholism
World Wide Web URL: http://www.thecoolspot.gov/

Anxiety Disorders
Discusses treatments available and resources to contact for more information on panic phobias, stress, obsessive compulsive, and other disorders.
Suggested Grade: 4-Adult
Format: Online Article; 24 pages
Special Notes: Use the on-site search engine to easily find this title. You may request a printed copy mailed to you for a fee.
Source: Federal Citizen Information Center
World Wide Web URL:
http://publications.usa.gov/USAPubs.php

Are Bioengineered Foods Safe?
Get the facts on what bioengineering is, how it affects humans, and what the FDA is doing to regulate the industry.
Suggested Grade: 7-Adult
Format: Online Article; 6 pages
Special Notes: Use the on-site search engine to easily find this title. You may request a printed copy mailed to you for a fee.
Source: Federal Citizen Information Center
World Wide Web URL:
http://publications.usa.gov/USAPubs.php

Ball Monster
A great indoor activity using basketballs.
Suggested Grade: 5-7
Format: Online Lesson Plan
Source: Kim Winters
World Wide Web URL: http://www.pecentral.org/lessonideas/ViewLesson.asp?ID=4986

Beanbag Freeze Tag
An exercise using swim noodles.
Suggested Grade: 6-8
Format: Online Lesson Plan
Source: Nick Jurman
World Wide Web URL:
http://www.pecentral.org/lessonideas/ViewLesson.asp?ID=5347

Best Bones Forever!
Information for girls on how to develop lifelong bone-healthy habits for a healthier future.
Suggested Grade: 3-8
Format: Web Site
Source: Centers for Disease Control and Prevention
World Wide Web URL: http://www.bestbonesforever.gov/

Building Leadership Skills in Middle School Girls Through Interscholastic Athletics
Discusses this issue.
Suggested Grade: Teacher Reference
Production Date: 2003
Format: Online Article
Source: Lawrence Hart et al.
World Wide Web URL:
http://www.ericdigests.org/2005-2/girls.html

Bulking Up Fiber's Healthful Reputation
Explains how a high fiber diet is associated with a reduced risk of certain cancers, digestive disorders, and other ailments.
Suggested Grade: 4-Adult
Format: Online Article; 5 pages
Special Notes: Use the on-site search engine to easily find this title. You may request a printed copy mailed to you for a fee.
Source: Federal Citizen Information Center
World Wide Web URL:
http://publications.usa.gov/USAPubs.php

Colds & Flu: Time Only Sure Cure
Explains the differences between a cold and the flu--and how to treat each of them.
Suggested Grade: 4-Adult
Format: Online Article; 5 pages
Special Notes: Use the on-site search engine to easily find this title. You may request a printed copy mailed to you for a fee.
Source: Federal Citizen Information Center
World Wide Web URL:
http://publications.usa.gov/USAPubs.php

Communicable Disease Fact Sheets
Lots of fact sheets about communicable diseases--from amebiasis to zoonoses.

All materials listed in this 2017-2018 edition are BRAND NEW!

HEALTH AND PHYSICAL EDUCATION

Suggested Grade: 6-Adult
Format: Downloadable Fact Sheets
Source: New York Department of Health
World Wide Web URL:
http://www.health.state.ny.us/diseases/communicable/

Dietary Guidelines for Americans
Discusses how to choose a diet that will taste good, be nutritious, and reduce chronic disease risks.
Suggested Grade: 4-Adult
Production Date: 2000
Format: Online Article; 44 pages
Special Notes: Use the on-site search engine to easily find this title. You may request a printed copy mailed to you for a fee.
Source: Federal Citizen Information Center
World Wide Web URL:
http://publications.usa.gov/USAPubs.php

Do I Have Arthritis?
Presents common sites of arthritis and tells how medications and exercise can help.
Suggested Grade: 6-Adult
Format: Online Article; 28 pages
Special Notes: Use the on-site search engine to easily find this title. You may request a printed copy mailed to you for a fee.
Source: Federal Citizen Information Center
World Wide Web URL:
http://publications.usa.gov/USAPubs.php

Do You Know the Health Risks of Being Overweight?
A guide to help you lose weight which also explains why, perhaps, you should.
Suggested Grade: 4-Adult
Format: Online Article; 10 pages
Special Notes: Use the on-site search engine to easily find this title. You may request a printed copy mailed to you for a fee.
Source: Federal Citizen Information Center
World Wide Web URL:
http://publications.usa.gov/USAPubs.php

Eating for Life
Explains how to make healthy and appetizing food choices.
Suggested Grade: 4-Adult
Format: Online Article; 23 pages
Special Notes: Use the on-site search engine to easily find this title. You may request a printed copy mailed to you for a fee.
Source: Federal Citizen Information Center
World Wide Web URL:
http://publications.usa.gov/USAPubs.php

Energy Safety
Tips from Smarty the Dog's Electric Safety coloring book.
Suggested Grade: preK-3
Format: Downloadable Coloring Book
Source: California Energy Commission
World Wide Web URL: http://www.energyquest.ca.gov/

15 Fantastic Id
Relay races can be a fun part of any field day--here are fifteen different ones.
Suggested Grade: preK-8
Format: Online Lesson Plan
Source: Gary Hopkins
World Wide Web URL:
http://www.educationworld.com/a_lesson/03/lp315-02.shtml

Fight BAC!: Four Simple Steps to Food Safety
Gives advice on how to handle food safely to avoid bacteria.
Suggested Grade: 4-Adult
Production Date: 1998
Format: Online Article; 5 pages
Special Notes: Use the on-site search engine to easily find this title. You may request a printed copy mailed to you for a fee.
Source: Federal Citizen Information Center
World Wide Web URL:
http://publications.usa.gov/USAPubs.php

Fitness Partner
Lots of information about physical fitness.
Suggested Grade: 6-12
Format: Web Site
Source: Vicki Pierson and Renee Cloe
World Wide Web URL:
http://primusweb.com/fitnesspartner

Growing Up Drug Free
Outlines what parents should know and can do to prevent or stop drug abuse, including alcohol and tobacco, at each age level.
Suggested Grade: 4-Adult
Format: Online Article; 46 pages
Special Notes: Use the on-site search engine to easily find this title. You may request a printed copy mailed to you for a fee.
Source: Federal Citizen Information Center
World Wide Web URL:
http://publications.usa.gov/USAPubs.php

Health Fact Sheets
Lots of informational fact sheets about many health issues.
Suggested Grade: 6-Adult
Format: Downloadable Fact Sheets
Source: Illinois Department of Public Health
World Wide Web URL:
http://www.idph.state.il.us/public/hbhome.htm

Health Fact Sheets
A large number of fact sheets with information of particular interest to the Hispanic community.
Suggested Grade: 6-Adult
Format: Downloadable Fact Sheets

All materials listed in this 2017-2018 edition are BRAND NEW!

HEALTH AND PHYSICAL EDUCATION

Source: National Alliance for Hispanic Health
World Wide Web URL:
http://www.hispanichealth.org/resource/healthfact.aspx

Health Fact Sheets
A large number of assorted fact sheet to help you learn more about important issues that can affect your health.
Suggested Grade: 6-Adult
Format: Downloadable Fact Sheets
Source: Tennessee Department of Health
World Wide Web URL:
http://health.state.tn.us/FactSheets/index.htm

Health Finder
A searchable database of health topics.
Suggested Grade: All ages
Format: Web Site
Source: U. S. Department of Health & Human Services
World Wide Web URL: http://www.healthfinder.gov/

KidsRunning.Com
A site devoted to help kids and their parents learn more about exercise--how to as well as the benefits.
Suggested Grade: preK-6
Format: Web Site
Source: Carol Goodrow
World Wide Web URL: http://www.kidsrunning.com/

Kids World
Dedicated to healthy teeth, here are interactive games, stories, and art projects.
Suggested Grade: preK-2
Format: Web Site
Source: Colgate-Palmolive Company
World Wide Web URL: http://kids-world.colgate.com/

Kid's World - Nutrition
Lots of information for youngsters about proper nutrition.
Suggested Grade: K-4
Format: Web Site
Source: North Carolina Department of Agriculture and Consumer Services
World Wide Web URL: http://www.agr.state.nc.us/cyber/kidswrld/nutrition/index.htm

Lacrosse Tag
Students will play tag using lacrosse sticks and balls.
Suggested Grade: 5-7
Format: Online Lesson Plan
Source: Heidi Qua
World Wide Web URL: http://www.pecentral.org/lessonideas/ViewLesson.asp?ID=5496

Landing
Includes many activities for practicing the skills of jumping and landing.
Suggested Grade: 2-5
Format: Online Lesson Plan

Source: Dan Carrigan
World Wide Web URL: http://www.lessonplanspage.com/PEJumpingAndLandingSkills25.htm

Making Healthy Food Choices
Teaches you how to choose and prepare healthy foods.
Suggested Grade: 4-Adult
Format: Online Article; 16 pages
Special Notes: Use the on-site search engine to easily find this title. You may request a printed copy mailed to you for a fee.
Source: Federal Citizen Information Center
World Wide Web URL:
http://publications.usa.gov/USAPubs.php

Protocols
A lesson that introduces the "go," "freeze," and "melt" protocols for gym class.
Suggested Grade: K-2
Format: Online Lesson Plan
Source: Lemeil Norman
World Wide Web URL: http://www.lessonplanspage.com/PEBeginSchoolFreezeMeltGoProtocalsK2.htm

RunStat 3
Enter the distance and time for your run and this program calculates your pace for your run.
Suggested Grade: 6-12
Format: Downloadable FULL PROGRAM
Special Notes: It is preferred that you download this program from the Web; if this does not work for you then you can send $5.00 to receive the program on disk.
Source: Scott Diamond & Cats
World Wide Web URL: http://ibiblio.org/drears/running/products/software/runstat.html

Safer Eggs: Laying the Groundwork
Explains the benefits of eggs in your diet as well as introducing new safety measures to make sure they are safe to eat.
Suggested Grade: 4-Adult
Format: Online Article; 6 pages
Special Notes: Use the on-site search engine to easily find this title. You may request a printed copy mailed to you for a fee.
Source: Federal Citizen Information Center
World Wide Web URL:
http://publications.usa.gov/USAPubs.php

Sheep and Wolves
A game for indoors or outdoors, giving students an opportunity to release pent-up energy.
Suggested Grade: K-5
Format: Online Lesson Plan
Source: Denis McCarthy
World Wide Web URL:
http://www.educationworld.com/a_tsl/archives/04-1/lesson019.shtml

*All materials listed in this 2017-2018 edition are **BRAND NEW!***

HEALTH AND PHYSICAL EDUCATION

Six Corner Locomotion/Six Corner Roll
Presents two activities that integrate locomotor movements with reading and listening skills.
Suggested Grade: 1-3
Format: Online Lesson Plan
Source: Jonathan Mazurczak
World Wide Web URL: http://www.lessonplanspage.com/PELASixCornerLocomotionAndRollActivities13.htm

Smoking and Your Digestive System
Think smoking only affects your lungs? Read these article to find out how smoking affects all parts of the body, including the digestive system.
Suggested Grade: 7-Adult
Format: Online Article
Source: National Digestive Diseases Information Clearinghouse
World Wide Web URL: http://digestive.niddk.nih.gov/ddiseases/pubs/smoking/index.htm

Sports and Nutrition: The Winning Connection
Explores the relationship between sports and exercise and the food you need to supply the energy needed.
Suggested Grade: 6-Adult
Format: Web Site
Source: University of Illinois Extension Urban Programs Resource Network
World Wide Web URL: http://www.urbanext.uiuc.edu/hsnut/index.html

Sun, UV, and You
Explains what the UV (ultraviolet radiation) index is and how you can use it to avoid skin cancer and other sun-related ailments.
Suggested Grade: 4-Adult
Format: Online Article; 12 pages
Special Notes: Use the on-site search engine to easily find this title. You may request a printed copy mailed to you for a fee.
Source: Federal Citizen Information Center
World Wide Web URL: http://publications.usa.gov/USAPubs.php

Swiss Ball Square Dance
A dance lesson.
Suggested Grade: 4-5
Format: Online Lesson Plan
Source: Laurie Hinman
World Wide Web URL: http://www.pecentral.org/lessonideas/ViewLesson.asp?ID=4356

Teens Health, Food & Fitness
Lots of articles about eating, dieting, strength training, and more, specifically targeted to teens.
Suggested Grade: 7-12
Format: Online Articles
Source: Nemours Foundation, The
World Wide Web URL: http://teenshealth.org/teen/food_fitness/

20 Field Day Activities Any Kid Can Do (And Do Well!)
Twenty great field day activities that emphasize fun over skill.
Suggested Grade: preK-8
Format: Online Lesson Plan
Source: Gary Hopkins
World Wide Web URL: http://www.educationworld.com/a_lesson/03/lp315-01.shtml

What Causes Tooth Decay
Uses vinegar and egg shells in a simulation of teeth decomposition.
Suggested Grade: 2-6
Format: Online Lesson Plan
Source: Melodie Hill
World Wide Web URL: http://youth.net/cec/cecmisc/cecmisc.50.txt

You Can Control Your Weight As You Quit Smoking
Offers help on how to avoid weight gain and adopt a healthier lifestyle when quitting smoking.
Suggested Grade: 4-Adult
Production Date: 1998
Format: Online Article; 10 pages
Special Notes: Use the on-site search engine to easily find this title. You may request a printed copy mailed to you for a fee.
Source: Federal Citizen Information Center
World Wide Web URL: http://publications.usa.gov/USAPubs.php

All materials listed in this 2017-2018 edition are BRAND NEW!

HISTORY

Actions and Reactions
Learn more about racial attitudes in the Mid-South area just before the Civil Rights movement began.
Suggested Grade: 7-8
Format: WebQuest
Source: Julia Meritt
World Wide Web URL:
http://web.archive.org/web/20030402015813/
www.memphis-schools.k12.tn.us/admin/
tlapages/civilrightswebquest.htm

Address to the Negroes in the State of New York, An
Here is a copy of a 1786 speech denouncing slavery, made by this black servant.
Suggested Grade: 6-12
Format: Online Article
Source: Jupiter Hammon
World Wide Web URL: http://www.blackpast.org/
?q=1787-jupiter-hammon-address-negroes-state-new-york

African American Odyssey
Showcases the incomparable African American collections of the Library of Congress. Gives a comprehensive picture of more than 200 years of African American struggle and achievement.
Suggested Grade: 3-Adult
Format: Web Site
Source: Library of Congress
World Wide Web URL:
http://memory.loc.gov/ammem/aaohtml/exhibit/aointro.html

Alaska's Gold
Designed to provide students and other learners with a unique way to understand Alaska's history and people.
Suggested Grade: 3-12
Format: Web Site
Source: Alaska Department of Education
World Wide Web URL:
http://library.state.ak.us/goldrush/HOME.HTM

All Hands on Deck
The online interdisciplinary curriculum provides educators with a video of "old ironsides" and integrates geography, math, social studies, arts and crafts, history, and more in 14 lessons.
Suggested Grade: K-12
Format: Online Curriculum
Source: USS Constitution Museum
World Wide Web URL: http://www.allhandsondeck.org/

American Civil War Webquest, The
You are a reporter whose job it is so report back to the President of the United States regarding the Civil War.
Suggested Grade: 4-8
Format: Web Quest
Source: Chris Koletzky
World Wide Web URL:
http://ck122.k12.sd.us/civilwar/index.htm

American Journeys
Provides eyewitness accounts of Northern American explorations.
Suggested Grade: 6-Adult
Format: Web Site
Source: Wisconsin Historical Society and National History Day
World Wide Web URL: http://www.americanjourneys.org/

American Revolution at a Glance
Learn about the major battles with colorful maps and informative descriptions.
Suggested Grade: 6-Adult
Production Date: 2001
Format: Online Article
Special Notes: Use the on-site search engine to easily find this title. You may request a printed copy mailed to you for a fee.
Source: Federal Citizen Information Center
World Wide Web URL:
http://publications.usa.gov/USAPubs.php

American Revolution Simulation
In order to understand why the American colonists declared their independence, students relate situations to life, liberty and the pursuit of happiness.
Suggested Grade: 6-8
Format: Online Lesson Plan
Source: Roseann Fox
World Wide Web URL:
http://youth.net/cec/cecsst/cecsst.137.txt

Ancient Egypt
Learn all about ancient Egyptian life and view artifacts from this time period.
Suggested Grade: 6-12
Format: Web Site
Source: British Museum, The
World Wide Web URL:
http://www.ancientegypt.co.uk/menu.html

Ancient Mesopotamia: The History, Our History
Tells the story of ancient Mesopotamia, now present-day Iraq.
Suggested Grade: 6-Adult
Format: Web Site
Source: Oriental Institute at the University of Chicago
World Wide Web URL:
http://mesopotamia.lib.uchicago.edu/

Anglo-Saxon and Viking Crafts--Textiles
This article details the weaving industry in Anglo-Saxon and Viking England and explains how woolen fabric was

HISTORY

created.
Suggested Grade: 4-Adult
Format: Online Article
Source: Roland Williamson
World Wide Web URL: http://www.regia.org/textiles.htm

Around the World in 1896
Students will plan, take, and document a trip around the world in 1896 using historic documents.
Suggested Grade: 6-9
Format: Web Site and Lesson Plans
Source: Eva L. Abbamonte and Della Barr Brooks
World Wide Web URL: http://www.loc.gov/teachers/classroommaterials/lessons/world/

Build Your Own Medieval Castle
Build a model castle and learn about the different parts of a castle and why they were constructed as they were.
Suggested Grade: 2-6
Format: Downloadable FULL PROGRAM
Source: Owl & Mouse Educational Software
World Wide Web URL: http://www.yourchildlearns.com/owlmouse.htm

Civil War Through a Child's Eye, The
Focuses on the use of historical fiction and primary sources to expand students' perceptions of the Civil War era.
Suggested Grade: 6-8
Format: WebQuest
Source: Micki M. Caskey and Paul Gregorio
World Wide Web URL: http://www.loc.gov/teachers/classroommaterials/lessons/childs-eye/

Egyptian Mummies
Students will study Egyptian Mummies while learning about Ancient Egypt.
Suggested Grade: 2-3
Format: WebQuest
Source: Melissa Armstrong
World Wide Web URL: http://members.tripod.com/~mbamca/egyptianmummies.html

18th Century History
Articles and information covering the 18th century.
Suggested Grade: 6-12
Format: Web Site
Source: Webseed.com
World Wide Web URL: http://www.history1700s.com

Erwin E. Smith: Teaching Guide
This guide provides a sampling of the vast number of photographs taken by Erwin E. Smith, AKA "the cowboy photographer." Throughout the guide are links to more than 700 images.
Suggested Grade: 4-7
Format: Online Teacher's Guide
Source: Amon Carter Museum
World Wide Web URL: http://www.cartermuseum.org/edu_guides/smith/index.htm

European Voyages of Exploration
Discusses the geography, politics, and culture of Portugal and Spain as they led explorations into other countries as they began the process of world globalization.
Suggested Grade: 6-12
Format: Web Site
Source: University of Calgary
World Wide Web URL: http://www.ucalgary.ca/applied_history/tutor/eurvoya/

Experience the Life
A complete and detailed overview of life in Colonial Williamsburg, Virginia.
Suggested Grade: 4-12
Format: Web Site
Source: Colonial Williamsburg Foundation
World Wide Web URL: http://www.history.org/Almanack/life/life.cfm

Face to Face--Stories from the Aftermath of Infamy
Explores the similarities in the thoughts and emotions of Japanese Americans after the bombing of Pearl Harbor and the Arab and Muslim Americans after the tragedy of September 11.
Suggested Grade: 6-12
Format: Web Site
Source: Rob Mikuriya
World Wide Web URL: http://archive.itvs.org/facetoface/intro.html

First Americans
Offers specific information on five tribes as well as activities.
Suggested Grade: K-8
Format: Web Site
Source: Karen Martin
World Wide Web URL: http://www.ic.arizona.edu/ic/kmartin/School/teacher.htm

First Person Narratives of the American South, 1860-1920
A compilation of printed texts of the 19th-century American South from the viewpoint of Southerners.
Suggested Grade: 4-12
Format: Web Site
Source: Library of Congress, American Memory (first)
World Wide Web URL: http://lcweb2.loc.gov/ammem/award97/ncuhtml/fpnashome.html

Great Depression and the 1990s, The
Asks students to research a modern government program having roots in the New Deal. Following their research,

*All materials listed in this 2017-2018 edition are **BRAND NEW!***

HISTORY

students participate in a congressional forum where they debate which programs should be continued.
Suggested Grade: 7-12
Format: Web Site and Lesson Plans
Source: Douglas Perry and Wendy Sauer
World Wide Web URL: http://www.loc.gov/teachers/classroommaterials/lessons/depression/

Gunfighters of the Old West
Sorting out what was real from what Hollywood has contributed is important to understanding the Old West.
Suggested Grade: 7-12
Format: Online Lesson Plan
Source: Jon Cohrs
World Wide Web URL: http://www.cbv.ns.ca/sstudies/soc/soc5.html

Hello, I Am Deborah Sampson
Students will identify important people and events from the America Revolution and learn more about how these things affect us even today.
Suggested Grade: 5
Format: Online Lesson Plan
Source: Cheryl McCauley
World Wide Web URL: http://lessonopoly.org/teacherslist?q=node/7582

History Happens
Sets the prominent stories of our history to music.
Suggested Grade: 3-8
Format: Web Site
Source: Electron Farm Publications
World Wide Web URL: http://ushistory.com/

History Textbook Controversies in Japan
Discusses the ongoing controversy in Japan about textbook treatments of Japanese military actions during World War II and the lesson for educators in the United States about this controversy.
Suggested Grade: Teacher Reference
Production Date: 2002
Format: Online Article
Source: Kathleen Woods Masalski
World Wide Web URL: http://www.ericdigests.org/2003-1/japan.htm

History Wired
View historic objects and learn more about them.
Suggested Grade: 3-12
Format: Web Site
Source: Smithsonian National Museum of American History
World Wide Web URL: http://historywired.si.edu/index.html

Illustrated History of the Roman Empire
Over 70 megabytes of information on the Roman empire.
Suggested Grade: 6-12
Format: Web Site
Source: Franco Cavazzi
World Wide Web URL: http://www.roman-empire.net/

Images of Native Americans
Presents artistic portrayals of Native Americans throughout history.
Suggested Grade: 6-12
Format: Web Site
Source: Bancroft Library, The
World Wide Web URL: http://bancroft.berkeley.edu/Exhibits/nativeamericans/index2.html

Jacques Lipetz
Tells the story of the author as a nine-year-old boy who escaped communism to hide in Manila.
Suggested Grade: 4-12
Format: Online Article
Source: Jacques Lipetz
World Wide Web URL: http://remember.org/witness/lipetz.htm

Making of America
Presents scanned images of original pages from texts written relating to the development of America from 1850-1877.
Suggested Grade: 6-Adult
Format: Web Site
Source: MoA
World Wide Web URL: http://www.hti.umich.edu/m/moagrp/

Mosaic America: Paths to the Present
Allows students to do a comparative examination of African American, Latino, and Native American history through the arts and hence become more aware of the ideologies of life, values, love, peace and struggle of these citizens of the United States.
Suggested Grade: 7
Format: Online Lesson Plan
Source: Ida Hickerson
World Wide Web URL: http://www.yale.edu/ynhti/curriculum/units/1995/4/95.04.07.x.html

Native Americans--Searching for Knowledge and Understanding
In this lesson students will study Native Americans in order to become familiar with the contributions to and influences on American society particularly, but not exclusively, in the Western region of the United States.
Suggested Grade: 6-8
Format: Online Lesson Plan
Source: B. J. Johnson
World Wide Web URL: http://www.thirteen.org/edonline/lessons/native_americans/index.html

*All materials listed in this 2017-2018 edition are **BRAND NEW!***

HISTORY

1900s, The
Presents a timeline of the last 100 years. Includes audio of music, famous speeches, and other noteworthy "sounds" of this 100 years in America.
Suggested Grade: 4-12
Format: Web Site
Source: Archer
World Wide Web URL:
http://members.tripod.com/archer2000/1900.html

Number the Stars: A WebQuest About the Holocaust
Based on the novel, Number the Stars, by Lois Lowry, this Webquest explores the holocaust.
Suggested Grade: 4-6
Format: WebQuest
Source: Lisa Hrubey
World Wide Web URL:
http://www.bgsu.edu/colleges/library/crc/webquest/number%20the%20stars/Homepage.html

Polar Postal History on the Web
Provides a history of stamp collecting and the history of the exploration of the South Pole.
Suggested Grade: 6-12
Format: Web Site
Source: Gary Pierson
World Wide Web URL: http://www.south-pole.com/

Relevant Approach to History, A
The purpose of this exercise is to assist the at-risk learner in gaining a perspective and impact to his environment.
Suggested Grade: 7-12
Format: Online Lesson Plan
Source: Missy J. Kasbaum
World Wide Web URL:
http://youth.net/cec/cecsst/cecsst.07.txt

Review of American History, A
Students will review the important historical events and time persons from discovery to the present.
Suggested Grade: 4-8
Format: Online Lesson Plan
Source: Dolores Carnahan
World Wide Web URL: http://ofcn.org/cyber.serv/academy/ace/soc/cecsst/cecsst003.html

Rise and Fall of Jim Crow, The
Offers simulations, lesson plans, essays, and other resources to help students learn about the Jim Crow era, from the end of the Civil War to the end of segregation.
Suggested Grade: 6-Adult
Format: Web Site
Source: New York Life
World Wide Web URL: http://www.pbs.org/wnet/jimcrow/

Seventy-First Came, The...To Gunskirchen Lager
Reproduces a pamphlet produced by the United States Army after they liberated a concentration camp in Austria. Recounts in detail, with very graphic photos, the tragedy they found in the camp.
Suggested Grade: 6-12
Format: Downloadable Book
Source: John Mooney
World Wide Web URL:
http://remember.org/mooney/gunskirchen-intro.html

Shields, Knights and Heraldry
Free software to print out shields and the elements of heraldry to make your own coat of arms.
Suggested Grade: 2-5
Format: Downloadable FULL PROGRAM
Source: Owl & Mouse Educational Software
World Wide Web URL:
http://www.yourchildlearns.com/owlmouse.htm

Shipwreck Island Adventure!
Travel the islands to find out the truth behind a mysterious message in a bottle.
Suggested Grade: 3-7
Format: WebQuest
Source: Candy Adams, Devon Fisher, and Amara Julian
World Wide Web URL: http://harrisburg.k12.mo.us/teacher/frittsn/mysteryisland.htm

Spartacus Encyclopedia of British History, The: British History
Contains a large amount of information about the Industrial Revolution in Great Britain.
Suggested Grade: 6-Adult
Format: Online Book
Source: John Simkin
World Wide Web URL:
http://www.spartacus.schoolnet.co.uk/Britain.html

Spiro Mounds; Oklahoma's Past Indian History
Students will learn about Native Americans in the history of Oklahoma.
Suggested Grade: 3-6
Format: Online Lesson Plan
Source: Ernestine Hightower
World Wide Web URL:
http://youth.net/cec/ceclang/ceclang.37.txt

Sworn to Serve
Your family seeks to become royalty--you need to find out what is required for you to do so.
Suggested Grade: 7
Format: WebQuest
Source: Colin Kenney
World Wide Web URL:
http://score.rims.k12.ca.us/score_lessons/sworntoserve/

All materials listed in this 2017-2018 edition are BRAND NEW!

HISTORY

Teacher's Guide to the Holocaust, A
An overview of the people and events of the Holocaust-- shown through text, documents, photographs, art, and literature.
Suggested Grade: Teacher Reference
Format: Web Site
Source: Florida Center for Instructional Technology
World Wide Web URL: http://fcit.coedu.usf.edu/holocaust/

Teaching History for Citizenship in the Elementary School
Discusses the research and curriculum development completed over the past two decades that can be used to improve the teaching of history to young children.
Suggested Grade: Teacher Reference
Production Date: 2003
Format: Online Article
Source: John D. Hoge
World Wide Web URL: http://www.ericdigests.org/2004-2/history.html

Teaching History with Technology
Here are examples of using technology in the history curriculum.
Suggested Grade: Teacher Reference
Production Date: 2003
Format: Online Article
Source: Tom Daccord
World Wide Web URL: http://thwt.org/

Team Approach to Oral History, A
Linking literature and history, students develop an appreciation for the people in the community who are the "living" history.
Suggested Grade: 8-10
Format: Online Lesson Plan
Source: Elaine Seavey
World Wide Web URL: http://youth.net/cec/cecsst/cecsst.45.txt

Time Traveller
Learn about the ancient Olympics.
Suggested Grade: 6
Format: WebQuest
Source: Leslie Blakeburn
World Wide Web URL: http://www.webquestuk.org.uk/Ancient%20Greece/olympics.htm

Trial of Standing Bear, The
Use the World Wide Web to find out more about the trial of this Ponca chief.
Suggested Grade: 5-8
Format: WebQuest
Source: Karen Harness
World Wide Web URL: http://score.rims.k12.ca.us/activity/standingbear/

WASP on the Web
Dedicated to the WASP (Women Airforce Service Pilots) of World War II. Lots of history.
Suggested Grade: 6-Adult
Format: Web Site
Source: Nancy Parrish
World Wide Web URL: http://wingsacrossamerica.us/wasp/

We Shall Overcome: Historic Places of the Civil Rights Movement National Register Travel Itinerary
This itinerary will take you, via the Internet, to 49 historic places associated with one of the most important chapters in our history.
Suggested Grade: 6-Adult
Format: Web Site
Source: National Park Service
World Wide Web URL: http://www.cr.nps.gov/nr/travel/civilrights/

What They Left Behind--Early Multi-National Influences in the United States
Explores the connections between European voyages of discovery, colonial spheres of influence, and various aspects of American culture.
Suggested Grade: 3-5
Format: Online Lesson Plan
Source: EDSITEment
World Wide Web URL: http://edsitement.neh.gov/lesson-plan/fairy-tales-around-world

Where I Come From
Students will examine their own family traditions to identify how beliefs, values, and customs vary from culture to culture and how those traditions influence their perception of other groups.
Suggested Grade: 6-9
Format: Online Lesson Plan
Source: Peace Corps
World Wide Web URL: http://www.peacecorps.gov/wws/publications/looking/index.cfm

World War I: Trenches on the Web
A comprehensive resource of World War I materials.
Suggested Grade: 6-12
Format: Web Site
Special Notes: This entire site is available on CD-ROM for a fee.
Source: Mike Iavarone
World Wide Web URL: http://www.worldwar1.com/

HOLIDAYS AND CEREMONIES

Cherokee Indians
Information about the ceremonies and history of these Native Americans.
Suggested Grade: 4-8
Format: Web Site
Special Notes: This URL will lead you to a subject page. Then click on the appropriate subject heading.
Source: ThinkQuest
World Wide Web URL:
http://www.thinkquest.org/pls/html/think.library

Christmas at the Cottage
Information about the Christmas holiday along with ideas for celebrating it.
Suggested Grade: All ages
Format: Web Site
Source: Beverly A. Qualheim
World Wide Web URL:
http://www.bevscountrycottage.com/christmas/

Christmas Celebration in the Black Culture, A
Incorporates a multicultural activity with scholastic activity while integrating the disciplines of computer literacy, social studies, and language arts.
Suggested Grade: 4-12
Format: Online Lesson Plan
Source: Chandra Thomas Jones
World Wide Web URL:
http://teachertech.rice.edu/Participants/cjones/lessons/kwanzaa/index.html

Christmas in Poland
Discusses Polish customs applied to the Christmas holiday.
Suggested Grade: All ages
Format: Web Site
Source: Polishworld.com
World Wide Web URL:
http://www.polishworld.com/christmas/

Christmas Traditions
Visit various websites and find out how people in different countries say Merry Christmas and how they refer to Santa Claus.
Suggested Grade: 2-4
Format: WebQuest
Source: Bunnie Brewer
World Wide Web URL:
http://its.guilford.k12.nc.us/webquests/hworld/chris.htm

Christmas--Where Did It Come From? Where Is It Going?
Presents the Christian story of Christmas.
Suggested Grade: All ages
Format: Web Site
Source: SOON Ministries
World Wide Web URL:
http://www.soon.org.uk/christmas.htm

Coffee Can Drum
Drums are an important part of life and ceremony in many cultures. Here is a simple method for creating a drum to celebrate the cultures of the world.
Suggested Grade: K-4
Format: Online Lesson Plan
Source: KinderArt
World Wide Web URL:
http://www.kinderart.com/multic/cofdrum.shtml

Easter
Brief information about this religious holiday.
Suggested Grade: All ages
Format: Web Site
Source: KU Medical Center
World Wide Web URL:
http://www3.kumc.edu/diversity/ethnic_relig/easter.html

Easter on the Net
Tells about this religious holiday.
Suggested Grade: All ages
Format: Web Site
Source: Studio Melizo
World Wide Web URL:
http://www.holidays.net/easter/index.htm

Festivals Around the World
Take a look at Christmas, Easter, New Year's and birthdays in Malaysia, England, Sweden, Germany, Australia, and the United States.
Suggested Grade: 4-12
Format: Web Site
Special Notes: This URL will lead you to a subject page. Then click on the appropriate subject heading.
Source: ThinkQuest
World Wide Web URL:
http://www.thinkquest.org/pls/html/think.library

For Whom the Clock Strikes
Students will learn about celebrations marking the new year in various cultures and countries around the world.
Suggested Grade: 6-12
Format: Online Lesson Plan
Source: Sierra Prasada Millman and Andrea Perelman
World Wide Web URL: http://learning.blogs.nytimes.com/2004/12/31/for-whom-the-clock-strikes/?scp=1&sq=For%20whom%20the%20clock%20strikes%20lesson%20plan&st=cse

Hawaiian Christmas Trees
Learn about the Christmas holiday celebration in Hawaii.
Suggested Grade: All ages
Format: Online Article
Source: Aloha from Hawaii
World Wide Web URL:
http://www.aloha-hawaii.com/dining/christmas+trees/

All materials listed in this 2017-2018 edition are BRAND NEW!

HOLIDAYS AND CEREMONIES

Holiday Traditions
Learn how Christmas is celebrated in Austria, England, Germany, Israel, Sweden, and many more countries.
Suggested Grade: All ages
Format: Web Site
Source: California Mall
World Wide Web URL:
http://www.californiamall.com/holidaytraditions/

How to Celebrate Chanukah
Ideas for celebrating this Jewish holiday are presented here along with an explanation of each night's religious meaning.
Suggested Grade: All ages
Format: Online Article
Source: Chabad.org
World Wide Web URL:
http://www.chabad.org/holidays/chanukah/

Kwanzaa
Students will create a mkeka (placemat) that has special meaning to the African American celebration of Kwanzaa.
Suggested Grade: 2-4
Format: Online Lesson Plan
Source: Kari Giles
World Wide Web URL:
http://teacherlink.ed.usu.edu/tlresources/units/byrnes-africa/kargil/index

Make a Multi-Cultural Calendar
In this activity, students research the traditions of different cultures.
Suggested Grade: All ages
Format: Downloadable Activity
Source: Houghton Mifflin Company
World Wide Web URL:
http://www.eduplace.com/ss/act/calend.html

Official & Religious Mexican Holidays
Learn about the many holidays celebrated in this country.
Suggested Grade: All ages
Format: Web Site
Source: Mexico Online
World Wide Web URL:
http://www.mexonline.com/holiday.htm

Paper Bag or Fabric Poncho
Here are the directions for making a replica of this traditional garment--perfect for a Cinco de Mayo festival.
Suggested Grade: K-3
Format: Online Lesson Plan
Source: KinderArt
World Wide Web URL:
http://www.kinderart.com/multic/poncho.shtml

Paper Mache Masks--Maskmania
A 4-part session of mask making that illustrates the importance of them to traditional civilizations.
Suggested Grade: K-8
Format: Online Lesson Plan
Source: KinderArt
World Wide Web URL:
http://www.kinderart.com/multic/machemask.shtml

Spanish Christmas, A
Explains how Christmas and New Years are celebrated in Spain.
Suggested Grade: 2-12
Format: Online Article
Source: tuSPAIN
World Wide Web URL:
http://www.tuspain.com/living/xmas.htm

Thanksgiving on the Net
Explains the tradition of this holiday celebrated in the United States.
Suggested Grade: All ages
Format: Web Site
Source: Studio Melizo
World Wide Web URL:
http://www.holidays.net/thanksgiving/index.htm

*All materials listed in this 2017-2018 edition are **BRAND NEW**!*

LANGUAGE ARTS

Adverbily
Students will learn more about using and identifying adverbs.
Suggested Grade: 4
Format: Online Lesson Plan
Source: Michael Burgoyne
World Wide Web URL:
http://youth.net/cec/ceclang/ceclang.41.txt

Aesop's Fables Online Collection
Presents more than 655 of these famous fables--including an explanation of the morals these fables provide.
Suggested Grade: All ages
Format: Online Stories
Source: John R. Long
World Wide Web URL: http://www.aesopfables.com/

Alex Catalogue of Electronic Texts
A collection of public domain documents from American and English literature as well as Western philosophy.
Suggested Grade: 6-Adult
Format: Downloadable Texts
Source: Eric Lease Morgan
World Wide Web URL: http://www.infomotions.com/alex/

Basic Grammar Review Using "Jabberwocky"
Written to help students identify where they are weak in their grammar skills (in a fun fashion).
Suggested Grade: 7-12
Format: Online Lesson Plan
Source: Monica R. Greene
World Wide Web URL:
http://youth.net/cec/ceclang/ceclang.04.txt

Become a Logophile
Students will learn to manipulate, explore, discover, and fall in love with words.
Suggested Grade: 4-8
Format: Online Lesson Plan
Source: Sandy Montgomery
World Wide Web URL:
http://youth.net/cec/ceclang/ceclang.12.txt

Bookhive
Presents reviews of hundreds of books for children ages birth through twelve.
Suggested Grade: Adult
Format: Web Site
Source: Public Library of Charlotte & Mecklenburg County
World Wide Web URL: http://www.bookhive.org/

Busy as a Bee
Exposes students to similes and how they can be used in writing.
Suggested Grade: 3-6
Format: Online Lesson Plan
Source: Lorraine Tanaka
World Wide Web URL:
http://youth.net/cec/ceclang/ceclang.42.txt

Carol Hurst's Children's Literature Site
A collection of reviews of books for kids and ideas of ways to use them in the classroom
Suggested Grade: Teacher Reference
Format: Web Site
Source: Carol Otis Hurst and Rebecca Otis
World Wide Web URL: http://www.carolhurst.com/

Character Education Through Children's Literature
Examines pertinent issues surrounding character education.
Suggested Grade: Teacher Reference
Production Date: 2003
Format: Online Article
Source: Shawna Brynildssen
World Wide Web URL:
http://www.ericdigests.org/2003-3/character.htm

Children's Literacy Development: Suggestions for Parent Involvement
Resources and information to help parents help their children to love reading and literature.
Suggested Grade: Parents
Production Date: 1994
Format: Online Article
Special Notes: This is a PDF file which will open automatically on your computer.
Source: Eleanor C. Macfarlane
World Wide Web URL:
http://www.eric.ed.gov/PDFS/ED365979.pdf

Children's Storybooks Online--Older Children
Two stories for young adults.
Suggested Grade: 7-9
Format: Online Books
Source: Carol Moore
World Wide Web URL:
http://www.magickeys.com/books/index.html

Children's Storybooks Online--Young Children
A good selection of short, illustrated stories for young children.
Suggested Grade: preK-2
Format: Online Books
Source: Carol Moore
World Wide Web URL:
http://www.magickeys.com/books/index.html

Collaborating on a Newspaper in the Elementary Classroom
Discusses the experience of publishing a classroom newspaper.

All materials listed in this 2017-2018 edition are BRAND NEW!

LANGUAGE ARTS

Suggested Grade: Teacher Reference
Production Date: 1998
Format: Online Article
  Source: Nola Kortner Aiex
  World Wide Web URL:
http://www.ericdigests.org/1998-2/newspaper.htm

Computer Assisted Writing Instruction
Discusses this issue.
Suggested Grade: Teacher Reference
Production Date: 1994
Format: Online Article
  Source: Marge Simic
  World Wide Web URL:
http://www.ericdigests.org/1995-2/computer.htm

Creative Dramatics in the Language Arts Classroom
Discusses the potential for using drama as a teaching method.
Suggested Grade: Teacher Reference
Production Date: 1988
Format: Online Article
Special Notes: This is a PDF file which will open automatically on your computer.
  Source: Bruce Robbins
  World Wide Web URL:
http://www.eric.ed.gov/PDFS/ED297402.pdf

Creative Strategies for Teaching Language Arts to Gifted Students
Here are strategies for helping students in K-8 classes.
Suggested Grade: Teacher Reference
Production Date: 2001
Format: Online Article
  Source: Joan Franklin Smutny
  World Wide Web URL:
http://www.hoagiesgifted.org/eric/e612.html

Database of Award-Winning Children's Literature
Allows you to search and create your own individualized reading lists.
Suggested Grade: Teacher Reference
Format: Web Site
  Source: Lisa R. Bartle
  World Wide Web URL: http://www.dawcl.com/

Decimal Search
Students will learn how to locate a book with the Dewey Decimal System.
Suggested Grade: 4-8
Format: Online Lesson Plan
  Source: Jean M. Beaird
  World Wide Web URL:
http://youth.net/cec/ceclang/ceclang.78.txt

Digital Divide and Its Implications for the Language Arts, The
Discusses this issue.
Suggested Grade: Teacher Reference
Production Date: 2000
Format: Online Article
  Source: Mila Stoicheva
  World Wide Web URL:
http://www.ericdigests.org/2001-1/divide.html

Effective Use of Student Journal Writing
Explores how to effectively use student journals for writing.
Suggested Grade: Teacher Reference
Production Date: 1995
Format: Online Article
Special Notes: This is a PDF file which will open automatically on your computer.
  Source: Gary R. Cobine
  World Wide Web URL:
http://www.eric.ed.gov/PDFS/ED378587.pdf

Einstein Club
An ongoing lesson to get students to learn the vocabulary that corresponds with core curriculum--students will learn vocabulary lists from science and social studies lessons.
Suggested Grade: 6
Format: Online Lesson Plan
  Source: Liz Cannon
  World Wide Web URL:
http://youth.net/cec/ceclang/ceclang.33.txt

English-Only Movement: Its Consequences for the Education of Language Minority Children
Examines the ideologies undergirding the English-Only movement and reviews the consequences of imposing this legislation on the language minority population.
Suggested Grade: Teacher Reference
Production Date: 1998
Format: Online Article
  Source: Mei-Yu Lu
  World Wide Web URL:
http://www.ericdigests.org/1999-4/english.htm

EverythingESL.net
A site devoted to helping teachers of English as a Second Language. Contains lesson plans, teaching tips, resource links, and more.
Suggested Grade: Teacher Reference
Format: Web Site
  Source: Judie Haynes
  World Wide Web URL: http://www.everythingesl.net/

Exploring the Function of Heroes and Heroines in Children's Literature from Around the World
Explores how heroes and heroines in children's literature from around the world help young learners understand and

*All materials listed in this 2017-2018 edition are **BRAND NEW**!*

LANGUAGE ARTS

appreciate different cultures.
Suggested Grade: Teacher Reference
Production Date: 2003
Format: Online Article
Source: Manjari Singh and Mei-Yu Lu
World Wide Web URL:
http://www.ericdigests.org/2004-1/heroes.htm

FableVision Place
Presents stories to read, hear, watch, and explore.
Suggested Grade: K-8
Format: Web Site
Source: FableVision Inc.
World Wide Web URL:
http://www.fablevision.com/place/index.html

Fairy Tales Around the World
Learn about these popular children's stories.
Suggested Grade: K-2
Format: Online Lesson Plan
Source: EDSITEment
World Wide Web URL: http://edsitement.neh.gov/lesson-plan/fairy-tales-around-world

Famous Quotes by Categories and Subjects
Lots of quotations.
Suggested Grade: 4-Adult
Format: Web Site
Source: Haythum R. Khalid
World Wide Web URL:
http://www.famous-quotations.com/asp/categories.asp

Gender Equity in Fairy Tales
The overall objective of this lesson is to create an awareness of fairy tale characters as a source of gender stereotyping.
Suggested Grade: 3-6
Format: Online Lesson Plan
Source: Kathleen E. van Noort
World Wide Web URL:
http://www.ricw.state.ri.us/lessons/142.htm

Gifted Readers and Reading Instruction
Discusses the issue of whether gifted readers require a different method of instruction.
Suggested Grade: Teacher Reference
Production Date: 1995
Format: Online Article
Source: Norma Decker Collins and Nola Kortner Aiex
World Wide Web URL:
http://www.education.com/reference/article/Ref_Gifted_Readers/

Giggle Poetry
Presents entertaining poems for reading or as inspiration. Includes lots of writing activities for budding poets.
Suggested Grade: 3-8
Format: Web Site
Source: Meadowbrook Press
World Wide Web URL: http://www.gigglepoetry.com

Helping Children Overcome Reading Difficulties
Helpful information for the reading teacher.
Suggested Grade: Teacher Reference
Production Date: 1992
Format: Online Article
Source: Carl B. Smith and Roger Sensenbaugh
World Wide Web URL:
http://www.ericdigests.org/1992-4/reading.htm

Helping Children Understand Literary Genres
Tips to help students understand the different types of literature.
Suggested Grade: Teacher Reference
Production Date: 1994
Format: Online Article
Source: Carl B. Smith
World Wide Web URL:
http://www.ericdigests.org/1994/genres.htm

Helping the Underachiever in Reading
Discusses how to help an underachieving student read better.
Suggested Grade: Teacher Reference
Production Date: 1999
Format: Online Article
Source: Diana J. Quatroche
World Wide Web URL:
http://www.ericdigests.org/2000-2/helping.htm

Helping Underachieving Boys Read Well and Often
Presents information on how schools and families can improve the reading skills of English-speaking children, particularly low-income elementary school boys.
Suggested Grade: Teacher Reference
Production Date: 2002
Format: Online Article
Source: Wendy Schwartz
World Wide Web URL:
http://www.ericdigests.org/2003-2/boys.html

Horrid Homonyms
This activity is designed to remind students of the specific meanings and correct usage of some of the most often confused words.
Suggested Grade: 6-8
Format: Online Lesson Plan
Source: Jerry Smith
World Wide Web URL:
http://youth.net/cec/ceclang/ceclang.54.txt

Integrating Literature into Middle School Reading Classrooms
Discusses how to use literature as a supplement to basal readers.

All materials listed in this 2017-2018 edition are BRAND NEW!

LANGUAGE ARTS

Suggested Grade: Teacher Reference
Production Date: 1990
Format: Online Article
Source: Jerry L. Johns and Susan J. Davis
World Wide Web URL:
http://www.ericdigests.org/pre-9214/middle.htm

Jeff's Poems for Kids
All sorts of poems--even ones labeled "yucky poems," written to entertain children.
Suggested Grade: preK-8
Format: Web Site
Source: Jeff Mondack
World Wide Web URL: http://www.jeffspoemsforkids.com/

Kids@Random
While this site offers information about books published by this source, it also offers lots of learning activities that do not require any book.
Suggested Grade: K-8
Format: Web Site
Source: Random House, Inc.
World Wide Web URL:
http://www.randomhouse.com/kids/home.pperl

KidsReads
Lots f information books--author interviews, book reviews, games, trivia, and more.
Suggested Grade: K-8
Format: Web Site
Source: KidsReads.com
World Wide Web URL: http://www.kidsreads.com/

Kim's Korner for Teacher Talk
Lots of ideas for the language arts teacher.
Suggested Grade: 5-8
Format: Web Site
Source: Kim Steele
World Wide Web URL:
http://www.kimskorner4teachertalk.com

Language Development in the Early Years
Discusses this issue.
Suggested Grade: Teacher Reference
Production Date: 2000
Format: Online Article
Source: Mei-Yu Lu
World Wide Web URL:
http://www.vtaide.com/png/ERIC/Language-Early.htm

Light in the Forest, The
Focuses on an extension of the teaching of the novel,"The Light in the Forest," by Conrad Richter.
Suggested Grade: 8
Format: WebQuest
Source: Linda Good
World Wide Web URL:
http://projects.edtech.sandi.net/lewis/litf/

Literature and Art Through Our Eyes: The African American Children
Designed to increase a students awareness of African Americans in literature and art.
Suggested Grade: 3
Format: Online Lesson Plan
Source: Patrice Flynn
World Wide Web URL: http://www.yale.edu/ynhti/curriculum/units/1995/4/95.04.02.x.html

Literature as Lessons on the Diversity of Culture
Reviews resources for teachers who wish to offer students varied literary and cultural experiences.
Suggested Grade: Teacher Reference
Production Date: 1989
Format: Online Article
Source: Nola Kortner Aiex
World Wide Web URL:
http://www.ericdigests.org/pre-9211/lessons.htm

Mathematics and Reading Connection, The
Discusses this issue.
Suggested Grade: Teacher Reference
Production Date: 1997
Format: Online Article
Source: Andrea K. Balas
World Wide Web URL:
http://www.ericdigests.org/2000-1/math.html

Motivating Low Performing Adolescent Readers
Focuses on motivating the low performing adolescent in a remedial reading or subject area classroom.
Suggested Grade: Teacher Reference
Production Date: 1996
Format: Online Article
Source: Norma Decker Collins
World Wide Web URL:
http://www.ericdigests.org/1997-1/low.html

New Look at Literature Instruction, A
Explores why literature instruction should be included in secondary schools and discusses how it should be taught.
Suggested Grade: Teacher Reference
Production Date: 1991
Format: Online Article
Source: Judith Langer
World Wide Web URL:
http://www.ericdigests.org/pre-9220/look.htm

Nursery Rhyme Mania
Students will learn nursery rhymes through creative activities.
Suggested Grade: 4-6
Format: Online Lesson Plan

All materials listed in this 2017-2018 edition are BRAND NEW!

LANGUAGE ARTS

Source: Carolyn Creger
World Wide Web URL:
http://youth.net/cec/ceclang/ceclang.30.txt

Oral Language Development Across the Curriculum, K-12
Answers many questions about how teachers can help students develop oral proficiency.
Suggested Grade: Teacher Reference
Production Date: 1995
Format: Online Article
Source: Zhang Hong and Nola Kortner Aiex
World Wide Web URL:
http://www.ericdigests.org/1996-3/oral.htm

OWL Handouts
You can select from well over one-hundred articles about writing, punctuation, spelling, sentence construction, and many more topics.
Suggested Grade: All ages
Format: Online Articles
Source: Purdue University Writing Lab, The
World Wide Web URL:
http://owl.english.purdue.edu/handouts/index.html

Paper Bag Book Report
Students will write book reports on grocery bags and the stores promote community literacy by using these bags to hold customers' purchases.
Suggested Grade: 3-8

Format: Online Lesson Plan
Source: Linda Bray
World Wide Web URL: http://www.educationworld.com/a_tsl/archives/02-1/lesson042.shtml

Parent Involvement in Elementary Language Arts: A Program Model
Organizational tips for getting parents involved in the language arts program.
Suggested Grade: Teacher Reference
Production Date: 1991
Format: Online Article
Source: Marge Simic
World Wide Web URL:
http://www.ericdigests.org/pre-9218/parent.htm

Parent Participation in Middle School Language Arts
Provides some ideas and suggestions about parental involvement in middle school education, focusing on language arts.
Suggested Grade: Teacher Reference
Production Date: 1996
Format: Online Article
Source: Nola Kortner Aiex
World Wide Web URL:
http://www.ericdigests.org/1997-2/parent.htm

Phonemic Awareness: An Important Early Step in Learning to Read
Discusses this issue.
Suggested Grade: Teacher Reference
Production Date: 1996
Format: Online Article
Source: Roger Sensenbaugh
World Wide Web URL:
http://www.kidsource.com/kidsource/content2/phoemic.p.k12.4.html

Photo Essay, A
Students will create a photo essay.
Suggested Grade: 2-4
Format: Online Lesson Plan
Source: Rebecca Sexson
World Wide Web URL:
http://youth.net/cec/ceclang/ceclang.20.txt

Poetry for Kids
Students will enjoy these funny poems so much they can't help but be inspired to write their own.
Suggested Grade: K-4
Format: Web Site
Source: Kenn Nesbitt
World Wide Web URL: http://www.poetry4kids.com/

Poetry Screen Saver
Displays quotes by English poets as a screensaver for your computer.
Suggested Grade: All ages
Format: Downloadable FULL PROGRAM
Source: Arro & Wartoft AB (poetry)
World Wide Web URL:
http://www.wartoft.nu/software/poetry/

Political Writings of George Orwell
Presents the political writings of this famous author.
Suggested Grade: 6-12
Format: Online Articles
Source: Patrick Farley
World Wide Web URL:
http://www.resort.com/~prime8/Orwell/

Punctuation: Less Is More?
Explores the evolution of using punctuation and discusses the degree to which it is used today.
Suggested Grade: Teacher Reference
Production Date: 1992
Format: Online Article
Special Notes: This is a PDF file which will open automatically on your computer.
Source: John Dawkins
World Wide Web URL:
http://www.eric.ed.gov/PDFS/ED347553.pdf

All materials listed in this 2017-2018 edition are BRAND NEW!

55

LANGUAGE ARTS

Pygmalion Effect, The: A Dramatic Study in the Classroom
This lesson deals with fantasies, feelings, and self-image through the study of Pygmalion.
Suggested Grade: 6-8
Format: Online Lesson Plan
Source: Elizabeth Lawrence
World Wide Web URL: http://www.yale.edu/ynhti/curriculum/units/1985/2/85.02.06.x.html

Reading and Writing in a Kindergarten Classroom
Helpful information for teaching young children to become readers and writers.
Suggested Grade: Teacher Reference
Production Date: 1991
Format: Online Article
Source: Bobbi Fisher
World Wide Web URL: http://www.ericdigests.org/pre-9219/reading.htm

Seussville University
Uses the popular Dr. Seuss characters to offer internet activities for people of all ages.
Suggested Grade: preK-5
Format: Web Site
Source: Random House, Inc. (seuss)
World Wide Web URL: http://www.randomhouse.com/seussville/university

Successful Paragraphs
Students will learn to write interesting, well-written paragraphs.
Suggested Grade: 4-6
Format: Online Lesson Plan
Source: Martha Adams
World Wide Web URL: http://youth.net/cec/ceclang/ceclang.01.txt

Teacher's Guide for a Midsummer Night's Dream
Contains a brief overview of this title by Shakespeare, followed by teaching suggestions to be used before, during, and after reading the play.
Suggested Grade: 6-12
Format: Online Teacher's Guide
Source: Penguin-Putnam Inc.
World Wide Web URL: http://us.penguingroup.com/static/html/services-academic/teachersguides.html

Teacher's Guide for Up From Slavery
Contains a brief overview of this Booker T. Washington title, with teaching suggestions to be used before, during, and after reading.
Suggested Grade: 6-12
Format: Online Teacher's Guide
Source: Penguin-Putnam Inc.
World Wide Web URL: http://us.penguingroup.com/static/html/services-academic/teachersguides.html

Teacher's Guide to As You Like It
Contains a brief overview of this title by Shakespeare, followed by teaching suggestions to be used before, during, and after reading the play.
Suggested Grade: 6-12
Production Date: 2000
Format: Online Teacher's Guide
Source: Penguin-Putnam Inc.
World Wide Web URL: http://us.penguingroup.com/static/html/services-academic/teachersguides.html

Teaching Creative Writing in the Elementary School
Information intended to help teachers build an emotionally involving and intellectually stimulating creative writing program.
Suggested Grade: Teacher Reference
Production Date: 1996
Format: Online Article
Source: Christopher Essex
World Wide Web URL: http://www.ericdigests.org/1996-3/writing.htm

Teaching Poetry: Generating Genuine, Meaningful Responses
Explores how to teach poetry to students at all age levels.
Suggested Grade: Teacher Reference
Production Date: 1989
Format: Online Article
Source: Charlie Frankenbach
World Wide Web URL: http://www.ericdigests.org/pre-9211/poetry.htm

Teaching Tips to Use with the Signet Classic Shakespeare Series
Tips to follow so that students actually get something out of Shakespeare.
Suggested Grade: 6-12
Format: Online Teacher's Guide
Source: Penguin-Putnam Inc.
World Wide Web URL: http://us.penguingroup.com/static/html/services-academic/teachersguides.html

Teaching Writing with Peer Response Groups Encouraging Revision
Explains why and how to implement peer writing groups.
Suggested Grade: Teacher Reference
Production Date: 1989
Format: Online Article

LANGUAGE ARTS

Source: Andrea W. Herrmann
World Wide Web URL:
http://www.ericdigests.org/pre-9211/peer.htm

TestDEN
Prepares students for the TOEFL test.
Suggested Grade: 4-Adult
Format: Online Course
Source: Act360 Media Ltd.
World Wide Web URL: http://www.actden.com/

Understanding Hispanic/Latino Culture and History Through the Use of Children's Literature
Uses children's literature as a way for studying about these cultures.
Suggested Grade: 3
Format: Online Lesson Plan
Source: Jean E. Sutherland
World Wide Web URL:
http://www.cis.yale.edu/ynhti/curriculum/units/1997/2/97.02.06.x.html

Very Bad Horrible No Good Day, The
A language arts lesson using this story we can all relate to!
Suggested Grade: 1
Format: WebQuest
Source: Amaki Ayikpa
World Wide Web URL:
http://projects.edtech.sandi.net/hawthorne/badday/

Vocabulary Building
Designed to help increase the vocabulary of students.
Suggested Grade: 1-3
Format: Online Lesson Plan
Source: Judy Ezell
World Wide Web URL:
http://youth.net/cec/ceclang/ceclang.13.txt

Writing Instruction: Changing Views Over the Years
Discusses changes and provides some background for dealing with questions that may remain unresolved.
Suggested Grade: Teacher Reference
Production Date: 2000
Format: Online Article
Source: Carl B. Smith
World Wide Web URL:
http://www.ericdigests.org/2001-3/views.htm

MATHEMATICS

AAA Math
Presents many, many online math exercises.
Suggested Grade: K-8
Format: Web Site
                Source: J. Banfill
    World Wide Web URL: http://www.aaamath.com/

Addition & Subtraction--Dyn-O-Sports
Learn math while playing a game. Correct answers are rewarded with a dinosaur making a basket, hitting a baseball, or scoring a soccer goal.
Suggested Grade: 1-4
Format: Downloadable FULL PROGRAM
             Source: School Express
             World Wide Web URL:
http://www.schoolexpress.com/compsoft/software02.php

AlgebraHelp.com
Lessons, calculators, worksheets, and resources for learning algebra.
Suggested Grade: 7-12
Format: Web Site
             Source: Algebrahelp.com
             World Wide Web URL:
       http://www.algebrahelp.com/index.jsp

A+ Math
Users can view flashcards for basic mathematical functions as well as more advanced ones. Math games are also available.
Suggested Grade: All ages
Format: Web Site
                Source: A+ Math
    World Wide Web URL: http://www.aplusmath.com

Area and Volume
This activity takes away the abstract idea and replaces it with a concrete model of area and volume.
Suggested Grade: 3
Format: Online Lesson Plan
             Source: Timothy Welch
             World Wide Web URL:
       http://youth.net/cec/cecmath/cecmath.30.txt

At Home with Math
This site offers activities to help students do math using everyday activities.
Suggested Grade: preK-5
Format: Web Site
                Source: TERC
    World Wide Web URL: http://athomewithmath.terc.edu/

Basic Skill Topics
An assortment of lessons on everything from basic arithmetic skills to beginning algebra.
Suggested Grade: 4-Adult
Format: Online Lessons

                Source: Dan Bach
             World Wide Web URL:
       http://home.earthlink.net/~djbach/basic.html

Birds, Fractions and Percentages
Students will learn fractions and percentages by applying them to real-life situations.
Suggested Grade: 6-12
Format: Online Lesson Plan
             Source: Regina Marsters
             World Wide Web URL:
         http://www.educationworld.com/a_tsl/
            archives/00-2/lesson0005.shtml

Brain Teasers and Math Puzzles
Contains brain teasers and math puzzles that are interactive with immediate scoring.
Suggested Grade: 4-Adult
Format: Web Site
             Source: Syvum Technologies Inc.
    World Wide Web URL: http://www.syvum.com/teasers/

Calculator Pattern Puzzles
There is growing awareness that children need experience with problem solving, math instruction can be inquiry-based, and the use of calculators should be applied at every level.
Suggested Grade: K-5
Format: Online Lesson Plan
             Source: Allison Holsten
             World Wide Web URL:
       http://youth.net/cec/cecmath/cecmath.06.txt

Convert
An easy to use unit conversion program that will convert the most popular units of distance, temperature, volume, time, speed, mass, power, density, and pressure.
Suggested Grade: 6-12
Format: Downloadable FULL PROGRAM
             Source: Joshua F. Madison
             World Wide Web URL:
       http://www.joshmadison.com/software/convert

Cool Math
Interactive games to help students learn math skills for all age levels.
Suggested Grade: All ages
Format: Web Site
             Source: coolmath.com
             World Wide Web URL:
       http://www.coolmath.com/home.htm

Count On
An online resource for elementary math classes.
Suggested Grade: K-8
Format: Web Site
             Source: Counton.org
    World Wide Web URL: http://www.mathsyear2000.co.uk/

58   *All materials listed in this 2017-2018 edition are* **BRAND NEW!**

MATHEMATICS

Cube Coloring Problem
Investigate what happens when different sized cubes are constructed from unit cubes with some surface areas painted.
Suggested Grade: 5-12
Format: Online Lesson Plan
Source: Linda Dickerson
World Wide Web URL: http://youth.net/cec/cecmath/cecmath.36.txt

Discovering Mathematical Talent
Some guidelines to follow to help you discover mathematical talent in children at an early age.
Suggested Grade: Teacher Reference
Production Date: 1990
Format: Online Article
Source: Richard C. Miller
World Wide Web URL: http://www.hoagiesgifted.org/eric/e482.html

Discovering Pi
This activity allows students to discover why pi works in solving problems dealing with finding circumference.
Suggested Grade: 5-7
Format: Online Lesson Plan
Source: Jack Eckley
World Wide Web URL: http://youth.net/cec/cecmath/cecmath.23.txt

Doing Mathematics With Your Child
Presents resources for parents to help their children with this important skill.
Suggested Grade: Parents
Production Date: 1994
Format: Online Article
Source: Martin D. Hartog and Patricia A. Brosnan
World Wide Web URL: http://www.math.com/parents/articles/domath.html

Easy Addition
This gives kids an alternative way of adding if they have trouble with "carrying." It is faster and more accurate for most kids.
Suggested Grade: 4-12
Format: Online Lesson Plan
Source: Lauren Evans
World Wide Web URL: http://youth.net/cec/cecmath/cecmath.35.txt

Estimating With Money
This activity can develop many different strategies to arrive at an answer, including estimates and guesstimates.
Suggested Grade: 1-5
Format: Online Lesson Plan
Source: Louise Murphy
World Wide Web URL: http://youth.net/cec/cecmath/cecmath.45.txt

Figure This! Math Challenges for Families
Presents problems requiring mathematical thinking, using patterns and logic to reach a solution.
Suggested Grade: 5-8
Format: Web Site
Source: Figurethis.org
World Wide Web URL: http://www.figurethis.org

Free Standing Structure
This activity shows students that cost, time, planning, modeling, designs, teamwork, and application are important in "real world" construction projects.
Suggested Grade: 4-8
Format: Online Lesson Plan
Source: Leslie Gonzales
World Wide Web URL: http://youth.net/cec/cecmath/cecmath.37.txt

Grey Labyrinth
A college of math and logic puzzles.
Suggested Grade: 6-12
Format: Web Site
Source: Kevin Lin
World Wide Web URL: http://www.greylabyrinth.com/

Growing, Growing, Graphing!
In this statistics lesson, students focus on China's population growth. They graph data on graph paper using a graphing calculator or spreadsheet software.
Suggested Grade: 7-12
Format: Online Lesson Plan
Source: Patricia M. Holmes
World Wide Web URL: http://www.thirteen.org/edonline/lessons/graphing/index.html

I Am the Greatest
A blend of skill and chance becomes motivation to understand the concept of place value.
Suggested Grade: 2-6
Format: Online Lesson Plan
Source: Katherine Beal
World Wide Web URL: http://youth.net/cec/cecmath/cecmath.18.txt

Interactive Mathematics Miscellany and Puzzles
Created to help users get over math anxiety, this site uses puzzles, games, and brain teasers to interest its audience in mathematics.
Suggested Grade: All ages
Format: Web Site
Special Notes: A subscription may be purchased on CD-ROM-- free only through the World Wide Web.
Source: CTK Software, Inc.
World Wide Web URL: http://www.cut-the-knot.com/content.shtml

All materials listed in this 2017-2018 edition are BRAND NEW!

MATHEMATICS

Ken White's Coin Flipping Page
Learn the probability of flipping coins--either one or multiple coins.
Suggested Grade: 4-12
Format: Online Demonstration
Source: Ken White
World Wide Web URL:
http://shazam.econ.ubc.ca/flip/index.html

Labyrinths & Mazes
Students will learn about labyrinths and mazes by taking information from the Internet, summarizing it, then design their own mazes.
Suggested Grade: 6-12
Format: Online Lesson Plan
Source: Valerie G. Olson
World Wide Web URL:
http://teachertech.rice.edu/Participants/volson/lessons/labrinthsandmazes/lessonplans.html

Learning About Ratios: A Sandwich Study
The purpose of this activity is to provide students with a concrete introduction to the concept of ratios.
Suggested Grade: 4-6
Format: Online Lesson Plan
Source: Sheryl Weinberg
World Wide Web URL:
http://youth.net/cec/cecmath/cecmath.17.txt

Linear Equations Game
Game cards help pair up students to solve linear equations for the value of a variable.
Suggested Grade: 6-12
Production Date: 2007
Format: Online Lesson Plan
Source: Madhavi Dhande
World Wide Web URL:
http://www.educationworld.com/a_tsl/archives/07-1/lesson016.shtml

Listening Practice/Team Review
Use this activity to build listening skills, encourage teamwork, and to review important math concepts.
Suggested Grade: 4-6
Format: Online Lesson Plan
Source: Karen Riggins
World Wide Web URL:
http://youth.net/cec/cecmath/cecmath.44.txt

Living on Your Own--Let's Calculate the Cost!
A fun way to review basic math skills, such as addition, subtraction, multiplication, division, finding averages, and working with percentages.
Suggested Grade: 7-8
Format: Online Lesson Plan
Source: Tracy Goodson-Espy, et al
World Wide Web URL:
http://www.thirteen.org/edonline/lessons/lifecost/index.html

Making Estimations in Measurement
This activity provides students an opportunity to utilize their knowledge of measurement in making accurate measurements and estimations.
Suggested Grade: 1-2
Format: Online Lesson Plan
Source: Debbie Ballard
World Wide Web URL:
http://youth.net/cec/cecmath/cecmath.21.txt

Making Mathematics
Provides the research results of a mentored research project for youth mathematicians.
Suggested Grade: 7-Adult
Format: Web Site
Source: Education Development Center, Inc.
World Wide Web URL: http://www2.edc.org/makingmath/

M&M Graphing and Probability
M&M graphing can be as simple as making a pictograph, or as involved as predicting and determining probability. A hands-on lesson.
Suggested Grade: 1-5
Format: Online Lesson Plan
Source: Karen Stewart
World Wide Web URL:
http://youth.net/cec/cecmath/cecmath.26.txt

Math Dice Review Game
This lesson can be used to review any math operation across the elementary to high school levels.
Suggested Grade: 3-12
Production Date: 2007
Format: Online Lesson Plan
Source: Kaitlin Kelly
World Wide Web URL:
http://www.educationworld.com/a_tsl/archives/07-1/lesson015.shtml

Math Fact Cafe
You'll find worksheets and flash cards for mathematics--there's even a game to play.
Suggested Grade: 1-4
Format: Web Site
Source: Math Fact Cafe, LLC
World Wide Web URL: http://www.mathfactcafe.com/

Mathnerds.com
MathNerds provides free, discovery-based, mathematical guidance via an international, volunteer network of mathematicians.
Suggested Grade: 6-12
Format: Web Site
Source: Mathnerds.com
World Wide Web URL: http://74.81.197.188/index.aspx

MATHEMATICS

Maths Dictionary for Kids, A
For all ages, this site defines and gives examples of more than 300 math terms.
Suggested Grade: All ages
Format: Web Site
Source: Jenny Eather
World Wide Web URL:
http://www.amathsdictionaryforkids.com/

Math Shortcuts
Math shortcuts will help students master some of the more difficult concepts by presenting a simpler method or helpful way of understanding the process.
Suggested Grade: 4-6
Format: Online Lesson Plan
Source: Randy Bartholomew
World Wide Web URL:
http://youth.net/cec/cecmath/cecmath.27.txt

Mixed-Up Math
A mathematical puzzle game where you must find the correct equations to solve the puzzle.
Suggested Grade: All ages
Format: Downloadable FULL PROGRAM
Source: Knowledge Probe Inc.
World Wide Web URL:
http://www.kprobe.com/kprobe/mu.htm

Multicultural Mathematics: A More Inclusive Mathematics
Explores multicultural mathematics.
Suggested Grade: Teacher Reference
Production Date: 1995
Format: Online Article
Source: Marilyn Strutchens
World Wide Web URL:
http://www.ericdigests.org/1996-1/more.htm

Multiplication Bingo
After students have mastered multiplication facts, this game can be introduced to reinforce learning.
Suggested Grade: 3-5
Format: Online Lesson Plan
Source: Elizabeth Lofties
World Wide Web URL:
http://youth.net/cec/cecmath/cecmath.49.txt

National Math Trail, The
An opportunity for K-12 teachers and students to discover and share the math that exists in their own environments.
Suggested Grade: K-12
Format: Web Site
Source: Kay Toliver
World Wide Web URL: http://www.nationalmathtrail.org/

Negative & Positive Numbers
These activities reinforce the idea that we work with positive and negative numbers all the time and that the concept is not difficult.
Suggested Grade: 4-12
Format: Online Lesson Plan
Source: Herb Colley
World Wide Web URL:
http://youth.net/cec/cecmath/cecmath.43.txt

Newton's Window
Presents games, puzzles, riddles, and more to help make learning math fun.
Suggested Grade: 3-12
Format: Web Site
Source: Newton's Window
World Wide Web URL: http://www.suzannesutton.com/

Numbers from 1 to 10 in Over 4500 Languages
Includes old world as well as new world languages.
Suggested Grade: All ages
Format: Web Site
Source: Mark Rosenfelder
World Wide Web URL:
http://www.zompist.com/numbers.shtml

Number Tick Tack Toe
By changing the rules and symbols slightly, you give the game new life, while giving students extended practice in basic addition and subtraction facts.
Suggested Grade: 1-3
Format: Online Lesson Plan
Source: Ann James
World Wide Web URL:
http://youth.net/cec/cecmath/cecmath.50.txt

Numeral Recognition, Matching, and Writing
This activity reinforces what many already know and teaches or reteaches numeral recognition to those who have not truly understood.
Suggested Grade: K-1
Format: Online Lesson Plan
Source: Chris Cox
World Wide Web URL:
http://youth.net/cec/cecmath/cecmath.05.txt

PlaneMath
Teaches mathematics through a set of highly interactive lessons on aeronautics.
Suggested Grade: 4-7
Format: Web Site
Source: InfoUse
World Wide Web URL: http://www.planemath.com/

Pop Clock
Students will review the Census Bureau's homepage on the Internet and gather data regarding trends in population.
Suggested Grade: 8-12
Format: Online Lesson Plan

MATHEMATICS

Source: Susan Boone
World Wide Web URL:
http://teachertech.rice.edu/Participants/sboone/Lessons/Titles/popclock.html

Probability: The Study of Chance
Written to help begin the process of helping students learn the basic principles of probability.
Suggested Grade: 5-12
Format: Online Lesson Plan
Source: Shirley LeMoine
World Wide Web URL:
http://youth.net/cec/cecmath/cecmath.15.txt

Problem Solving--A Part of Everyday Thinking
Students will master the process of applying critical thinking to each and every problem/task that confronts them in their daily understandings (well, that is the plan anyway).
Suggested Grade: 4-12
Format: Online Lesson Plan
Source: Octaviano Garcia
World Wide Web URL:
http://youth.net/cec/cecmath/cecmath.29.txt

Quarks to Quasars, Powers of Ten
"A study of the effect of adding another zero."
Suggested Grade: 6-12
Format: Web Site
Source: Bruce Bryson
World Wide Web URL:
http://www.wordwizz.com/pwrsof10.htm

Reading, Writing, and Math in Daily Living
Learning to make cookies is a fun activity, teaching basic reading, math, and writing.
Suggested Grade: 4-6
Format: Online Lesson Plan
Source: Marlene Reed
World Wide Web URL:
http://youth.net/cec/cecmath/cecmath.20.txt

Rectangle: Area, Perimeter, Length, and Width
What is the largest area of a rectangle if it's perimeter is 20?
Suggested Grade: 8-12
Format: Online Applet
Source: Kristen Carvell
World Wide Web URL:
http://www.mste.uiuc.edu/carvell/rectperim/RetPerim2.html

Roman Numerals
Explains how Roman numerals "work."
Suggested Grade: 5-12
Format: Online Lesson Plan
Source: Bess Kuzma
World Wide Web URL:
http://youth.net/cec/cecmath/cecmath.41.txt

Running to Conclusions
Explores the processing of finding the best fitting exponential curve to sets of data.
Suggested Grade: 8-12
Format: Online Lesson Plan
Source: Ed Malczewski
World Wide Web URL:
http://www.mste.uiuc.edu/malcz/ExpFit/INTRO.html

Shopping
This lesson provides children with realistic practice opportunities using money skills prior to going into the community to shop.
Suggested Grade: K-2
Format: Online Lesson Plan
Source: Cheryl J. Pembroke-Webster
World Wide Web URL:
http://youth.net/cec/cecmath/cecmath.09.txt

Smile Metric Style
Using metrics can be difficult for many students. This activity provides practice.
Suggested Grade: 4-8
Format: Online Lesson Plan
Source: Deana Metzler
World Wide Web URL:
http://youth.net/cec/cecmath/cecmath.11.txt

Sports and Hobby Math
Students will write about the role math plays in a favorite sport or hobby.
Suggested Grade: 3-12
Format: Online Lesson Plan
Source: Melissa Thomas
World Wide Web URL:
http://www.educationworld.com/a_tsl/archives/04-1/lesson021.shtml

Sports and Geometry
Understand why geometry is important by seeing the connections between sports and geometry.
Suggested Grade: 6-12
Production Date: 2007
Format: Online Lesson Plan
Source: Debbie Miskiel
World Wide Web URL: http://www.education-world.com/a_tsl/archives/07-1/lesson018.shtml

Squares of Numbers in Multiplication, The
This gives students a visual image for simple patterns that will facilitate learning other patterns and extend to later math concepts.
Suggested Grade: 2-3
Format: Online Lesson Plan
Source: Glenda Lazenby
World Wide Web URL:
http://youth.net/cec/cecmath/cecmath.10.txt

*All materials listed in this 2017-2018 edition are **BRAND NEW!***

MATHEMATICS

Taking America's Measure
Word finds, puzzles, hidden pictures and many more fun activities for kids about measurement.
Suggested Grade: 3-8
Format: Web Site
Source: National Institute of Standards and Technology
World Wide Web URL: http://www.nist.gov/public_affairs/kids/kidsmain.htm

Tangrams
A lesson plan using these shapes.
Suggested Grade: 4-12
Format: Online Lesson Plan
Source: Fay Zenigami
World Wide Web URL: http://youth.net/cec/cecmath/cecmath.12.txt

Usage and Interpretation of Graphs
This lesson involves problem solving and will demonstrate how useful graphs are.
Suggested Grade: 3-6
Format: Online Lesson Plan
Source: Gary Malsam
World Wide Web URL: http://youth.net/cec/cecmath/cecmath.03.txt

Valentine Candy Count
This is a fun and exciting method through which children can explore and internalize graphing skills by sorting colored Valentine conversation hearts.
Suggested Grade: 1-4
Format: Online Lesson Plan
Source: Judy Dale
World Wide Web URL: http://youth.net/cec/cecmath/cecmath.07.txt

Visual Fractions
A collection of activities that illustrate fraction operations.
Suggested Grade: 3-8
Format: Web Site
Source: Richard E. Rand
World Wide Web URL: http://visualfractions.com/

WebMath
A homework help site that generates answers to specific math problems that students input. Also provides the steps for solving the problems so that students learn how the answer was achieved--not just what the answer is.
Suggested Grade: All ages
Format: Web Site
Source: Webmath.com
World Wide Web URL: http://www.webmath.com/

Word Problems for Kids
Word problems designed to help students improve problem solving skills.
Suggested Grade: 5-12
Format: Web Site
Source: St. Francis Xavier University
World Wide Web URL: http://www.stfx.ca/special/mathproblems/welcome.html

World of Math Online, The
Provides math tips and lessons, quizzes, and games for all levels of mathematics.
Suggested Grade: K-12
Format: Web Site
Source: Math.com
World Wide Web URL: http://www.math.com/

All materials listed in this 2017-2018 edition are BRAND NEW!

SAFETY

Automobile Safety Articles
Here are a number of articles about automobile safety.
Suggested Grade: 6-Adult
Format: Online Articles
   Source: Center for Auto Safety, The
   World Wide Web URL: http://www.autosafety.org/

Babysitter Handbook, The
Useful information to know when you are asked to babysit.
Suggested Grade: 6-12
Format: Web Site
Special Notes: This URL will lead you to a subject page. Then click on the appropriate subject heading.
   Source: ThinkQuest
   World Wide Web URL:
   http://www.thinkquest.org/pls/html/think.library

Cartooning to Teach Safety
Uses original cartoon animals and text to teach elementary age students about making safe choices.
Suggested Grade: 1-5
Format: Web Site
Special Notes: This URL will lead you to a subject page. Then click on the appropriate subject heading.
   Source: ThinkQuest
   World Wide Web URL:
   http://www.thinkquest.org/pls/html/think.library

Crool Zone?
A series of activities designed to help people explore issues related to school safety.
Suggested Grade: All ages
Format: WebQuest
   Source: Tom March
   World Wide Web URL:
   http://tommarch.com/webquests/croolzone/group.htm

Disaster Strikes!
Provides general and safety information for nine natural disasters.
Suggested Grade: 4-12
Format: Web Site
Special Notes: This URL will lead you to a subject page. Then click on the appropriate subject heading.
   Source: ThinkQuest
   World Wide Web URL:
   http://www.thinkquest.org/pls/html/think.library

Electrical Safety World
Information, experiments, games, and activities to teach students the principles and practices of electrical safety.
Suggested Grade: 2-8
Format: Web Site
   Source: Central Hudson Gas & Electric Corporation
   World Wide Web URL:
   http://www.centralhudson.com/kids/electric/html/kids2c.html

Electrical Safety World
Features information, experiments, games, and activities to teach students the principles of electricity and the practices of electrical safety.
Suggested Grade: K-8
Format: Web Site
   Source: Wisconsin Public Service
   World Wide Web URL:
   http://www.wisconsinpublicservice.com/safetyforkids/landing.html

Farm Safety 4 Just Kids
All sorts of activities to help teach kids about being safe on the farm.
Suggested Grade: preK-4
Format: Web Site
   Source: Farm Safety 4 Just Kids
   World Wide Web URL: http://www.fs4jk.org/

Fire Safety & Education Factsheets
A collection of fact sheets that offer important safety tips on a wide variety of topics.
Suggested Grade: All ages
Format: Downloadable Fact Sheets
   Source: United States Fire Administration
   World Wide Web URL: http://www.usfa.dhs.gov/citizens/

Fire Safety for Young Children
Students will learn about the role of a fire fighter along with important fire safety tips.
Suggested Grade: preK-K
Format: Online Lesson Plan
Special Notes: This is a PDF file which will open automatically on your computer.
   Source: Sue Bouchard and Claire Gerin Buell
   World Wide Web URL:
   http://assets.freeprintable.com/pdfs/2695.pdf

Fire Safety WebQuest
Help a youngster overcome his fear that his house is not safe from a fire.
Suggested Grade: 2-5
Format: WebQuest
   Source: Joanne Groff and Bev Crouch
   World Wide Web URL:
   http://www.hobart.k12.in.us/bcrouch/fire2/FSintro.html

Indoor Electrical Safety Check
Quick and easy tips to make your home safe from electrical hazards.
Suggested Grade: 4-Adult
Production Date: 2004
Format: Online Article; 21 pages
Special Notes: Use the on-site search engine to easily find this title. You may request a printed copy mailed to you for a fee.
   Source: Federal Citizen Information Center
   World Wide Web URL:
   http://publications.usa.gov/USAPubs.php

*All materials listed in this 2017-2018 edition are **BRAND NEW!***

SAFETY

Making Your Home Safe from Fire and Carbon Monoxide
Tips on preventing fires, creating an emergency exit plan, what types of safety equipment you should have, and more.
Suggested Grade: 4-Adult
Format: Online Article; 6 pages
Special Notes: Use the on-site search engine to easily find this title. You may request a printed copy mailed to you for a fee.
Source: Federal Citizen Information Center
World Wide Web URL:
http://publications.usa.gov/USAPubs.php

Natural Gas Safety World
Features information, experiments, games, and activities to teach students natural gas science and safety principles.
Suggested Grade: K-8
Format: Web Site
Source: Wisconsin Public Service
World Wide Web URL:
http://www.wisconsinpublicservice.com/safetyforkids/landing.html

RiskWatch
This site is a companion to the RiskWatch project, an injury-prevention program for children.
Suggested Grade: preK-8
Format: Web Site
Source: National Fire Protection Association
World Wide Web URL:
http://www.nfpa.org/riskwatch/home.html

SAFE: Safety Always for Everyone
Explains how and why kids should be safe. Includes a safety quiz.
Suggested Grade: 2-6
Format: Web Site
Special Notes: This URL will lead you to a subject page. Then click on the appropriate subject heading.
Source: ThinkQuest
World Wide Web URL:
http://www.thinkquest.org/pls/html/think.library

Safety
Students will learn safety measures.
Suggested Grade: 2-4
Format: Online Lesson Plan
Source: Kim-Scott Miller
World Wide Web URL:
http://youth.net/cec/cecmisc/cecmisc.44.txt

Sparky the Fire Dog
Young children will learn about fire education and other safety issues with Sparky as their guide.
Suggested Grade: K-5
Format: Web Site
Source: National Fire Protection Association
World Wide Web URL:
http://www.sparky.orghttp://www.sparky.org

Stay Alive! Do You Know How?
Learn about first aid, navigational skills, and survival training.
Suggested Grade: 6-12
Format: Web Site
Special Notes: This URL will lead you to a subject page. Then click on the appropriate subject heading.
Source: ThinkQuest
World Wide Web URL:
http://www.thinkquest.org/pls/html/think.library

SunSmart
Students will learn how to protect themselves from the dangers of the sun.
Suggested Grade: K-1
Format: Online Lesson Plan
Source: Bo Campbell
World Wide Web URL:
http://assets.freeprintable.com/pdfs/2697.pdf

Survival Kit
Allows students to become aware of what they think should be in a survival kit.
Suggested Grade: 5-6
Format: Online Lesson Plan
Source: Patti Emley
World Wide Web URL:
http://youth.net/cec/cecmisc/cecmisc.49.txt

All materials listed in this 2017-2018 edition are BRAND NEW!

SCIENCE

Aeronautics Educator Guide
An educator's guide full of activities for teaching about aeronautics.
Suggested Grade: K-4
Format: Downloadable Teacher's Guide
Source: NASA Spacelink
World Wide Web URL:
http://www.nasa.gov/audience/foreducators/
topnav/materials/listbytype/Aeronautics.html

Alaska Wildlife Notebook Series
Includes descriptions of more than 100 of Alaska's wild fish and game animals.
Suggested Grade: All ages
Format: Downloadable Fact Sheets
Special Notes: May be purchased, in print form, for $12.50.
Source: Alaska Department of Fish & Game
World Wide Web URL: http://www.adfg.alaska.gov/
index.cfm?adfg=educators.notebookseries

Aluminum Beverage Cans: The ABCs of Environmental Education
Includes information, in-class experiments, and extracurricular activities about environmental education-- using the aluminum beverage can as a case study.
Suggested Grade: 5-8
Format: Online Curriculum
Source: Can Manufacturers Institute
World Wide Web URL:
http://www.cancentral.com/canc/abc.htm

Amateur Entomologist
Information about the preservation of moths and butterflies.
Suggested Grade: All ages
Format: Web Site
Source: Laurent Lecerf
World Wide Web URL: http://butterflies.freeservers.com/

Amazing Space: Explorations
Interactive lessons about space.
Suggested Grade: All ages
Format: Web Site
Source: Space Telescope Science Institute
World Wide Web URL: http://amazing-
space.stsci.edu/resources/explorations/

Animal Diversity Web
An online database of animal natural history, distribution, classification, and conservation biology.
Suggested Grade: 6-12
Format: Online Database
Source: University of Michigan Museum of Zoology
World Wide Web URL:
http://animaldiversity.ummz.umich.edu/site/index.html

Animal Info--Endangered Animals
Searchable information on rare, threatened and endangered mammals.
Suggested Grade: 4-12
Format: Web Site
Source: Animal Info
World Wide Web URL: http://www.animalinfo.org/

Anthropology on the Internet for K-12
Provides links to a great number of resources for studying anthropology.
Suggested Grade: All ages
Format: Web Site
Source: Margaret R. Dittemore
World Wide Web URL: http://www.sil.si.edu/
SILPublications/Anthropology-K12/index.htm

Archeology Dig
This plan provides students with experience in analyzing artifacts and relics and constructing a hypothetical scenario describing a prehistoric culture.
Suggested Grade: 5-7
Format: Online Lesson Plan
Source: Sharin Manes
World Wide Web URL:
http://youth.net/cec/cecsst/cecsst.72.txt

ASPCA Kids
Here are games, contests, and lots of information on caring for pets.
Suggested Grade: K-5
Format: Web Site
Source: American Society for the Prevention of Cruelty to Animals
World Wide Web URL: http://www.aspca.org/aspcakids/

Astronomy Picture of the Day
Each day a different image or photograph of our fascinating universe is featured, along with a brief explanation written by a professional astronomer.
Suggested Grade: All ages
Format: Web Site
Source: Robert Nemiroff and Jerry Bonnell
World Wide Web URL:
http://antwrp.gsfc.nasa.gov/apod/astropix.html

Astro-Venture
An interactive multimedia site that asks students to search for and create a planet suitable for human habitation while they act as NASA employees.
Suggested Grade: 5-8
Format: Web Site
Source: NASA Quest
World Wide Web URL: http://quest.arc.nasa.gov/projects/
astrobiology/astroventure/avhome.html

Atom's Family, The
Teaching units and online activities for learning about energy, light, electricity, and other "atomic" matters.
Suggested Grade: All ages
Format: Web Site

66 *All materials listed in this 2017-2018 edition are BRAND NEW!*

SCIENCE

Source: Miami Museum of Science/Science Learning Network
World Wide Web URL: http://www.miamisci.org/af/sln

Auroras: Paintings in the Sky
Shows what auroras look like on Earth and explains how they are created.
Suggested Grade: All ages
Format: Web Site
Source: Mish Denlinger
World Wide Web URL: http://www.exploratorium.edu/learning_studio/auroras/

Backyard Nature
All sorts of activities and ideas for learning about and celebrating nature in your own backyard.
Suggested Grade: All ages
Format: Web Site
Source: Jim Conrad
World Wide Web URL: http://www.backyardnature.net/

Becoming Human
An online documentary that traces one point of view regarding the evolution of humankind.
Suggested Grade: 6-12
Format: Online Documentary
Source: Institute of Human Origins, The
World Wide Web URL: http://www.becominghuman.org/

BioInteractive
Includes interactive activities, videos, animations, and virtual labs for students to learn about biology.
Suggested Grade: 6-Adult
Format: Web Site
Source: Howard Hughes Medical Institute (bio)
World Wide Web URL: http://www.hhmi.org/biointeractive/

Birds at the National Zoo
Learn all about the birds at the National Zoo.
Suggested Grade: All ages
Format: Downloadable Fact Sheets
Source: Smithsonian National Zoological Park
World Wide Web URL: http://nationalzoo.si.edu/Animals/Birds/Index/

Birthday Moons
Students will become familiar with lunar phases by locating and then graphing the Moon phase of their own birthdays. After listening to and discussing lunar myths and legends they create their own Birthday Moon stories.
Suggested Grade: 4-8
Format: Online Teacher's Guide
Source: NASA/MSU-Bozeman CERES Project
World Wide Web URL: http://btc.montana.edu/ceres/html/Birthday/birthday1.htm

Birthday Moons: It's Just a Phase You're Going Through
Learn the phases of the moon by taking a virtual trip to the Moon for your birthday!
Suggested Grade: 4-12
Format: Online Lesson Plan
Source: Walter Sanford
World Wide Web URL: http://www.wsanford.com/~wsanford/exo/b-day_moons.html

Bizarre Stuff You Can Make in Your Kitchen
"...sort of a warped semi-scientific cookbook for tricks, gimmicks, and pointless experimentation, concoctions, and devices, using, for the most part, things found in the house." "If you happen to learn something in the process, consider yourself a better person for it."
Suggested Grade: All ages
Format: Web Site
Source: Brian Carusella
World Wide Web URL: http://bizarrelabs.com/

Bluebird Quest, A
Find out more about bluebirds.
Suggested Grade: All ages
Format: WebQuest
Source: Nancy Bocian, Christi Guptill, and Barbara Grollimund
World Wide Web URL: http://www2.lhric.org/kat/BLUE.HTM

Build-a-Prairie
Choose the best plants and animals to bring to your prairie restoration site and be sure to avoid dangerous exotic species! Then watch the prairie come to life.
Suggested Grade: All ages
Format: Online Game
Source: Bell Live!
World Wide Web URL: http://www.bellmuseum.umn.edu/games/prairie/build/index.html

ButterflySite.com
Explore 12 butterfly topics with pages packed full of butterfly information.
Suggested Grade: All ages
Format: Web Site
Source: Randi Jones
World Wide Web URL: http://www.thebutterflysite.com/

Camp Silos
Explore the history and development of agriculture in America.
Suggested Grade: K-6
Format: Web Site
Source: Silos & Smokestacks National Heritage Area
World Wide Web URL: http://www.campsilos.org

All materials listed in this 2017-2018 edition are BRAND NEW!

SCIENCE

Carolina Coastal Science
A study of coastal life and the challenges we face in maintaining the ecological balance of these areas.
Suggested Grade: 6-12
Format: Web Site
Source: Alec M. Bodzin
World Wide Web URL: http://www.ncsu.edu/coast/

Center for History of Physics, The
Provides exhibits, sample syllabi, and many other resources for physics history and its allied fields.
Suggested Grade: 6-12
Format: Web Site
Source: American Institute of Physics
World Wide Web URL: http://aip.org/history/index.html

Cetacean Fact Packs
Facts sheets about whales and dolphins.
Suggested Grade: All ages
Format: Downloadable Fact Sheets
Source: American Cetacean Society
World Wide Web URL: http://acsonline.org/education/fact-sheets/

Changing Faces: A Study of Solar and Planetary Rotation Rates
Students will work as NASA scientists to make repeated observations of our Sun and the planets to determine their rotation rates.
Suggested Grade: 5-8
Format: Online Teacher's Guide
Source: NASA/MSU-Bozeman CERES Project
World Wide Web URL: http://btc.montana.edu/ceres/html/Faces/faces1.html

Classroom Energy!
Provides activities and resources for learning all about energy.
Suggested Grade: 6-8
Format: Web Site
Source: American Petroleum Institute
World Wide Web URL: http://www.classroom-energy.org/

Coal Science Fair Ideas
Numerous ideas for using coal in a science fair project.
Suggested Grade: 4-12
Format: Online Article
Special Notes: This is a PDF file which will open automatically on your computer.
Source: American Coal Foundation
World Wide Web URL: http://teachcoal.org/wp-content/uploads/2011/11/ScienceFair_Revision.pdf

Comets
Discover what elements make up comets and learn more about Halley's Comet.
Suggested Grade: 3-6
Format: WebQuest
Source: Carolyn Starmer
World Wide Web URL: http://can-do.com/uci/lessons98/Comets.html

Conserving America's Fisheries
Find out what is being done to restore our fisheries and what you can do to help.
Suggested Grade: 6-Adult
Production Date: 2002
Format: Online Article; 7 pages
Special Notes: Use the on-site search engine to easily find this title. You may request a printed copy mailed to you for a fee.
Source: Federal Citizen Information Center
World Wide Web URL: http://publications.usa.gov/USAPubs.php

Constellations, The
Here you will find all kinds of information relating to the 88 constellations.
Suggested Grade: All ages
Format: Web Site
Source: Richard Dibon-Smith
World Wide Web URL: http://www.dibonsmith.com/stars.htm

Cool Science for Curious Kids
An interactive site created to help kids appreciate science.
Suggested Grade: All ages
Format: Web Site
Source: Howard Hughes Medical Institute
World Wide Web URL: http://www.hhmi.org/coolscience/

Dan's Wild, Wild Weather Page
Information and activities for studying the weather.
Suggested Grade: All ages
Format: Web Site
Source: Dan Satterfield
World Wide Web URL: http://www.wildwildweather.com/

Dig--The Archaeology Magazine for Kids!
Supplement to Dig Magazine, this website introduces students to archaeology, paleontology, and earth sciences. Site includes teacher's guides.
Suggested Grade: 2-7
Format: Web Site
Source: Cobblestone Publishing Company
World Wide Web URL: http://digonsite.com/

DNA for Dinner?
Students assess information on the genetic engineering of food and then present what laws they believe should be enacted regarding this treatment of food.
Suggested Grade: 6-12
Format: WebQuest
Source: William E. Peace
World Wide Web URL: http://dnafordinner.blogspot.com/

*All materials listed in this 2017-2018 edition are **BRAND NEW!***

SCIENCE

Earth Force
Invites children to make a difference in the quality of the environment in their communities by presenting things they can do themselves.
Suggested Grade: K-8
Format: Web Site
Source: Earth Force
World Wide Web URL: http://www.earthforce.org/

Ecology Data Tip Archives
Data activities to help learn more about our environment and ecology.
Suggested Grade: 6-12
Format: Online Lesson Plans
Source: Bridge
World Wide Web URL:
http://www.vims.edu/bridge/ecologyarchives.html

Ecosystems
Students will learn more about biodiversity and ecosystems as they visit a small part of the school grounds, a local park, or even a National Park.
Suggested Grade: 6-8
Format: Online Lesson Plan
Source: R. Mark Herzog
World Wide Web URL:
http://www.discoveryeducation.com/teachers/
free-lesson-plans/ecosystems.cfm

Edible/Inedible Experiments Archive
Some of these experiments may be eaten before, during or after the experiment, and some definitely should not be eaten at all.
Suggested Grade: All ages
Format: Web Site
Source: MAD Scientist Network, The
World Wide Web URL:
http://www.madsci.org/experiments/

Educational Poster on Water Pollution
Learn where our drinking water comes from, potential threats to the safety of our water, and what is being done to protect it.
Suggested Grade: All ages
Production Date: 2002
Format: Downloadable Poster
Special Notes: Use the on-site search engine to easily find this title. You may request a printed copy mailed to you for a fee.
Source: Federal Citizen Information Center
World Wide Web URL:
http://publications.usa.gov/USAPubs.php

Electric Universe, The
A wealth of information about electricity, how it affects our lives, and how to harness its power safely. This site is really a group of individual sites, each of specific interest for a specific grade level.

Suggested Grade: All ages
Format: Web Site
Source: American Electric Power
World Wide Web URL: http://aep.electricuniverse.com/

Endangered/Threatened Species
A listing of the mollusks, fish, amphibians, reptiles, birds, mammals, and crustaceans declared by this agency to be endangered or threatened.
Suggested Grade: All ages
Format: Online Article
Special Notes: This is a PDF file which will open automatically on your computer.
Source: Tennessee Wildlife Resources Agency
World Wide Web URL:
http://tennessee.gov/twra/pdfs/endangered.pdf

Endeavour Views the Earth Electronic Picture Book
An electronic picture book.
Suggested Grade: All ages
Format: Downloadable eBook
Special Notes: Macintosh requires HyperCard Player 2.1; Windows requires WinPlus Runtime.
Source: Exploration in Education
World Wide Web URL: http://www.stsci.edu/exined/

Eyes on the Sky, Feet on the Ground
Provides a wealth of hands-on astronomy explorations.
Suggested Grade: 2-6
Format: Online Book
Source: Smithsonian Institution
World Wide Web URL:
http://hea-www.harvard.edu/ECT/the_book/index.html

Farm Animals
Helps kids learn about farm life when they don't have access to one.
Suggested Grade: preK-4
Format: Web Site
Source: Kids Farm
World Wide Web URL: http://www.kidsfarm.com/farm.htm

Fear of Physics
Demonstrates physics in action.
Suggested Grade: All ages
Format: Web Site
Source: FearOfPhysics.com
World Wide Web URL: http://www.fearofphysics.com/

Finding Funding for Environmental Education Efforts
Presents steps in identifying potential sources for funding and how to apply for those funds.
Suggested Grade: Teacher Reference
Production Date: 1993
Format: Online Article

All materials listed in this 2017-2018 edition are BRAND NEW!

SCIENCE

Source: Joe E. Heimlich and Dawn D. Puglisi
World Wide Web URL:
http://www.ericdigests.org/1993/funding.htm

Five Senses
Activities and lessons for teaching about the five senses.
Suggested Grade: 1-4
Format: Online Activities
Source: Southwest Educational Development Laboratory
World Wide Web URL: http://www.sedl.org/scimath/pasopartners/senses/welcome.html

Florida Panther Net
A complete web site devoted to teaching students about the state animal of Florida. Includes games, activities, lesson plans, and more.
Suggested Grade: All ages
Format: Web Site
Source: Florida Panther Net
World Wide Web URL: http://www.floridapanthernet.org/

Forest Stewardship
Children will learn that a forest is made up of many different working parts.
Suggested Grade: K
Format: Online Lesson Plan
Source: Marguerite Wills
World Wide Web URL:
http://sftrc.cas.psu.edu/LessonPlans/Forestry/ForestStewardship.html

Friction, Forces and Motion
Here are some activities and websites to use when teaching and learning about friction, forces, and motion.
Suggested Grade: 4-8
Format: Online Lesson Plans
Source: Robin Ann Henry
World Wide Web URL: http://teachertech.rice.edu/Participants/rhenry/Lessons/frfomo/index.html

Frogland
Includes frog facts, frogs in the news, frog jokes and much more.
Suggested Grade: All ages
Format: Web Site
Source: Dorota
World Wide Web URL:
http://allaboutfrogs.org/froglnd.shtml

FT Exploring
Provides basic information on how energy controls the way things work in nature.
Suggested Grade: 6-8
Format: Web Site
Source: Flying Turtle Company
World Wide Web URL: http://www.ftexploring.com/

Genetic Science Learning Center
Activities and information about genetics.
Suggested Grade: 3-5
Format: Web Site
Source: Genetic Science Learning Center
World Wide Web URL: http://learn.genetics.utah.edu/

Geothermal Energy
Explains this form of energy.
Suggested Grade: 4-12
Format: Online Article
Source: California Energy Commission
World Wide Web URL: http://www.energyquest.ca.gov/

Global Issues and Environmental Education
Discusses this topic.
Suggested Grade: Teacher Reference
Production Date: 1993
Format: Online Article
Source: Carmen E. Trisler
World Wide Web URL:
http://www.ericdigests.org/1993/issues.htm

Great Plant Escape, The
An upper elementary program for teaching about plant science.
Suggested Grade: 4-8
Format: Web Site
Source: University of Illinois Extension Urban Programs Resource Network
World Wide Web URL:
http://urbanext.illinois.edu/gpe/index.html

Healthy Forests
Students learn what makes a healthy forest.
Suggested Grade: 4-5
Format: Online Lesson Plan
Source: Julia Gordon
World Wide Web URL: http://sfr.psu.edu/youth/sftrc/lesson-plans/forestry/k-5/healthy-forests

Hello Dolly: A WebQuest
Students will explore the impact of cloning on agriculture.
Suggested Grade: 6-12
Format: WebQuest
Source: Keith Nuthall
World Wide Web URL:
http://www.pusd.info/projects/dolly/agriculture.htm

How Fast Are You Going?
Students will learn about speed and motion.
Suggested Grade: 6-12
Format: WebQuest
Source: William Chavez
World Wide Web URL:
http://www.can-do.com/uci/ssi2002/motion.html

All materials listed in this 2017-2018 edition are BRAND NEW!

SCIENCE

How Stuff Works
A place to learn about how all sorts of things work in the world around you--from how the engine in the car works to what makes the refrigerator cold. A new article is added every week.
Suggested Grade: All ages
Format: Web Site
Source: HowStuffWorks, Inc.
World Wide Web URL: http://www.howstuffworks.com/

How to View an Eclipse
Provides illustrated, step-by-step directions for making a pinhole projector for viewing an eclipse.
Suggested Grade: 6-12
Format: Online Article
Source: Ron Hipschman
World Wide Web URL: http://www.exploratorium.edu/eclipse/how.html

Human Anatomy Online
Here is a great reference for students studying human anatomy and for those who just want to know more about the medical descriptions commonly used by doctors and nurses.
Suggested Grade: 6-12
Format: Online Tutorial
Source: Inner Learning On-line
World Wide Web URL: http://www.innerbody.com/http://www.innerbody.com/

Hurricane Hunters, The
Here is where you will find information gathered from pilots who have actually flown into hurricanes.
Suggested Grade: 6-12
Format: Web Site
Source: Major Val Salva
World Wide Web URL: http://www.hurricanehunters.com/

Hurricanes and Tropical Storms
Explains how hurricanes work, hurricane safety, how hurricanes are named, and more.
Suggested Grade: K-8
Format: Web Site
Source: Environment Canada
World Wide Web URL: http://www.ns.ec.gc.ca/weather/hurricane/kids.html

I Can Do That!
Learn about DNA, RNA, cells, protein, and cloning.
Suggested Grade: 6-12
Format: Web Site
Source: Eureka!Science
World Wide Web URL: http://www.eurekascience.com/ICanDoThat/

Infection, Detection, Protection
Through the use of interactive stories and games, students will learn about what causes infection, how to detect if you have one, and how to prevent getting one.
Suggested Grade: K-5
Format: Web Site
Source: American Museum of Natural History
World Wide Web URL: http://www.amnh.org/nationalcenter/infection/

Investigating Plants
Find the answers to these many questions about plants, by visiting listed web sites.
Suggested Grade: 4
Format: WebQuest
Source: Gerald Robillard and Dee Charbonneau
World Wide Web URL: http://www.swlauriersb.qc.ca/english/edservices/pedresources/webquest/plants.htm

It's So Simple
An introduction to simple machines.
Suggested Grade: 6-12
Format: Online Lesson Plan
Source: Kimberly Baker-Brownfield and Jacques Marquette Branch
World Wide Web URL: http://www.iit.edu/~smile/mp0298.htm

Jefferson Lab--Science Education
Lesson plans, activities, worksheets, games, and more are found on this site to help teachers and students in the study of math and science.
Suggested Grade: 3-8
Format: Web Site
Source: Jefferson Office of Science Education
World Wide Web URL: http://education.jlab.org/index.html

Journey North, The
Track spring's Journey North and the migratory patterns of a dozen species. Students can share their own field observations and have discussions with scientists online.
Suggested Grade: K-12
Format: Web Site
Source: Annenberg/CPB Math and Science Project, The
World Wide Web URL: http://www.learner.org/jnorth/

Journey Through the Galaxy
Information and resources for teaching and learning about the solar system.
Suggested Grade: 6-12
Format: Web Site
Source: Stuart Robbins and David McDonald
World Wide Web URL: http://jtg.sjrdesign.net/index.html

Kentucky Bug Connection Teaching Resources
Entomology resources for parents and educators.
Suggested Grade: 6-12
Format: Online Lesson Plans and Curriculum Guides

All materials listed in this 2017-2018 edition are BRAND NEW!

SCIENCE

Source: University of Kentucky Entomology
World Wide Web URL:
http://www.uky.edu/Agriculture/CritterFiles/casefile/bugconnection/teaching/teaching.htm

Leaf ID and Leaf Bingo
Kids will learn to identify various leaves.
Suggested Grade: 3
Format: Online Lesson Plan
Source: Kelly Garthwaite
World Wide Web URL:
http://sfr.psu.edu/youth/sftrc/lesson-plans/forestry/k-5/leaf-bingo

Lewis and Clark as Naturalists
Learn about the plants and animals Lewis and Clark found along their great journey.
Suggested Grade: 3-8
Format: Web Site
Source: Smithsonian National Museum of Natural History
World Wide Web URL:
http://www.mnh.si.edu/lewisandclark/index.html?loc=/lewisandclark/home.html

Magnets
Teaches students all about magnets and how they attract.
Suggested Grade: 4-12
Format: Online Lesson Plan
Source: Consuela Llamas
World Wide Web URL:
http://teachertech.rice.edu/Participants/cllamas/lessons/science/magnets/studentmagnets.htm

Making a Comet in the Classroom
A dramatic and effective way to begin a unit on comets is to make your own comet right in front of the class. Here's how.
Suggested Grade: All ages
Format: Web Site
Source: Dennis Schatz
World Wide Web URL:
http://www.noao.edu/education/crecipe.html

Mammals of Texas, The
Presents information on the distribution, physical characteristics and life histories of the 181 species of Texas mammals.
Suggested Grade: 6-12
Format: Online Book
Source: William B. Davis and David J. Schmidly
World Wide Web URL:
http://www.nsrl.ttu.edu/tmot1/Default.htm

"Me? Live in a Rainforest?"
Learn all about the rainforest.
Suggested Grade: 3-6
Format: WebQuest
Source: Bill Byles
World Wide Web URL:
http://www.internet4classrooms.com/tropical_rain.htm

Minerals by Name
Just click on the name of a mineral and you will learn more about that mineral.
Suggested Grade: 7-Adult
Format: Web Site
Source: Amethyst Galleries, Inc.
World Wide Web URL:
http://www.galleries.com/minerals/byname.htm

Modeling Eclipses
Build a model to understand what occurs when there is an eclipse.
Suggested Grade: 4-8
Format: Online Activity
Source: Dennis Schatz
World Wide Web URL: http://solar-center.stanford.edu/eclipse/model.html

Mousetrap Racer!!!
Learn about and have fun with mousetrap cars.
Suggested Grade: 6-12
Format: WebQuest
Source: Robert Valadez
World Wide Web URL:
http://www.can-do.com/uci/ssi2002/mousetrap-racer.html

Mutualism and Co-evolution
A unit of lessons that uses a variety of methods and approaches to teach flowering plant biology.
Suggested Grade: 8
Format: Online Lesson Plan
Source: Roxane J. Johnson
World Wide Web URL: http://biology.arizona.edu/sciconn/lessons2/Roxane/page1.htm

My Day As an Insect
Learn more about insects.
Suggested Grade: K-2
Format: WebQuest
Source: Lisa Price, Walda Brooks, and Ann Abbuhl
World Wide Web URL:
http://projects.edtech.sandi.net/sessions/insects/

Nine Planets, The: A Multimedia Tour of the Solar System
Here is an overview of the history, mythology, and current scientific knowledge of each of the planets and moons in our solar system.
Suggested Grade: All ages
Format: Online Tutorial
Source: Bill Arnett
World Wide Web URL: http://www.nineplanets.org/

All materials listed in this 2017-2018 edition are **BRAND NEW!**

SCIENCE

Nonindigenous Species: Activities for Youth
A detailed manual of activities for helping students to learn about exotic species of plants and animals.
Suggested Grade: 2-8
Format: Downloadable Book; 55 pages
Special Notes: This is a PDF file which will open automatically on your computer.
Source: John Guyton, Dave Burrage and Rick Kastner
World Wide Web URL:
http://msucares.com/pubs/publications/p2286.pdf

North American Skies
A monthly guide to astronomical phenomena occurring over North America.
Suggested Grade: 6-12
Format: Web Site
Source: Larry Sessions
World Wide Web URL:
http://home.comcast.net/~sternmann/

Nova--Science in the News
Provides information to help explain current events in the field of science.
Suggested Grade: 6-12
Format: Web Site
Source: Australian Academy of Science
World Wide Web URL: http://www.science.org.au/nova/

Official Seed Starting Home Page, The
A site started simply for the love of gardening. Information about how to grow flowers, vegetables, and herbs is found here.
Suggested Grade: All ages
Format: Web Site
Source: Weekend Gardener, The
World Wide Web URL:
http://www.chestnut-sw.com/seedhp.htm

Owl Pellets
As students dissect an owl pellet, this lesson will help them learn more about the food chain as well as skeletal parts of animals ingested by owls.
Suggested Grade: 4-12
Format: Online Lesson Plan
Source: Jeanette Vratil
World Wide Web URL:
http://hub.colonialsd.org/curriculum/Science/Documents/Owl%20in%20the%20Shower%20K-3%20Science%20Enrichment/Owl%20in%20the%20Shower%20-%20Owl%20Pellet%20Dissection.PDF

Physical Science Activity Manual
This book contains 34 hands-on activities to bring excitement to your classroom.
Suggested Grade: Teacher Reference
Format: Downloadable Book
Source: Center of Excellence for Science and Mathematics Education, The
World Wide Web URL:
http://www.utm.edu/departments/cece/cesme/psam/psam.shtml

PhysicsFront.org
Lesson plans, activities, teacher resources, and much more. For high school students learning physics, but the sight contains a great section of physical science in grades K-8.
Suggested Grade: K-12
Format: Web Site
Special Notes: You must register, but registration is free.
Source: American Association of Physics Teachers
World Wide Web URL:
http://www.compadre.org/precollege/index.cfm

Planet Pals
Activities and projects for celebrating Earth Day.
Suggested Grade: K-5
Format: Web Site
Source: Planet Pals
World Wide Web URL:
http://www.planetpals.com/earthday.html

Planets or Not, Here We Come!
Students will develop their research skills as they find information about a specific planet in our solar system.
Suggested Grade: 3-4
Format: WebQuest
Source: Stephanie Sirvent
World Wide Web URL:
http://projects.edtech.sandi.net/king/planets

Plant Parts
After students learn about the 6 basic plant parts, they will create a game or activity so that others may learn the same thing.
Suggested Grade: 4-8
Format: WebQuest
Source: Colleen Boyea
World Wide Web URL:
http://its.guilford.k12.nc.us/webquests/plantquest/

POP Goes Antarctica?
Follow this teacher as she joins a team of scientists to research the effects of persistent organic pollutants on the food web of Antarctica.
Suggested Grade: 6-12
Format: Web Site
Source: Susan Cowles
World Wide Web URL:
http://literacynet.org/polar/pop/html/project.html

Que Tal in the Current Skies
Useful information about observing the visible planets, our moon, and other moons, the sun, and other "things" celestial.

All materials listed in this 2017-2018 edition are **BRAND NEW!**

SCIENCE

Suggested Grade: All ages
Format: Online Newsletter
Source: Bob Riddle
World Wide Web URL: http://currentsky.com/

Recycling Lesson Plan
Students will learn more about recycling.
Suggested Grade: 3
Format: Online Lesson Plan
Source: Hope Wenzel
World Wide Web URL:
http://sftrc.cas.psu.edu/LessonPlans/Forestry/Recycling.html

Research Vessels
Information about these vessels which give us so much information.
Suggested Grade: 4-12
Format: Online Articles
Source: Office of Naval Research
World Wide Web URL:
http://www.onr.navy.mil/focus/ocean/vessels/default.htm

Rocks For Kids
Lots of information as well as additional links concerning rocks and minerals.
Suggested Grade: 3-12
Format: Web Site
Source: GMB Services
World Wide Web URL: http://www.rocksforkids.com/

ROVer Ranch
Presents resources for teaching and learning about robotic engineering and more about robotic systems.
Suggested Grade: K-12
Format: Web Site
Source: NASA Johnson Space Center
World Wide Web URL: http://prime.jsc.nasa.gov/ROV/

Salmon Homing Instincts
Follows the interesting lifestyle of the salmon and how they find their way back to the stream in which they were hatched.
Suggested Grade: 3-9
Format: Online Lesson Plan
Source: Deborah A. Werner
World Wide Web URL:
http://ofcn.org/cyber.serv/academy/ace/sci/cecsci/cecsci002.html

Sammy Soil--A Downloadable Coloring Book
A very cute coloring book that teaches youngsters about soil.
Suggested Grade: preK-2
Format: Downloadable Coloring book
Source: Mississippi Soil and Water Conservation Commission
World Wide Web URL:
http://www.epa.gov/gmpo/edresources/ssoil.html

Save the Rainforest
Provides a virtual tour of the rainforest and lots of information about why we need them and why they are becoming endangered ecosystems.
Suggested Grade: All ages
Format: Web Site
Source: Save the Rainforest.org
World Wide Web URL: http://www.savetherainforest.org/

Science Fair Home Page
A project of the Eastern Newfoundland Science Fairs Council, this site lists hundreds of topics for science fair projects. Broken down by grade level and subject.
Suggested Grade: All ages
Format: Web Site
Source: Science Fairs
World Wide Web URL: http://eastern.scifairs.k12.nf.ca/

Science is Fun
This chemistry professional shares the fun of science through home science activities, demonstration shows, and more.
Suggested Grade: All ages
Format: Web Site
Source: Bassam Z. Shakhashiri
World Wide Web URL: http://scifun.chem.wisc.edu/

ScienceMaster
News, homework help, links, articles, and more in all major areas of science.
Suggested Grade: 6-12
Format: Web Site
Source: KGM Group, Inc., The
World Wide Web URL: http://www.ScienceMaster.com/

Science Role Plays
An interesting experiment in which students role play the scientific processes.
Suggested Grade: 5-8
Format: Online Lesson Plan
Source: Janet Weaver
World Wide Web URL: http://ofcn.org/cyber.serv/academy/ace/sci/cecsci/cecsci175.html

Sea Turtle Migration-Tracking Education Program
Information about sea turtle species, biology, habitat, and migration patterns.
Suggested Grade: All ages
Format: Web Site
Special Notes: Teachers in the United States only can send for a free Educator's Guide which includes lesson plans and activities.
Source: Caribbean Conservation Corporation
World Wide Web URL: http://www.cccturtle.org/

All materials listed in this 2017-2018 edition are **BRAND NEW!**

SCIENCE

SET Toolkit
Lots of activities for learning science.
Suggested Grade: 3-6
Format: Series of downloadable science activities
Source: Cornell University, Cooperative Extension
World Wide Web URL: http://nys4h.cce.cornell.edu/about%20us/Pages/SETToolkit.aspx

Simply Sharks!
An interactive, interdisciplinary unit that leads you into the deep blue sea.
Suggested Grade: K-1
Format: WebQuest
Source: Shelby Madden, et al
World Wide Web URL: http://projects.edtech.sandi.net/encanto/simplysharks/

Single-Use Foodservice Packaging--Facts and Fun Teacher's Kit
A curriculum to help students learn about the benefits of foodservice disposable products.
Suggested Grade: 6-9
Format: Downloadable Teacher's Kit
Special Notes: Includes lesson plans, activities, glossary, and a new interactive game. May also be downloaded from web site.
Source: Foodservice Packaging Institute, Inc.
World Wide Web URL: http://www.fpi.org/dms/dm_browse.asp?pid=97

SkyDEN
Offers a visually stunning introduction to astronomy.
Suggested Grade: All ages
Format: Online Course
Source: Act360 Media Ltd.
World Wide Web URL: http://www.actden.com/

Snakes of Massachusetts
Lots of information on snakes.
Suggested Grade: All ages
Format: Web Site
Source: University of Massachusetts Extension
World Wide Web URL: http://www.masnakes.org/

Soda Play
Practice your creativity as well as learn a little physics by building animated models online.
Suggested Grade: 6-Adult
Format: Web Site
Source: Sodaplay
World Wide Web URL: http://www.sodaplay.com/

Solar System Bowl
Learn all about the vast solar system.
Suggested Grade: 3-5
Format: Online Lesson Plan
Source: Jane Whaling
World Wide Web URL: http://youth.net/cec/cecmisc/cecmisc.29.txt

StarChild
Lots of information about the solar system and the universe.
Suggested Grade: 3-8
Format: Web Site
Source: Joyce Dejoie and Elizabeth Truelove
World Wide Web URL: http://starchild.gsfc.nasa.gov/docs/StarChild/StarChild.html

Studying Watersheds: A Confluence of Important Ideas
Ideas and resources for teaching about this valuable resource.
Suggested Grade: Teacher Reference
Production Date: 2000
Format: Online Article
Source: David L. Haury
World Wide Web URL: http://www.ericdigests.org/2003-1/ideas.htm

Switch ZoO
Students can take parts of one animal and place them on another to create a brand new animal. Not only fun, but the site encourages them to then write a story about their new animal. Information about each animal as they really exist is also presented.
Suggested Grade: K-8
Format: Web Site
Source: Tubehead.com
World Wide Web URL: http://www.switcheroozoo.com/

Talk About Trees
Activities, lesson plans, newsletters, and more about trees.
Suggested Grade: All ages
Format: Online Lesson Plans and activities
Source: Forest Foundation, The
World Wide Web URL: http://www.talkabouttrees.org/

Teachers' Domain
Focuses on life sciences and provides a free multimedia digital library of resources for teachers and students alike.
Suggested Grade: All ages
Format: Web Site
Source: WGBH Educational Foundation
World Wide Web URL: http://www.teachersdomain.org/

Teaching Science in the Field
Explains how to successfully take students "outside" to learn science.
Suggested Grade: Teacher Reference
Production Date: 1996
Format: Online Article
Source: Carol Landis
World Wide Web URL: http://www.ericdigests.org/1998-1/field.htm

All materials listed in this 2017-2018 edition are BRAND NEW!

SCIENCE

Temperature and Water Density
Teaches students about the density of water as it relates to temperature and helps them identify the forces governing convection in liquids.
Suggested Grade: 7-8
Format: Online Lesson Plan
Source: Steve McFarland
World Wide Web URL: http://ofcn.org/cyber.serv/academy/ace/sci/cecsci/cecsci212.html

There Are Algae in Your House!
Students will be surprised to learn that seaweed is not only found in the ocean.
Suggested Grade: 4-12
Format: Online Lesson Plan
Source: Beth Nalker and Doug Casey
World Wide Web URL: http://seawifs.gsfc.nasa.gov/OCEAN_PLANET/HTML/education_lesson1.html

Thinking Fountain
Presents ideas from A to Z for science lessons, activities, and resources.
Suggested Grade: All ages
Format: Web Site
Source: Science Museum of Minnesota
World Wide Web URL: http://www.thinkingfountain.org/

Toilet Paper Solar System
This activity will help students to describe the relative distances of planets from our sun.
Suggested Grade: All ages
Format: Online Lesson Plan
Source: Elizabeth Roettger
World Wide Web URL: http://www.nthelp.com/eer/HOAtpss.html

Tox Town
Provides an introduction to toxic chemicals and environmental health risks you might encounter in everyday life, in everyday places.
Suggested Grade: All ages
Format: Web Site
Source: U. S. National Library of Medicine
World Wide Web URL: http://toxtown.nlm.nih.gov/

Under the Weather
Students will learn to identify measurable characteristics about the weather and learn how they are monitored. They then will research and propose the construction of a weather monitoring station on their school's grounds.
Suggested Grade: 6-12
Format: Online Lesson Plan
Source: Priscilla Chan and Andrea Perelman
World Wide Web URL: http://www.nytimes.com/learning/teachers/lessons/20041230thursday.html

Universe in the Classroom, The
An electronic newsletter for teachers, youth group leaders, librarians, and anybody else who wants to help children of all ages learn more about the wonders of the universe.
Suggested Grade: All ages
Format: Online Newsletter
Source: Astronomical Society of the Pacific
World Wide Web URL: http://www.astrosociety.org/education/publications/tnl/tnl.html

Volcanoes of the United States
Describes the principal volcanoes in the U. S. that have erupted during the last few hundred years.
Suggested Grade: 4-12
Format: Online Booklet; 44 pages
Source: USGS Information Services
World Wide Web URL: http://pubs.usgs.gov/gip/volcus/

Water Conservation Lesson Plan
Students will learn the importance of water in everyday living, how we use it, and how to conserve it.
Suggested Grade: 3
Format: Online Lesson Plan
Source: Hope Wenzel
World Wide Web URL: http://sfr.psu.edu/youth/sftrc/lesson-plans/water/k-5/conservation-2

Waterford Press Free Games, Activities & More
Games, activities, and quizzes that can be downloaded and printed easily in support of the natural science curriculum.
Suggested Grade: K-12
Format: Web Site
Special Notes: Requires registration, but registration is free.
Source: Waterford Press Ltd.
World Wide Web URL: http://www.waterfordpress.com/index.php/Educator-Resources/Waterford-Activity-Zone.html

Wetland Ecosystems II--Interactions and Ecosystems
Units include wetland types, energy pyramids, abiotic factors, and more.
Suggested Grade: 7-8
Format: Downloadable Teacher's Guide and Lessons.
Source: Ducks Unlimited
World Wide Web URL: http://www.greenwing.org/dueducator/lesson_plans.html

Whale Songs
A resource for teachers, students, and whale lovers.
Suggested Grade: All ages
Format: Web Site
Source: Lance Leonhardt
World Wide Web URL: http://www.whalesongs.org

Whales on the Net
Lots of resources for learning about whales.

*All materials listed in this 2017-2018 edition are **BRAND NEW**!*

SCIENCE

Suggested Grade: 4-12
Format: Web Site
Source: Whales on the Net
World Wide Web URL:
http://www.whales.org.au/index.html

Who Dunnit?
Learn how to be a crime solver by studying how forensic scientists analyze evidence.
Suggested Grade: 6-8
Format: Web Site
Source: Linda C. Joseph and Linda D. Resch
World Wide Web URL:
http://www.cyberbee.com/whodunnit/crime.html

WildFinder
A map-driven, searchable database of more than 26,000 species worldwide, with a powerful search tool that allows users to discover where species live or explore wild places to find out what species live there.
Suggested Grade: 6-12
Format: Web Site
Source: World Wildlife Fund
World Wide Web URL:
http://www.worldwildlife.org/wildfinder/

YES I Can! Science
Provides teacher resources, classroom activities, and lesson plans that support the Canadian science curriculum.
Suggested Grade: K-12
Format: Web Site
Source: York University
World Wide Web URL: http://www.yesican-science.ca/

All materials listed in this 2017-2018 edition are BRAND NEW!

SPECIAL EDUCATION

ADHD eBook
Here is the complete text of this book which discusses this disorder and presents solutions and treatment for coping.
Suggested Grade: Adult
Format: Downloadable Book
Source: Martin L. Kutscher, M.D.
World Wide Web URL:
http://www.pediatricneurology.com/adhd.htm

Alternatives to Behaviorism
Summarizes the research of Dr. Stanley Greenspan which demonstrates the superiority of relationship-based approaches to early intervention when working with autistic children.
Suggested Grade: Teacher Reference
Format: Online Article
Source: Autism National Committee
World Wide Web URL:
http://www.autcom.org/articles%5CBehaviorism.html

American Sign Language Browser
Offers movies showing SL gestures conveying concepts and phrases.
Suggested Grade: All ages
Format: Web Site
Special Notes: Available on CD-ROM for $19.95.
Source: Michigan State University, Communication Technology Laboratory
World Wide Web URL:
http://commtechlab.msu.edu/sites/aslweb/browser.htm

Applications of Participatory Action Research with Students Who Have Disabilities
Offers several examples of how researchers and practitioners are using participatory action research data to select effective practices and support change and innovation.
Suggested Grade: Teacher Reference
Production Date: 2003
Format: Online Article
Source: Cynthia Warger and Jane Burnette
World Wide Web URL:
http://www.ericdigests.org/2004-2/action.html

Chatback Trust, The
This project helps special-needs schools communicate using email.
Suggested Grade: 6-12
Format: Web Site
Source: Chatback Trust, The
World Wide Web URL:
http://atschool.eduweb.co.uk/chatback/

Everything You Always Wanted to Know About Dyslexia
Explains this learning disorder.
Suggested Grade: All ages
Format: Web Site
Special Notes: This URL will lead you to a subject page. Then click on the appropriate subject heading.
Source: ThinkQuest
World Wide Web URL:
http://www.thinkquest.org/pls/html/think.library

General Information About Blindness
Provides an overview of blindness and tells things you should know about blind people.
Suggested Grade: Teacher Reference
Format: Online Article
Source: Blind Net, A
World Wide Web URL:
http://www.blind.net/general-information/

Hard of Hearing and Deaf Students: A Resource Guide to Support Classroom Teachers
Provides lots of information to help teachers be effective educators to students who suffer hearing loss.
Suggested Grade: Teacher Reference
Format: Online Article
Source: British Columbia Ministry of Education
World Wide Web URL:
http://www.bced.gov.bc.ca/specialed/hearimpair/

Integrating Children with Disabilities Into Preschool
Examines research on preschool programs that include children both with and without disabilities.
Suggested Grade: Teacher Reference
Production Date: 1994
Format: Online Article
Source: Karen E. Diamond, Linda L. Hestenes, and Caryn O'Connor
World Wide Web URL:
http://www.ericdigests.org/1994/preschool.htm

See What I Say: Connecting the Hearing with the Hearing Impaired
Info on communication between hearing and hearing impaired.
Suggested Grade: 6-8
Format: Web Site
Special Notes: This URL will lead you to a subject page. Then click on the appropriate subject heading.
Source: ThinkQuest
World Wide Web URL:
http://www.thinkquest.org/pls/html/think.library

SIGNhear
Learn American Sign Language, practice, or look up a word.
Suggested Grade: 4-12
Format: Web Site

*All materials listed in this 2017-2018 edition are **BRAND NEW!***

SPECIAL EDUCATION

Special Notes: This URL will lead you to a subject page. Then click on the appropriate subject heading.
Source: ThinkQuest
World Wide Web URL:
http://www.thinkquest.org/pls/html/think.library

Sign Language
Provides the viewer with a history of American Sign Language and shows how to make each of the letter signs.
Suggested Grade: All ages
Format: Web Site
Special Notes: This URL will lead you to a subject page. Then click on the appropriate subject heading.
Source: ThinkQuest
World Wide Web URL:
http://www.thinkquest.org/pls/html/think.library

Sounds of Silence
To educate hearing people about deafness and the deaf community.
Suggested Grade: 2-Adult
Format: Web Site
Special Notes: This URL will lead you to a subject page. Then click on the appropriate subject heading.
Source: ThinkQuest
World Wide Web URL:
http://www.thinkquest.org/pls/html/think.library

Students with Intellectual Disabilities: A Resource Guide for Teachers
Explains how to approach and effectively teach students who have intellectual disabilities.
Suggested Grade: Teacher Reference
Format: Online Article
Source: British Columbia Ministry of Education
World Wide Web URL:
http://www.bced.gov.bc.ca/specialed/sid/

Students with Visual Impairments
Tips to help you effectively teach students with sight impairments.
Suggested Grade: Teacher Reference
Format: Online Article
Source: British Columbia Ministry of Education
World Wide Web URL:
http://www.bced.gov.bc.ca/specialed/visimpair/

Understanding Disabilities
Describes the characteristics and causes of autism, deafness, and blindness.
Suggested Grade: All ages
Format: Web Site
Special Notes: This URL will lead you to a subject page. Then click on the appropriate subject heading.
Source: ThinkQuest
World Wide Web URL:
http://www.thinkquest.org/pls/html/think.library

What the Blind Can See
Describes the many methods that blind people use "to see" that helps them lead productive lives.
Suggested Grade: All ages
Format: Web Site
Special Notes: This URL will lead you to a subject page. Then click on the appropriate subject heading.
Source: ThinkQuest
World Wide Web URL:
http://www.thinkquest.org/pls/html/think.library

All materials listed in this 2017-2018 edition are BRAND NEW!

TEACHER REFERENCE

Action Research in Early Childhood Education
Explores this issue in a concise report.
Suggested Grade: Teacher Reference
Production Date: 1996
Format: Online Article
    Source: Eileen T. Borgia and Dorothy Schuler
    World Wide Web URL:
    http://www.ericdigests.org/1997-2/action.htm

Adopted Children in the Early Childhood Classroom
Discusses this issue.
Suggested Grade: Parents
Production Date: 1999
Format: Online Article
    Source: Judith E. Stroud, James C. Stroud, and Lynn M. Staley
    World Wide Web URL:
    http://www.ericdigests.org/1999-3/adopted.htm

Americans with Disabilities Act: Questions and Answers
Explains how the civil rights of persons with disabilities are protected at work and in public places.
Suggested Grade: Teacher Reference
Format: Online Article; 31 pages
Special Notes: Use the on-site search engine to easily find this title. You may request a printed copy mailed to you for a fee.
    Source: Federal Citizen Information Center
    World Wide Web URL:
    http://publications.usa.gov/USAPubs.php

Are You With It?
Discusses a discipline model effective for dealing with students in physical education classes.
Suggested Grade: Teacher Reference
Format: Online Article
    Source: Deb Wuest
    World Wide Web URL:
    http://www.pecentral.org/climate/april99article.html

Assessing Bilingual Students for Placement and Instruction
Discusses how to evaluate bilingual students for proper classroom placement.
Suggested Grade: Teacher Reference
Production Date: 1990
Format: Online Article
    Source: Carol Ascher
    World Wide Web URL:
    http://www.ericdigests.org/pre-9217/placement.htm

Assessing Young Children's Social Competence
Provides information to help educators evaluate a child's social competence.
Suggested Grade: Teacher Reference
Production Date: 2001
Format: Online Article
    Source: Diane E. McClellan and Lilian G. Katz
    World Wide Web URL:
    http://www.ericdigests.org/2001-4/assessing.html

Attending to Learning Styles in Mathematics and Science Classrooms
Discusses learning styles and how to teach science and mathematics.
Suggested Grade: Teacher Reference
Production Date: 1997
Format: Online Article
    Source: Barbara S. Thomson and John R. Mascazine
    World Wide Web URL:
    http://www.ericdigests.org/2000-1/attending.html

Back to the Agora: Workable Solutions for Small Urban School Facilities
Suggests adapting Socrates' model of agora to meet modern needs in small urban school settings.
Suggested Grade: Teacher Reference
Production Date: 2003
Format: Online Article
    Source: Barbara Kent Lawrence
    World Wide Web URL:
    http://www.ericdigests.org/2004-1/back.htm

Behind the Scenes Look at the Landrum News Network, A
Overview of a television production class at Landrum Middle School as they produce their own news show.
Suggested Grade: 6-12
Format: Web Site
Special Notes: This URL will lead you to a subject page. Then click on the appropriate subject heading.
    Source: ThinkQuest
    World Wide Web URL:
    http://www.thinkquest.org/pls/html/think.library

Blind Men and the Elephant, The
Through the retelling of a traditional story from India, students will learn how "dangerous" it is to come to conclusions without adequate information.
Suggested Grade: 3-5
Format: Online Lesson Plan
    Source: Peace Corps
    World Wide Web URL: http://www.peacecorps.gov/wws/publications/looking/index.cfm

Boy/Girl Pieces
Maintains a focus on talking about issues from one's own experience instead of their perceptions of the experiences of "those people." Adaptable for race, sexual orientation, socioeconomic class, religion, and other identifiers.
Suggested Grade: Teacher Reference
Format: Online Lesson Plan

*All materials listed in this 2017-2018 edition are **BRAND NEW!***

TEACHER REFERENCE

Source: Paul Gorski
World Wide Web URL:
http://www.edchange.org/multicultural/activities/boygirl.html

Can Failing Schools Be Fixed?
Examines, at length, this current issue.
Suggested Grade: Teacher Reference
Format: Online Article
Source: Ronald C. Brady
World Wide Web URL:
http://www.edexcellence.net/publications/canfailingschools.html

Can Performance-Based Assessments Improve Urban Schooling?
Attempts to answer this question.
Suggested Grade: Teacher Reference
Production Date: 1990
Format: Online Article
Source: Carol Ascher
World Wide Web URL:
http://www.ericdigests.org/pre-9218/urban.htm

Capitalizing on Small Class Size
Discusses this topic.
Suggested Grade: Teacher Reference
Production Date: 2000
Format: Online Article
Source: Jessica O'Connell and Stuart C. Smith
World Wide Web URL:
http://www.kidsource.com/education/money.small.class.html

Catch the Spirit: A Student's Guide to Community Service
Ideas and information on how young people can make their community a better place.
Suggested Grade: All ages
Production Date: 2005
Format: Downloadable Booklet; 15 pages
Special Notes: Use the on-site search engine to easily find this title. You may request a printed copy mailed to you for a fee.
Source: Federal Citizen Information Center
World Wide Web URL:
http://publications.usa.gov/USAPubs.php

Changing Face of Racial Isolation and Desegregation in Urban Schools
Focuses on several issues in school desegregation that stem from recent changes in demography, policy, and research.
Suggested Grade: Teacher Reference
Production Date: 1993
Format: Online Article
Source: Carol Ascher
World Wide Web URL:
http://www.ericdigests.org/1993/face.htm

Chapter I Schoolwide Projects: Advantages and Limitations
Discusses this issue.
Suggested Grade: Teacher Reference
Production Date: 1993
Format: Online Article
Source: Gary Burnett
World Wide Web URL:
http://www.ericdigests.org/1994/chapter.htm

Charter Schools: An Approach for Rural Education?
Describes characteristics of charter schools, outlines some tentative research findings, discusses advantages and shortcomings, and summarizes challenges rural communities might face in starting such a school.
Suggested Grade: Teacher Reference
Production Date: 1999
Format: Online Article
Source: Timothy Collins
World Wide Web URL:
http://www.ericdigests.org/1999-3/charter.htm

Child-Initiated Learning Activities for Young Children Living in Poverty
Discusses the findings of empirical students on teacher-directed and child-initiated preschool programs for this group.
Suggested Grade: Teacher Reference
Production Date: 1997
Format: Online Article
Source: Lawrence J. Schweinhart
World Wide Web URL:
http://www.ericdigests.org/1998-1/poverty.htm

Children, Stress, and Natural Disasters: School Activities for Children
Lots of activities for students of all ages.
Suggested Grade: Teacher Reference
Format: Online Articles
Source: University of Illinois Extension Disaster Resources
World Wide Web URL:
http://web.extension.uiuc.edu/disaster/teacher/teacher.html

Choosing Instructional Materials for Environmental Education
Helpful information for finding and evaluating these materials.
Suggested Grade: Teacher Reference
Production Date: 1998
Format: Online Article
Source: David L. Haury and Linda A. Milbourne
World Wide Web URL:
http://www.ericdigests.org/2000-2/materials.htm

Conflict Resolution Programs in Schools
Discusses how to set up these programs.

All materials listed in this 2017-2018 edition are BRAND NEW!

TEACHER REFERENCE

Suggested Grade: Teacher Reference
Production Date: 1991
Format: Online Article
Source: Morton Inger
World Wide Web URL:
http://www.ericdigests.org/1992-5/conflict.htm

Creating an A+++ Classroom Library
A veteran teacher explains his foolproof method for setting up a classroom library where students literally plead for more silent reading time.
Suggested Grade: Teacher Reference
Format: Online Article
Source: Jeff Lowe
World Wide Web URL:
http://teacher.scholastic.com/professional/classmgmt/classroomlib.htm

Cultural Liberation: East-West Biculturalism for a New Century
Explains how and why we should embrace the cultures of other countries and denominations.
Suggested Grade: Teacher Reference
Format: Online Article
Source: Steve McCarty
World Wide Web URL:
http://edchange.org/multicultural/papers/mccarty.html

Custom Addressbook 0.7.2
Store and manage all your address data.
Suggested Grade: Teacher Reference
Format: Downloadable FULL PROGRAM
Source: Henk Hagedoorn
World Wide Web URL: http://www.freebyte.com/freeware/

Data Inquiry and Analysis for Educational Reform
Outlines the most useful types of data to drive the process of school improvement, the steps that must be taken to collect and analyze the data, the role of administrations in guiding the data-driven reform process, and the results that can be expected.
Suggested Grade: Teacher Reference
Production Date: 2001
Format: Online Article
Source: Howard H. Wade
World Wide Web URL:
http://www.ericdigests.org/2002-4/data-inquiry.html

Determining the Existence of Gender Bias in Daily Tasks
Demonstrates how role responsibilities in the every day environment of home remain based in stereotyping to a great degree.
Suggested Grade: 3-6
Format: Online Lesson Plan
Source: Kathleen E. van Noort
World Wide Web URL:
http://www.ricw.state.ri.us/lessons/135.htm

Developing a School District Web Presence
Walks you through the organizational process of creating a district web site.
Suggested Grade: Teacher Reference
Format: Online Article
Source: TeAch-nology.com
World Wide Web URL:
http://www.teach-nology.com/tutorials/district_web/

Developing Language Proficiency and Connecting School to Students's Lives: Two Standards for Effective Teaching
Helpful information for teachers.
Suggested Grade: Teacher Reference
Production Date: 1998
Format: Online Article
Source: Center for Research on Education, Diversity & Excellence
World Wide Web URL:
http://www.cal.org/resources/digest/daltoneric.html

Diversity is About Change and Leadership
Discusses how to adapt to the ever increasing diversity of the United States.
Suggested Grade: Teacher Reference
Format: Online Article
Special Notes: The author is Vice-President for Affirmative Action/Diversity at the Southeast Community College System in Lincoln, Nebraska.
Source: Jose Soto
World Wide Web URL:
http://www.edchange.org/multicultural/papers/diversity_soto.html

Diversity Within Unity: Essential Principles for Teaching and Learning in a Multicultural Society
What do we know about education and diversity and how do we know it? Twelve essential principles are explained in this publication, which includes a checklist for educational practitioners.
Suggested Grade: Teacher Reference
Format: Online Article
Source: Dr. James Banks
World Wide Web URL:
http://education.washington.edu/cme/dwu.htm

Dr. Mac's Amazing Behavior Management Advice Site
Offers thousands of tips on managing student behavior, and provides step-by-step directions for implementing a great number of standard interventions. Also contains a bulletin board.

TEACHER REFERENCE

Suggested Grade: Adult
Format: Web Site
Source: Thomas McIntyre
World Wide Web URL: http://www.behavioradvisor.com/

Education of Immigrant Children in New York City, The
Discusses a program already in place that might help other educators.
Suggested Grade: Teacher Reference
Production Date: 1996
Format: Online Article
Source: Francisco L. Rivera-Batiz
World Wide Web URL: http://www.ericdigests.org/1997-3/nyc.html

Encouraging Creativity in Early Childhood Classrooms
Explores this issue in a concise report.
Suggested Grade: Teacher Reference
Production Date: 1995
Format: Online Article
Source: Carolyn Pope Edwards and Kay Wright Springate
World Wide Web URL: http://www.kidsource.com/kidsource/content2/Creativity.html

Exploring Language: Definitions Activity
Considers language as a vital aspect of multicultural education and awareness. Participants discuss how they define words such as prejudice, discrimination, racism, sexism, and more.
Suggested Grade: Teacher Reference
Format: Online Lesson Plan
Source: Paul Gorski
World Wide Web URL: http://www.edchange.org/multicultural/activities/activity4.html

Family Diversity in Urban Schools
Identifies several common types of nontraditional families and presents a few of their characteristics relevant to their children's education.
Suggested Grade: Teacher Reference
Production Date: 1999
Format: Online Article
Source: Wendy Schwartz
World Wide Web URL: http://www.ericdigests.org/2000-2/urban.htm

Family Finding: Exploring Multicultural Families Using Film
Created so children entering kindergarten can learn about families all over the world.
Suggested Grade: K
Format: Downloadable Curriculum Unit
Source: Kathleen C. Rende
World Wide Web URL: http://www.yale.edu/ynhti/curriculum/units/2005/1/05.01.07.x.html

Family Involvement in Early Multicultural Learning
Explores this issue in a concise report.
Suggested Grade: Teacher Reference
Production Date: 1995
Format: Online Article
Source: Kevin J. Swick, Gloria Boutte, and Irma van Scoy
World Wide Web URL: http://www.ericdigests.org/1996-1/family.htm

First Impressions
When working on this unit, students will recognize that a single observation can be misleading.
Suggested Grade: 3-5
Format: Online Lesson Plan
Source: Peace Corps
World Wide Web URL: http://www.peacecorps.gov/wws/publications/looking/index.cfm

Four Directions
Represents the partnership of 19 Bureau of Indian Affairs schools and 11 private and public universities and organizations. The participants are working to build an online community of practice for people interested in promoting the education of Native Americans. The Cache section has a lot of research resources and information on native cultures.
Suggested Grade: 6-Adult
Format: Web Site
Source: 4Directions Project
World Wide Web URL: http://4directions.org/

4th Grade Treasure Trove
Not only provides links of interest to second graders, but provides networking opportunities for teachers of this grade.
Suggested Grade: 4
Format: Web Site
Source: Karen Walkowiak
World Wide Web URL: http://www.karensclassroom.com/treasuretrove/gradefour/index.htm

Full-Day Kindergarten Programs
Explores this issue in a concise report.
Suggested Grade: Teacher Reference
Production Date: 1995
Format: Online Article
Source: Dianne Rothenberg
World Wide Web URL: http://www.ericdigests.org/1996-1/full.htm

Gangs in the Schools
Discusses this issue.

All materials listed in this 2017-2018 edition are BRAND NEW!

TEACHER REFERENCE

Suggested Grade: Teacher Reference
Production Date: 1994
Format: Online Article
Source: Gary Burnett and Garry Walz
World Wide Web URL:
http://www.ericdigests.org/1995-1/gangs.htm

Gangs the Foster Family
Find out what role apparel, hand signals, and graffiti play in gangs and ways to make a dent in the problem of gang violence.
Suggested Grade: 6-12
Format: Web Site
Special Notes: This URL will lead you to a subject page. Then click on the appropriate subject heading.
Source: ThinkQuest
World Wide Web URL:
http://www.thinkquest.org/pls/html/think.library

Gender Differences in Educational Achievement within Racial and Ethnic Groups
Discusses this issue.
Suggested Grade: Teacher Reference
Production Date: 2001
Format: Online Article
Source: ERIC Clearinghouse on Urban Education
World Wide Web URL:
http://www.ericdigests.org/2002-1/gender.html

Geo-Images Project
A database of images (mostly photographs) for using in teaching geography.
Suggested Grade: Teacher Reference
Format: Web Site
Source: G. Donald Bain
World Wide Web URL: http://GeoImages.Berkeley.edu/

Getting Started--Respect Activity
Introduces the first crucial step in discussing multicultural issues: building a community of respect.
Suggested Grade: Teacher Reference
Format: Online Lesson Plan
Source: Paul Gorski
World Wide Web URL:
http://www.edchange.org/multicultural/activities/activity1.html

Help for "They Won't Let Me Play with Them!"
A useful guide for setting standards and expectations with students and how to follow up on them all year.
Suggested Grade: Teacher Reference
Format: Online Article
Source: William Kreidler
World Wide Web URL: http://teacher.scholastic.com/professional/classmgmt/playhelp.htm

Homeschooling
Answers the questions, "What are the origins of home schooling?," "How many children are home schooled today?," and more.
Suggested Grade: Teacher Reference
Production Date: 2001
Format: Online Article
Special Notes: This is a PDF file which will open automatically on your computer.
Source: Patricia M. Lines
World Wide Web URL:
http://www.eric.ed.gov/PDFS/ED457539.pdf

Hunger Site, The
Click on the button on this Web site to make a free donation of food to hungry people around the world. Sponsors pay for the donation, which you can make once every day.
Suggested Grade: All ages
Format: Web Site
Source: Hunger Site, The
World Wide Web URL:
http://www.thehungersite.com/cgi-bin/WebObjects/CTDSites

Iceberg, The
Upon completion of this unit, students will be able to identify features that all cultures have in common and understand that culture includes both visible and invisible features.
Suggested Grade: All ages
Format: Online Lesson Plan
Source: Peace Corps
World Wide Web URL: http://www.peacecorps.gov/wws/publications/looking/index.cfm

Identification and Recruitment of Migrant Students: Strategies and Resources
Provides an overview of how to develop a realistic and workable system for quickly finding and enrolling eligible students.
Suggested Grade: Teacher Reference
Production Date: 2002
Format: Online Article
Source: Ray Melecio and Thomas J. Hanley
World Wide Web URL:
http://www.ericdigests.org/2003-4/migrant-students.html

I Love That Teaching Idea
Although a site that sells things, this site also presents a number of free teaching ideas and reproducibles for elementary classrooms.
Suggested Grade: Teacher Reference
Format: Web Site
Source: I Love That Teaching Idea
World Wide Web URL:
http://www.ILoveThatTeachingIdea.com/

TEACHER REFERENCE

Implementing the Multiage Classroom
Explains what teachers and administrators need to know about implementing the multiage classroom.
Suggested Grade: Teacher Reference
Production Date: 1995
Format: Online Article
   Source: Joan Gaustad
   World Wide Web URL:
   http://www.ericdigests.org/1996-1/multiage.htm

Implementing Whole-School Reform
Examines some of the key issues surrounding the implementation of schoolwide reform and the factors that can lead to failure or success.
Suggested Grade: Teacher Reference
Production Date: 1999
Format: Online Article
   Source: Elizabeth Hertling
   World Wide Web URL:
   http://www.ericdigests.org/2002-1/reform.html

Instructional Models for Early Childhood Education
Discusses the knowledge base on the differential effects of various approaches to early education.
Suggested Grade: Teacher Reference
Production Date: 2002
Format: Online Article
   Source: Susan L. Golbeck
   World Wide Web URL:
   http://www.ericdigests.org/2003-3/early.htm

Integrated Curriculum in the Middle School
Discusses three critical concepts about middle school curriculum.
Suggested Grade: Teacher Reference
Production Date: 1992
Format: Online Article
   Source: James Beane
   World Wide Web URL:
   http://www.ericdigests.org/1992-1/middle.htm

Internet and Early Childhood Educators, The: Some Frequently Asked Questions
Answers questions which explain the usefulness of the Internet in early childhood education.
Suggested Grade: Teacher Reference
Production Date: 1995
Format: Online Article
   Source: Dianne Rothenberg
   World Wide Web URL:
   http://www.ericdigests.org/1996-1/internet.htm

INTIME
INTIME stands for Integrating New Technologies Into the Methods of Education. This site provides research, information, and online videos about integrating technology into proven research-based methods of teaching and learning.
Suggested Grade: Teacher Reference
Format: Web Site
   Source: INTIME
   World Wide Web URL: http://www.intime.uni.edu/

Involving Migrant Families in Education
Describes parent involvement in the education process from the perspective of parents and educators and offers strategies to enhance the experience of schooling for migrant students and their families.
Suggested Grade: Teacher Reference
Production Date: 2000
Format: Online Article
   Source: Yolanda G. Martinez and Jose A. Velazquez
   World Wide Web URL:
   http://www.ericdigests.org/2001-3/migrant.htm

Issues in the Education of American Indian and Alaska Native Students with Disabilities
Presents information on this topic.
Suggested Grade: Teacher Reference
Production Date: 2000
Format: Online Article
   Source: Susan Faircloth and John W. Tippeconnic
   World Wide Web URL:
   http://www.ericdigests.org/2001-3/alaska.htm

Key Characteristics of Middle Level Schools
Explores this issue in a concise report.
Suggested Grade: Teacher Reference
Production Date: 1996
Format: Online Article
   Source: John H. Lounsbury
   World Wide Web URL:
   http://www.ericdigests.org/1997-2/key.htm

Language and Literacy Environments in Preschools
Discusses this issue.
Suggested Grade: Teacher Reference
Production Date: 1999
Format: Online Article
   Source: Catherine E. Snow, M. Susan Burns, and Peg Griffin
   World Wide Web URL:
   http://www.kidsource.com/education/lang.lit.preschool.html

Lasting Benefits of Preschool Programs
Explores this issue in a concise report.
Suggested Grade: Teacher Reference
Production Date: 1994
Format: Online Article
   Source: Lawrence J. Schweinhart
   World Wide Web URL:
   http://www.ericdigests.org/1994/lasting.htm

*All materials listed in this 2017-2018 edition are **BRAND NEW!***

TEACHER REFERENCE

Latinos in School: Some Facts and Findings
Discusses this issue.
Suggested Grade: Teacher Reference
Production Date: 2001
Format: Online Article
Source: ERIC Clearinghouse on Urban Education
World Wide Web URL:
http://www.ericdigests.org/2001-3/facts.htm

Multicultural Person, The
Useful for teaching elementary school children about the many groups to which they belong.
Suggested Grade: 3-5
Format: Online Lesson Plan
Source: Peace Corps
World Wide Web URL: http://www.peacecorps.gov/wws/publications/looking/index.cfm

New Patterns of School Governance
Explains why public school governance is the subject of increasing scrutiny, identifies who is held accountable for results in the current governance system, and describes several recent proposals for transforming governance structures.
Suggested Grade: Teacher Reference
Production Date: 2000
Format: Online Article
Source: Ron Renchler
World Wide Web URL:
http://www.eric.ed.gov/PDFS/ED363914.pdf

Our Creative Diversity
Compiled by the World Commission for Culture and Development, this report discusses the relationship between culture and development.
Suggested Grade: Teacher Reference
Format: Online Article
Source: Power of Culture
World Wide Web URL:
http://kvc.minbuza.nl/uk/archive/report/inleiding.html

Overcrowding in Urban Schools
Explores the effects of too many students in the school.
Suggested Grade: Teacher Reference
Production Date: 1995
Format: Online Article
Source: Gary Burnett
World Wide Web URL:
http://www.ericdigests.org/1996-1/overcrowding.htm

Parent Engagement as a School Reform Strategy
Discusses this issue.
Suggested Grade: Teacher Reference
Production Date: 1998
Format: Online Article
Source: Hollyce C. Giles
World Wide Web URL:
http://www.ericdigests.org/1998-3/reform.html

Peer Conflicts in the Classroom
Examines the structure of peer conflicts and the implications for teachers.
Suggested Grade: Teacher Reference
Production Date: 1994
Format: Online Article
Source: Edyth J. Wheeler
World Wide Web URL:
http://www.ericdigests.org/1995-1/conflicts.htm

Planning for Parent Participation in Schools for Young Children
Helpful guidelines for working with parents.
Suggested Grade: Teacher Reference
Format: Online Article
Source: Mick Coleman
World Wide Web URL:
http://www.ericdigests.org/1992-4/parent.htm

Poverty and Learning
Discusses the relationship between poverty and learning.
Suggested Grade: Adult
Production Date: 1993
Format: Online Article
Special Notes: This is a PDF file which will automatically open on your computer.
Source: Ron Renchler
World Wide Web URL:
http://www.eric.ed.gov/PDFS/ED357433.pdf

Project Appleseed
Focuses on parental involvement as a means for improving public schools and provides parents with information and resources to help them work on school improvement.
Suggested Grade: Parents
Format: Web Site
Source: National Campaign for Public School Improvement, The
World Wide Web URL: http://www.projectappleseed.org/

Promoting Diversity in Elementary School Curricula
Focuses on how to study the many ethnic groups found in the United States in order to promote an understanding of them, and therefore eliminate racism.
Suggested Grade: 3
Format: Online Lesson Plan
Source: Johanna Wilson
World Wide Web URL: http://www.cis.yale.edu/ynhti/curriculum/units/1997/4/97.04.10.x.html

All materials listed in this 2017-2018 edition are BRAND NEW!

TEACHER REFERENCE

Prospects for Education Vouchers After the Supreme Court Ruling, The
Examines this issue.
Suggested Grade: Teacher Reference
Production Date: 2002
Format: Online Article
Source: Clive Belfield
World Wide Web URL:
http://www.ericdigests.org/2003-4/vouchers.html

Recent Evidence on Preschool Programs
Presents the results of studies conducted on the educational value of preschool programs.
Suggested Grade: Teacher Reference
Production Date: 2001
Format: Online Article
Source: Lawrence J. Schweinhart
World Wide Web URL:
http://www.ericdigests.org/2002-2/preschool.htm

Recent Research on All-Day Kindergarten
Explores research done on the value of all-day kindergarten.
Suggested Grade: Teacher Reference
Production Date: 2001
Format: Online Article
Source: Patricia Clark
World Wide Web URL:
http://www.ericdigests.org/2002-1/kindergarten.html

Recess in Elementary School: What Does the Research Say?
Discusses this issue.
Suggested Grade: Teacher Reference
Production Date: 2002
Format: Online Article
Source: Olga S. Jarrett
World Wide Web URL:
http://www.ericdigests.org/2003-2/recess.html

Resource Rooms for Children: An Innovative Curricular Tool
Explores this issue in a concise report.
Suggested Grade: Teacher Reference
Production Date: 1994
Format: Online Article
Source: Sonja de Groot Kim
World Wide Web URL:
http://www.ericdigests.org/1994/rooms.htm

Retaining Good Teachers in Urban Schools
Tells ways to keep good teachers in what can sometimes be, bad schools.
Suggested Grade: Teacher Reference
Production Date: 1991
Format: Online Article
Source: Carol Ascher
World Wide Web URL:
http://www.ericdigests.org/1992-4/good.htm

Retaining Principals
Discusses this topic.
Suggested Grade: Teacher Reference
Production Date: 2001
Format: Online Article
Source: Elizabeth Hertling
World Wide Web URL:
http://www.ericdigests.org/2002-1/principals.html

Role of Online Communications in Schools, The: A National Study
Presents the results of a study conducted that shows the value of online access for students.
Suggested Grade: Teacher Reference
Format: Online Article
Source: Center for Applied Special Technology
World Wide Web URL:
http://www.empowermentzone.com/ol_study.txt

Safer Schools Through Environmental Design
Discusses this topic.
Suggested Grade: Teacher Reference
Production Date: 2001
Format: Online Article
Source: Tod Schneider
World Wide Web URL:
http://www.ericdigests.org/2001-4/safer.html

School-Based Budgeting
Discusses this issue--the facilitative arm of school-based management.
Suggested Grade: Teacher Reference
Production Date: 1999
Format: Online Article
Special Notes: This is a PDF file which will open automatically on your computer.
Source: Margaret Hadderman
World Wide Web URL:
http://www.eric.ed.gov/PDFS/ED434401.pdf

School Calendars
Discusses this topic.
Suggested Grade: Teacher Reference
Production Date: 2002
Format: Online Article
Source: Bill Metzker
World Wide Web URL:
http://www.ericdigests.org/2003-2/calendars.html

Schooling for Self-Determination: Research on the Effects of Including Native Language and Culture in the Schools
Briefly reviews the educational effects of assimilationist schooling and later efforts to create schools supportive of American Indian and Alaska Native self-determination.
Suggested Grade: Teacher Reference
Production Date: 2001
Format: Online Article

All materials listed in this 2017-2018 edition are BRAND NEW!

TEACHER REFERENCE

Source: Jerry Lipka
World Wide Web URL:
http://www.ericdigests.org/2002-3/effects.htm

School Productivity
Explains how schools can be productive--that is, make the most out of the resources available to them.
Suggested Grade: Teacher Reference
Production Date: 1998
Format: Online Article
Special Notes: This is a PDF file which will open automatically on your computer.
Source: Margaret Hadderman
World Wide Web URL:
http://chiron.valdosta.edu/whuitt/files/schoolprod.html

School Programs for African American Male Students
Explains some programs that can be set up to specifically help these students.
Suggested Grade: Teacher Reference
Production Date: 1991
Format: Online Article
Source: Carol Ascher
World Wide Web URL:
\http://www.ericdigests.org/pre-9220/males.htm

School Violence Prevention
Explores how schools can prevent violence in their midst.
Suggested Grade: Teacher Reference
Production Date: 1995
Format: Online Article
Source: Dean Walker
World Wide Web URL:
http://www.ericdigests.org/1996-1/violence.htm

2nd Grade Treasure Trove
Not only provides links of interest to second graders, but provides networking opportunities for teachers of this grade.
Suggested Grade: 2
Format: Web Site
Source: Karen Walkowiak
World Wide Web URL: http://www.karensclassroom.com/treasuretrove/gradetwo/index.htm

Self-Esteem and Narcissism: Implications for Practice
Explores this issue in a concise report.
Suggested Grade: Teacher Reference
Production Date: 1993
Format: Online Article
Source: Lilian G. Katz
World Wide Web URL:
http://www.ericdigests.org/1993/esteem.htm

September 11: What Our Children Need to Know
Presents advice on what schools should teach and children should learn about this date in history.
Suggested Grade: Teacher Reference
Format: Downloadable Report
Source: John Agresto, et al
World Wide Web URL:
http://www.edexcellence.net/publications/sept11.html

Sexual Misconduct by School Employees
Discusses this topic seen often in today's news.
Suggested Grade: Teacher Reference
Production Date: 1999
Format: Online Article
Source: Brad Goorian
World Wide Web URL:
http://www.ericdigests.org/2000-3/sexual.htm

Shared Decision-Making
Explores the complexities of shared decision-making.
Suggested Grade: Teacher Reference
Production Date: 1994
Format: Online Article
Source: Lynn Balster Liontos
World Wide Web URL:
http://www.ericdigests.org/1994/shared.htm

Should You Be the Boss?
Soul searching questions for teachers considering administration.
Suggested Grade: Teacher Reference
Format: Online Article
Source: Roberta Bernstein
World Wide Web URL: http://teacher.scholastic.com/professional/teachertoteacher/boss.htm

6th Grade Treasure Trove
Not only provides links of interest to sixth graders, but provides networking opportunities for teachers of this grade.
Suggested Grade: 6
Format: Web Site
Source: Karen Walkowiak
World Wide Web URL:
http://www.karensclassroom.com/treasuretrove/gradesix/index.htm

Small Schools and Teacher Professional Development
Reviews some of the recent research on professional development issues in small schools and smaller learning communities.
Suggested Grade: Teacher Reference
Production Date: 2002
Format: Online Article

*All materials listed in this 2017-2018 edition are **BRAND NEW**!*

TEACHER REFERENCE

Source: Michael Klonsky
World Wide Web URL: http://www.ericdigests.org/2003-4/small-schools.html

Southeast Asian Adolescents: Identity and Adjustment
Provides information to help teachers work effectively with these students.
Suggested Grade: Teacher Reference
Production Date: 1989
Format: Online Article
Source: Carol Ascher
World Wide Web URL:
http://www.ericdigests.org/pre-9211/southeast.htm

SSSH--Successful, Simple Simulation, Hassle-Free
A game to be used in introducing conflict situations and resolving them.
Suggested Grade: 5
Format: Online Lesson Plan
Source: Joy C. Blanton
World Wide Web URL:
http://youth.net/cec/cecsst/cecsst.53.txt

Starting Early: Environmental Education During the Early Childhood Years
Discusses the rationale for environmental education during the early years.
Suggested Grade: Teacher Reference
Production Date: 1996
Format: Online Article
Source: Ruth A. Wilson
World Wide Web URL:
http://www.ericdigests.org/1998-1/early.htm

Strategies for Teaching the Value of Diversity
Presents strategies that teachers can use to help children value the diversity that exists in the world around them.
Suggested Grade: preK-3
Format: Online Lesson Plan
Source: Christine Elmore
World Wide Web URL: http://www.yale.edu/ynhti/curriculum/units/1997/4/97.04.02.x.html

Student Diversity and Learning Needs
Discusses how to reach students based on varying learning needs.
Suggested Grade: Teacher Reference
Production Date: 1997
Format: Online Article
Source: Joseph Sanacore
World Wide Web URL:
http://www.ericdigests.org/1998-1/needs.htm

Student-Led Conferences at the Middle Level
Explores this alternative to the traditional middle level parent-teacher conference.
Suggested Grade: Teacher Reference
Production Date: 1997
Format: Online Article
Source: Donald G. Hackmann
World Wide Web URL:
http://www.ericdigests.org/1997-4/middle.htm

Student Mobility and Academic Achievement
Discusses this issue.
Suggested Grade: Teacher Reference
Production Date: 2002
Format: Online Article
Source: Russell W. Rumberger
World Wide Web URL:
http://www.ericdigests.org/2003-2/mobility.html

Student Truancy
Examines some of the ways truancy affects both individuals and society, and identifies factors that may place students at greater risk of becoming truant.
Suggested Grade: Teacher Reference
Production Date: 1999
Format: Online Article
Source: Jay DeKalb
World Wide Web URL:
http://www.eric.ed.gov/PDFS/ED429334.pdf

Substance Abuse Policy
Presents information for schools on how to develop a substance abuse policy, and why it is so necessary.
Suggested Grade: Teacher Reference
Production Date: 1993
Format: Online Article
Special Notes: This is a PDF file which will open automatically on your computer.
Source: Kelly Markham
World Wide Web URL:
https://scholarsbank.uoregon.edu/xmlui/bitstream/handle/1794/3301/digest080.pdf?sequence=1

Substitute Teaching: An Insider's View
Provides guidance to current and potential substitute teachers so they know what to expect--and how to handle it.
Suggested Grade: Teacher Reference
Format: Online Article
Source: Deborah Bouley
World Wide Web URL:
http://www.teach-nology.com/tutorials/teaching/sub/

Success for All: A Summary of Evaluations
Summarizes research on this school wide research-based reform model.
Suggested Grade: Teacher Reference
Production Date: 1998
Format: Online Article
Source: Jeanne Weiler
World Wide Web URL:
http://www.ericdigests.org/1999-3/success.htm

All materials listed in this 2017-2018 edition are BRAND NEW!

TEACHER REFERENCE

Synthesis of Scholarship in Multicultural Education, A
Presents guidelines for action to implement multicultural education programs.
Suggested Grade: Teacher Reference
Production Date: 1994
Format: Online Article
Source: Geneva Gay
World Wide Web URL: http://www.ncrel.org/sdrs/areas/issues/educatrs/leadrshp/le0gay.htm

Teacher Files
Resources, ideas, activities, lessons plans, and more for teachers.
Suggested Grade: All ages
Format: Web Site
Source: Shayni Tokarczyk
World Wide Web URL:
http://www.teacherfiles.com/http://www.teacherfiles.com/

Teacher Preparation and Teacher-Child Interaction in Preschools
Discusses this issue.
Suggested Grade: Teacher Reference
Production Date: 2002
Format: Online Article
Source: Susan Kontos and Amanda Wilcox-Herzog
World Wide Web URL:
http://www.ericdigests.org/2003-4/preschool.html

Teaching Young Children About Native Americans
Explores this issue in a concise report.
Suggested Grade: Teacher Reference
Production Date: 1996
Format: Online Article
Source: Debbie Reese
World Wide Web URL:
http://www.ericdigests.org/1996-4/native.htm

Ten C's for Evaluating Internet Sources
Presents "ten c's" to consider in evaluating Internet resources.
Suggested Grade: 6-Adult
Format: Web Site
Special Notes: This is a PDF file which will open automatically on your computer.
Source: McIntyre Library, UW-Eau Claire
World Wide Web URL:
http://www.montgomerycollege.edu/Departments/writegt/htmlhandouts/Ten%20C%20internet%20sources.htm

Theoretical Perspectives, Research Findings, and Classroom Implications of the Learning Styles of American Indian and Alaska Native Students
Begins with a brief discussion of two prominent definitions of learning styles and then describes studies that have found differences between the learning styles of American Indian students and students of other cultural groups.
Suggested Grade: Teacher Reference
Production Date: 2002
Format: Online Article
Source: R. Soleste Hilberg and Roland G. Tharp
World Wide Web URL:
http://www.ericdigests.org/2003-3/alaska.htm

Thirteen Ed Online
A web service for K-12 teachers that offers lesson plans for core curriculum topics and lots more.
Suggested Grade: Teacher Reference
Format: Web Site
Source: Thirteen Ed Online
World Wide Web URL: http://www.thirteen.org/edonline/

Threads: Computers, Music, and a Little Theory
Explore how music theory, math, and computer science intersect. Highly technical.
Suggested Grade: Teacher Reference
Format: Web Site
Special Notes: This URL will lead you to a subject page. Then click on the appropriate subject heading.
Source: ThinkQuest
World Wide Web URL:
http://www.thinkquest.org/pls/html/think.library

Turning It Around for All Youth: From Risk to Resilience
Explains how to reach at-risk students.
Suggested Grade: Teacher Reference
Production Date: 1997
Format: Online Article
Source: Bonnie Benard
World Wide Web URL:
http://resilnet.uiuc.edu/library/dig126.html

Urban Policies and Programs to Reduce Truancy
Explains how to combat the truancy problem in urban schools.
Suggested Grade: Teacher Reference
Production Dae: 1997
Format: Online Article
Source: ERIC Clearinghouse on Urban Education
World Wide Web URL:
http://www.ericdigests.org/1998-2/urban.htm

Urban School Finance: The Quest for Equal Educational Opportunity
Provides ideas to gain urban school financing so that all schools can be equal.
Suggested Grade: Teacher Reference
Production Date: 1989
Format: Online Article

All materials listed in this 2017-2018 edition are **BRAND NEW!**

TEACHER REFERENCE

Source: Carol Ascher
World Wide Web URL:
http://www.ericdigests.org/pre-9213/urban.htm

Urban Youth in Community Service: Becoming Part of the Solution
Explains how youth involvement in community service is beneficial to the community, as well as the student.
Suggested Grade: Teacher Reference
Production Date: 1992
Format: Online Article
Source: Anne Lewis
World Wide Web URL:
http://www.ericdigests.org/1992-1/urban.htm

Using Culturally and Linguistically Appropriate Assessments to Ensure that American Indian and Alaska Native Students Receive the Special Education Programs and Services They Need
Discusses this issue.
Suggested Grade: Teacher Reference
Production Date: 2002
Format: Online Article
Source: John W. Tippeconnic and Susan C. Faircloth
World Wide Web URL:
http://www.ericdigests.org/2003-4/special-education.html

Using Federal Funds to Improve Child Care
Explores this issue in a concise report.
Suggested Grade: Teacher Reference
Production Date: 1994
Format: Online Article
Source: Helen Blank
World Wide Web URL:
http://www.ericdigests.org/1994/federal.htm

Using Film, Video, and TV in the Classroom
Explores how these media can be used in the language arts classroom.
Suggested Grade: Teacher Reference
Production Date: 1988
Format: Online Article
Source: Nola Kortner Aiex
World Wide Web URL:
http://www.ericdigests.org/pre-929/film.htm

Using Primary Sources in the Primary Grades
Discusses how simple artifacts--primary sources--can stimulate young interests in the social studies.
Suggested Grade: Teacher Reference
Production Date: 1998
Format: Online Article
Source: Evelyn Holt Otten
World Wide Web URL:
http://www.ericdigests.org/1999-1/primary.html

Video Games and Children
Provides some ideas about the effect of video games on children--slightly out-of-date.
Suggested Grade: Teacher Reference
Production Date: 1994
Format: Online Article
Source: Bernard Cesarone
World Wide Web URL:
http://www.ericdigests.org/1994/video.htm

Virtual Classroom, The
Tools to help you create and administer tests using multiple choice, true or false, or mix and match answers.
Suggested Grade: Teacher Reference
Format: Web Site
Special Notes: This URL will lead you to a subject page. Then click on the appropriate subject heading.
Source: ThinkQuest
World Wide Web URL:
http://www.thinkquest.org/pls/html/think.library

What Federal Statistics Reveal About Migrant Farmworkers: A Summary for Education
Summarizes recent federal reports on this issue in order to help educators reach children of migrant farmworkers effectively.
Suggested Grade: Teacher Reference
Production Date: 2002
Format: Online Article
Source: Gary G. Huang
World Wide Web URL:
http://www.ericdigests.org/2003-4/migrant-farmworkers.html

"Who I Am" Poems
Begins an active introspective process while continuing to provide opportunities for individuals to make connections with each other.
Suggested Grade: Teacher Reference
Format: Online Lesson Plan
Source: Paul Gorski
World Wide Web URL:
http://www.edchange.org/multicultural/activities/poetry.html

Whole-School Reform
Discusses this concept.
Suggested Grade: Teacher Reference
Production Date: 1998
Format: Online Article
Source: Jim McChesney
World Wide Web URL:
http://www.ericdigests.org/1999-4/reform.htm

Why Files?, The
Presents news articles twice a month in the areas of science, math, engineering, and technology.
Suggested Grade: All ages
Format: Online Articles
Source: University of Wisconsin--Madison
World Wide Web URL: http://whyfiles.org/

All materials listed in this 2017-2018 edition are BRAND NEW!

TEACHER REFERENCE

Working with Perfectionist Students
Explores this issue in a concise report.
Suggested Grade: Teacher Reference
Production Date: 1996
Format: Online Article
    Source: Jere Brophy
    World Wide Web URL:
    http://www.ericdigests.org/1997-2/students.htm

Working with Shy or Withdrawn Students
Explores this issue in a concise report.
Suggested Grade: Teacher Reference
Production Date: 1996
Format: Online Article
    Source: Jere Brophy
    World Wide Web URL:
    http://www.ericdigests.org/1997-3/shy.html

"World-Class Standards" and Local Pedagogies: Can We Do Both?
Attempts to answer this question.
Suggested Grade: Teacher Reference
Production Date: 2000
Format: Online Article
    Source: Thomas J. Gibbs and Aimee Howley
    World Wide Web URL:
    http://www.ericdigests.org/2001-3/world.htm

Year-Round Education: A Strategy for Overcrowded Schools
Explores this issue.
Suggested Grade: Teacher Reference
Production Date: 1994
Format: Online Article
    Source: Morton Inger
    World Wide Web URL:
    http://www.ericdigests.org/1995-2/year.htm

Young Children's Emotional Development and School Readiness
Discusses this issue.
Suggested Grade: Teacher Reference
Production Date: 2003
Format: Online Article
    Source: C. Cybele Raver
    World Wide Web URL:
    http://www.ericdigests.org/2004-1/young.htm

*All materials listed in this 2017-2018 edition are **BRAND NEW!***

TITLE INDEX

-A-

Abacus, The--The Art of Calculating with Beads	58
ABC's of Legal Terms	10
ABC's of Snacking, The	12
ABCteach	23
Aboriginal English	19
Abraham Lincoln Online	15
Accentuate the Positive	58
Achievements and Challenges of Peru, The	26
Acronym Finder	10
Across the USA	26
Action Research in Early Childhood Education	80
Actions and Reactions	44
Addition & Subtraction Concentration Game	58
Addition and Subtraction Game	58
Address to the Negroes in the State of New York, An	44
ADHD eBook	78
Adolescent & School Health	40
Adopted Children in the Early Childhood Classroom	80
Adverbily	51
Aeronautics Educator Guide	66
Aesop's Fables Online Collection	51
Afghanistan: The Harrison Forman Collection	26
Africa: Eating Senegal Style	26
AfriCam	26
African American Odyssey	44
African Art and Culture	26
African Flags Archive	26
African Folk Tales	26
African Languages at the K-12 Level	19
Africa--South of the Sahara	26
AgMag	26
Ah Choo!	40
Ainsworth Computer Seminar	6
Alan Cooper's Homonym List	10
Alaska's Gold	44
Alaska Wildlife Notebook Series	66
Alcohol, Peer Pressure and Underage Drinking Info for Young Teens	40
Alex Catalogue of Electronic Texts	51
ALFY: The Web Portal for Kids	12
Algebra--One on One	58
Algebra Through Problem Solving	58
Alien Language	19
All Hands on Deck	44
AllWords.com	10
Alphabet Soup	12
Alternatives to Behaviorism	78
Aluminum Beverage Cans: The ABCs of Environmental Education	66
Amateur Entomologist	66
Amazing Space: Explorations	66
American Civil War Webquest, The	44
American Journeys	44
American Revolution at a Glance	44
American Revolution Simulation	44
American Sign Language as a Foreign Language	19
American Sign Language Browser	78
Americans with Disabilities Act: Questions and Answers	80
America's Career InfoNet	36
Ancient Egypt	44
Ancient Mesopotamia: The History, Our History	44
Anglo-Saxon and Viking Crafts--Textiles	44
Animal Diversity Web	66
Animal Info--Endangered Animals	66
Anne Frank in the World Teacher Workbook	15
Annenberg Classroom	33
Another Face--Masks Around the World	26
Anthropology on the Internet for K-12	66
Anxiety Disorders	40
Applications of Participatory Action Research with Students Who Have Disabilities	78
Appomattox Court House Teacher's Packet	26
Appreciating African Languages	19
Archeology Dig	66
Are Bioengineered Foods Safe?	40
Are You With It?	80

TITLE INDEX

Around the World in 1896	45
Artist Research Poster Lesson	1
Artists of the Renaissance	15
Artists: The Good, the Bad, and the Ugly	15
ArtMagick	1
Ask Dr. Math	58
Ask the Presidents	33
ASPCA Kids	66
Assessing Bilingual Students for Placement and Instruction	80
Assessing Young Children's Social Competence	80
Astronaut Biographies	15
Astronomy Picture of the Day	66
Astro-Venture	66
Atom's Family, The	66
Attending to Learning Styles in Mathematics and Science Classrooms	80
Aunty Math	58
Auroras: Paintings in the Sky	67
Australian Folk Songs	1
Automobile Safety Articles	64
Awareness of Pre-Algebra Concepts	58

-B-

Babysitter Handbook, The	64
Back to the Agora: Workable Solutions for Small Urban School Facilities	80
Backyard Nature	67
Ball Monster	40
Baltimore Curriculum Project Lesson Plans	23
Banner Generator, The	6
Baroque Reference, The	10
Baseball Hall of Fame and Museum	15
Basic Grammar Review Using Jabberwocky	51
Beanbag Freeze Tag	40
Bean Toss	58
Become a Logophile	51
Becoming Human	67
Becoming Webwise	6

Behind the Scenes Look at the Landrum News Network, A	80
Ben's Guide to U. S. Government for Kids	33
Best Bones Forever!	40
Biographical Dictionary	10
Biographies of Explorers and Associated People	15
Biography-Center	15
Biography.com	15
BioInteractive	67
Bird Cross Stitch Patterns	1
Birds at the National Zoo	67
Birthday Moons	67
Birthday Moons: It's Just a Phase You're Going Through	67
Bizarre Stuff You Can Make in Your Kitchen	67
Blind Men and the Elephant, The	80
Bluebird Quest, A	67
bNetS@vvy	6
Bookhive	51
Box of Crayons, A	36
Boy/Girl Pieces	80
Brain Food	23
Brain Research: Implications for Second Language Learning	19
Brush with Wildlife, A	1
Buen Viaje a Espana!	27
Build-a-Prairie	67
Building an African Compound	27
Building a School Web Site	6
Building Leadership Skills in Middle School Girls Through Interscholastic Athletics	40
Build Your Own Medieval Castle	45
Bulking Up Fiber's Healthful Reputation	40
Busy as a Bee	51
ButterflySite.com	67

-C-

Calculators On-Line Center	58
Camp Silos	67
Canada on Postcards	27
Can Failing Schools Be Fixed?	81

TITLE INDEX

Can Performance-Based Assessments Improve Urban Schooling?	81
Capitalizing on Small Class Size	81
Career Development for All Students	36
Career Guide for the Atmospheric Sciences, A	36
Careers and Industries Overview	36
Careers in Accounting	36
Careers in Aging	36
Careers in Psychology	36
Careers in the Genetics Field	36
Career WebQuest	36
Carol Hurst's Children's Literature Site	51
Carolina Coastal Science	68
Cartooning to Teach Safety	64
Catch the Spirit: A Student's Guide to Community Service	81
Center for History of Physics, The	68
Cetacean Fact Packs	68
CGI Made Really Easy	6
CGI Resource Index, The	6
Challenges of Our Changing Atmosphere: Careers in Atmospheric Research and Applied Meteorology	36
Changing Attitudes in America	36
Changing Face of Racial Isolation and Desegregation in Urban Schools	81
Changing Faces: A Study of Solar and Planetary Rotation Rates	68
Chapter I Schoolwide Projects: Advantages and Limitations	81
Character Education Through Children's Literature	51
Charter Schools: An Approach for Rural Education?	81
Chatback Trust, The	78
Cherokee Indians	49
Child-Initiated Learning Activities for Young Children Living in Poverty	81
Children's Literacy Development: Suggestions for Parent Involvement	51
Children's Storybooks Online--Older Children	51
Children's Storybooks Online--Young Children	51
Children, Stress, and Natural Disasters: School Activities for Children	81
Child's Daily Life in South Africa, A	27
Chinese Dragon	27
Choosing Instructional Materials for Environmental Education	81
Christmas at the Cottage	49
Christmas Celebration in the Black \Culture, A	49
Christmas in Poland	49
Christmas Traditions	49
Christmas--Where Did It Come From? Where Is It Going?	49
Chubbie Cubbie's Activity Ideas	12
Citizenship and the Constitution	33
Civilisation Francaise	19
Civil War Through a Child's Eye, The	45
C-Language Course	6
Classroom Energy!	68
Classroom Learning 2.0	6
Coal Science Fair Ideas	68
Coffee Can Drum	49
Colds & Flu: Time Only Sure Cure	40
Collaborating on a Newspaper in the Elementary Classroom	51
Colomusic	1
Colonial Hall	15
Color Code Writing	12
Comets	68
Common African Food, A: Fou-Fou	27
Communication Strategies for Employment Interviews	37
Communicable Disease Fact Sheets	40
Communicating Values and History Through Masks	27
Computer Almanac	6
Computer and Internet Use by Children and Adolescents in 2001: Statistical Analysis Report	6
Computer Assisted Writing Instruction	52
Computers and How They Work	6

95

TITLE INDEX

Computers: History and Development	6
Conflict Resolution Programs in Schools	81
Confucius--His Life and Times	15
Conserving America's Fisheries	68
Constellations, The	68
Constitution of the United States and the Declaration of Independence	33
Constitution, The: Our Plan for Government	33
Contemporary Art Experience, The	15
Cool Science for Curious Kids	68
Coping with Death and Dying	37
Coptic Language, The	19
Country Reports on Human Rights Practices	27
Craftplace	1
Create-a-Composition	1
Creating a Blog: A Workshop for Teens	7
Creating an A+++ Classroom Library	82
Creating Music	1
Creative Dramatics in the Language Arts Classroom	52
Creative Strategies for Teaching Language Arts to Gifted Students	52
Crool Zone?	64
Cuisine and Etiquette in Sierra Leone, Uganda, and Zambia	27
Cultural Liberation: East-West Biculturalism for a New Century	82
Cultural Plunge, A	37
Cultural Spaces	27
Culture of the Frisians	27
Cultures of the Andes	27
Custom Addressbook 0.7.2	82

-D-

Dan's Wild, Wild Weather Page	68
Database of Award-Winning Children's Literature	52
Data Inquiry and Analysis for Educational Reform	82
Decimal Search	52
Declare the Causes: The Declaration of Independence	33

Derivation of Pi, The	58
Design a Track	58
Determining the Existence of Gender Bias in Daily Tasks	82
Deutsch Plus	19
Developing a School District Web Presence	82
Developing Language Proficiency and Connecting School to Students's Lives: Two Standards for Effective Teaching	82
Dictionary.com	10
Dietary Guidelines for Americans	41
Digital Divide and Its Implications for the Language Arts, The	52
Dig--The Archaeology Magazine for Kids!	68
Disaster Strikes!	64
Diversity is About Change and Leadership	82
Diversity Within Unity: Essential Principles for Teaching and Learning in a Multicultural Society	82
DNA for Dinner?	68
Do I Have Arthritis?	41
Do You Know the Health Risks of Being Overweight?	41
Do You Know Van Gogh?	15
Dramatic Education, A	1
Draw and Color with Uncle Fred	1
Drawing for Children	12
Dr. Mac's Amazing Behavior Management Advice Site	82
Dr. Martin Luther King, Jr.	16

-E-

Early American Weaving	1
Early Childhood Art Lessons	1
Earth Force	69
Easter	49
Easter on the Net	49
Eating for Life	41
Ecology Data Tip Archives	69
Ecosystems	69
Edible/Inedible Experiments Archive	69

TITLE INDEX

Edible State Map	28
EducatingJane.com	23
Educational Poster on Water Pollution	69
Education of Immigrant Children in New York City, The	83
Effective Use of Student Journal Writing	52
Egyptian Mummies	45
18th Century History	45
Einstein Club	52
Einstein: Man in Spacetime	16
Electrical Safety World	64
Electrical Safety World	64
Electric Universe, The	69
Electronic Mapping	28
Elementary Art Lesson Plans	1
Elizabeth Cady Stanton & Susan B. Anthony Papers Project Online, The	16
Enchanted Learning Web Site	12
Encouraging Creativity in Early Childhood Classrooms	83
Encyclopedia.com	10
Endangered/Threatened Species	69
Endeavour Views the Earth Electronic Picture Book	69
Energy Safety	41
English-Only Movement: Its Consequences for the Education of Language Minority Children	52
Entertainment Careers	37
ePALS Classroom Exchange	28
Equal Mathematics Education for Female Students	59
Erwin E. Smith: Teaching Guide	45
EspanOle!	19
Ethnic Art: African, Mexican and Caribbean Perspectives	2
European Voyages of Exploration	45
Everyday Life in Africa	28
Everyone Has a Culture--Everyone Is Different	28
EverythingESL.net	52
Everything Preschool	12
Everything You Always Wanted to Know About Dyslexia	78
Expanding Fifth Grade Ethnic Awareness (Latino and Native American) Through Literature	28
Experience the Life	45
Exploring African Music	28
Exploring Caves	28
Exploring Language: Definitions Activity	83
Exploring Occupations: Getting You Started on Your Career Path!	37
Exploring the Function of Heroes and Heroines in Children's Literature from Around the World	52
Eyes on the Sky, Feet on the Ground	69

-F-

FableVision Place	53
Face to Face--Stories from the Aftermath of Infamy	45
Fact Monster	10
Factoring Large Numbers	59
Fairy Tales Around the World	53
Familiar Quotations--Passages, Phrases and Proverbs Traced to Their Sources	10
Family Diversity in Urban Schools	83
Family Finding: Exploring Multicultural Families Using Film	83
Family Involvement in Early Multicultural Learning	83
Famous Canadians	16
Famous Hispanics in the World and History	16
Famous People with Perfect Pitch	16
Famous Person--Who Am I?	16
Famous Quotes by Categories and Subjects	53
Farm Animals	69
Farm Safety 4 Just Kids	64
FastMIDI Player	2
Fear of Physics	69
Festivals Around the World	49
Few Scanning Tips, A	7
15 Fantastic Id	41
50 Careers in Trees	37

97

TITLE INDEX

Fight BAC!: Four Simple Steps to Food Safety	41
FILExt	7
Finding Funding for Environmental Education Efforts	69
Find Lost Files and Folders	7
Fire Safety & Education Factsheets	64
Fire Safety for Young Children	64
Fire Safety WebQuest	64
First Americans	45
First Guide to PostScript, A	7
First Impressions	83
First Person Narratives of the American South, 1860-1920	45
First-School	12
Fitness Partner	41
Five Senses	70
Florida Panther Net	70
Football Review	23
Forest Stewardship	70
For Whom the Clock Strikes	49
Four Directions	83
4Kids2Play	12
4th Grade Treasure Trove	83
4000 Years of Women in Science	16
Fraction Conversion Bingo	59
Fraction Fun	59
Free Animated GIFs	7
Free Education on the Internet	23
Free Online Pronunciation Guide	19
French Language Course	19
French Online Grammar Quiz	20
Friction, Forces and Motion	70
Frogland	70
FT Exploring	70
Full-Day Kindergarten Programs	83
Funbrain.com	12
Fun Facts, Amazing Animal Facts, World Facts and More!	23
Funschool.com	12
Fun With Estimation	59

-G-

Gallery of Achievers	16
Game Goo	12
Games and Toys Reflect Resouces	28
Gangs in the Schools	83
Gangs the Foster Family	84
GardenWeb Glossary	10
Gender Differences in Educational Achievement within Racial and Ethnic Groups	84
Gender Equity in Fairy Tales	53
Gender Stereotypes and Advertisements	37
General Information About Blindness	78
Genetic Science Learning Center	70
Geo-Critters	59
Geographia	28
Geo-Images Project	84
Geothermal Energy	70
German American Contributions to Mainstream Culture	20
German for Music Lovers	20
GetNetWise	7
Getting Started--Respect Activity	84
Gifted Readers and Reading Instruction	53
Giggle Poetry	53
Girlstart	23
Global Issues and Environmental Education	70
Global Online Adventure Learning Site	28
Glossary of Internet & Web Terms	10
Goetz's Programming Kit	7
Grand Pantheon, The	2
Graphing from a 5th Grader's Point of View	59
Great Depression and the 1990s, The	45
Great Plant Escape, The	70
Great Thinkers: A Study in Philosophy	16
Green Bean's Treehouse	12
Growing Up Drug Free	41
Guidelines for Starting an Elementary School Foreign Language Program	20
Guide to British Life, Culture and Customs	29
Gunfighters of the Old West	46

TITLE INDEX

-H-

H-AfrTeach	29
Handbook of Texas Online	29
Handouts and Information Guides	37
Hard of Hearing and Deaf Students: A Resource Guide to Support Classroom Teachers	78
Harmonica Lessons	2
Hausa Online Grammar	20
Hawaiian Christmas Trees	49
Health Fact Sheets	41
Health Fact Sheets	41
Health Fact Sheets	42
Health Finder	42
Healthy Forests	70
Helen Keller Biography	16
Hello Dolly: A WebQuest	70
Hello, I Am Deborah Sampson	46
Help for They Won't Let Me Play with Them!	84
Helping Children Overcome Reading Difficulties	53
Helping Children Understand Literary Genres	53
Helping the Underachiever in Reading	53
Helping Underachieving Boys Read Well and Often	53
Helping Your Child Learn Geography	29
Helping Your Child Learn Math	59
Heroism in Action	16
History Happens	46
History Textbook Controversies in Japan	46
History Wired	46
Hitler & Stalin	17
HJ-Install 2.9	7
Hoagies' Gifted Education Page	23
Holiday Traditions	50
Homes Around the World	29
Homeschooling	84
Honoring the Animal Spirits	29
Hoover Dam Learning Packet	29
Horrid Homonyms	53
How a Bill Becomes a Law	33
How Do They Do That with HTML?	7
How Fast Are You Going?	70
How Our Laws Are Made	33
How Stuff Works	71
How the Internet Came to Be	7
How to Celebrate Chanukah	50
How to Earn Commendable Marks in Fourth Grade	23
How to View an Eclipse	71
HTML Goodies	7
HTML Imager Version 1.2a	7
Human Anatomy Online	71
Hunger Site, The	84
Hungry for Math	59
Hurricane Hunters, The	71
Hurricanes and Tropical Storms	71
HymnSite.Com	2

-I-

I Can Do That!	71
Iceberg, The	84
ICT Games	13
Idea Box	13
Ideas for Exploring Our City and State	29
Identification and Recruitment of Migrant Students: Strategies and Resources	84
Illustrated History of the Roman Empire	46
I Love That Teaching Idea	84
Images of Native Americans	46
Implementing the Multiage Classroom	85
Implementing Whole-School Reform	85
Indexes of Biographies	17
Indoor Electrical Safety Check	64
Infection, Detection, Protection	71
In My Other Life	37
Instructional Models for Early Childhood Education	85
Integrated Curriculum in the Middle School	85
Integrating Children with Disabilities Into Preschool	78
Integrating Language and Content: Lessons from Immersion	20

99

TITLE INDEX

Integrating Literature into Middle School Reading Classrooms	53
Interactive Constitution	33
Interactive Demos 1	59
Interactive Demos 2	59
Interactive On-Line Reference Grammar, An	20
Internet Acronym Server	10
Internet and Early Childhood Educators, The: Some Frequently Asked Questions	85
Internet Glossary of Soil Science Terms	10
INTIME	85
Invention Dimension	17
Investigating Patterns: Symmetry and Tessellations	60
Investigating Plants	71
Involving Community Members, Parents, and Community Agencies in Student Learning.	23
Involving Migrant Families in Education	85
Irish Lessons	20
Issue-Centered Civic Education in Middle Schools	33
Issues in the Education of American Indian and Alaska Native Students with Disabilities	85
Italian Electronic Classroom, The	20
It's So Simple	71
Ivy's Coloring Page Search Engine	13

-J-

Jack's Harmonica Page	2
Jacques Lipetz	46
Jambo Means Hello: An Introduction to Swahili	20
Jan's Illustrated Computer Literacy 101	8
Japanese Education in Grades K-12	29
JazClass	2
Jefferson Lab--Science Education	71
Jeff's Poems for Kids	54
Job Genie	37
Journey North, The	71
Journey Through the Galaxy	71

Justice	34
Justice for Kids and Youth	34

-K-

Kameshi Ne Mpuku: An African Game	29
Kamusi Project, The	20
Kanienkehaka Language Homepage	20
Karbosguide.com	8
Keep the Traffic Moving!	60
Kentucky Bug Connection Teaching Resources	71
Key Characteristics of Middle Level Schools	85
Kids@Random	54
Kids Farm	13
Kids Heart, A	13
KidsKonnect	23
Kids Next Door	34
KidsPsych	13
KidsReads	54
KidsRunning.Com	42
Kids World	42
Kid's World - Nutrition	42
Kim's Korner for Teacher Talk	54
KinderArt Littles	13
Knowledge Master	23
Know Your Local Government	34
Kwanzaa	50

-L-

Lacrosse Tag	42
Landing	42
Language and Literacy Environments in Preschools	85
Language Development in the Early Years	54
Language in Classroom Texts	37
Languages Across the Curriculum	20
Larry's Animals-n-Things	13
Larry's Count	13
Larry's Songs	13
Lasting Benefits of Preschool Programs	85
Latinos in School: Some Facts and Findings	86

TITLE INDEX

Laura Ingalls Wilder	17
Laws--Who Needs Them?	34
Leaf ID and Leaf Bingo	72
Learning the Compass	29
Learn Letters	13
Learn to Read Bengali	21
Learn to Read Punjabi	21
Learn to Read Sanskrit	21
Learn to Read Spanish	21
Learn to Read Tamil	21
Learn to Read Urdu	21
Learn 2 Type	8
Leonardo Da Vinci: A Man of Both Worlds	17
Lesson #29: Textured Pottery Using Self-Hardening Clay and Multicultural Designs	2
Lesson Plans	2
Let Me Tell You About My State!	29
Let's Get Along	37
Letter Sounds	13
Lewis and Clark as Naturalists	72
Life of Abraham Lincoln, The: An Illustrated Timeline for Young Readers	17
LifeWorks	38
Lift Every Voice and Sing	2
Lighting the Perimeter	60
Light in the Forest, The	54
Lissa Explains It All	8
Literacy Center	13
Literature and Art Through Our Eyes: The African American Children	54
Literature as Lessons on the Diversity of Culture	54
Little Czech Primer in Pictures	21
Little Red House, The	14
Living Gulf, The: A Place to Treasure	29
Logical Games and Puzzles 1	60
Logical Games and Puzzles 2	60
Logical Games and Puzzles 3	60
LOGOS Multilingual Portal	11

-M-

Magnets	72
Make a Multi-Cultural Calendar	50
Make a Papier Mache Bowl	2
Make a Splash with Color	2
Make a Village	30
Making a Comet in the Classroom	72
Making an Illustrated Dictionary with Geographic Terms	30
Making a Pinata	2
Making Healthy Food Choices	42
Making Mathematical Connections in Middle School	60
Making of America	46
Making the Connection: How to Go Online	8
Making Your Home Safe from Fire and Carbon Monoxide	65
Mammals of Texas, The	72
M&M Math	60
Marinecareers	38
Mars Fraction Hunt	60
Masai and I: A Cultural Comparison	30
Matching Yourself with the World of Work	38
Math Cats	60
Math Cove	60
MathDEN	60
Mathematical Quotations Server	61
Mathematics and Reading Connection, The	54
Mathematics of Cartography	30
Mathematics Standards for Pre-Kindergarten Through Grade 2	61
Math Function Mania	61
Math Jeopardy	61
Math League Help Topics	61
MathMol Hypermedia Textbook	61
Math of Geography, The	61
Meet Amazing Americans	17
MegaMaps--Walk Through the Continents	30
Me? Live in a Rainforest?	72
Menuz	8
Metrics Matter	61
Mexican WebQuest	30

TITLE INDEX

Middle Schools and Foreign Languages: A View for the Future	21
Military Careers	38
Minerals by Name	72
Mini-Unit Topic: Native Americans	30
Minnesota State Highway Map	30
Mix 'n Match	3
Modeling Eclipses	72
Mop Top the Hip Hop Scientist	17
Mosaic America: Paths to the Present	46
Motivating Low Performing Adolescent Readers	54
Mouse Club, The	14
Mousetrap Racer!!!	72
Mr. Dowling's Electronic Passport	30
Mr. Pitonyak's Pyramid Puzzle	61
Mrs. Glosser's Math Goodies	61
Multiage-Educators Home Page, The	23
Multicultural Person, The	86
Museum of Musical Instruments, The	3
Music from Across America	3
Music of Yesterday and Today	3
Mutualism and Co-evolution	72
My Day As an Insect	72
Mystery Pictures	14

-N-

National Geographic GeoBee Challenge	30
National Women's Hall of Fame	17
Native American Geometry	61
Native Americans--Searching for Knowledge and Understanding	46
Native American Technology and Art	3
Natural Gas Safety World	65
NCTM Illuminations	61
New Look at Literature Instruction, A	54
New Patterns of School Governance	86
NewsDEN	24
NFBkids	24
Nile Adventure	30
Nine Planets, The: A Multimedia Tour of the Solar System	72
1900s, The	47

Nonindigenous Species: Activities for Youth	73
Noodle Tools	24
North American Skies	73
Not Indians, Many Tribes: Native American Diversity	30
Nova--Science in the News	73
Number the Stars: A WebQuest About the Holocaust	47
Nursery Rhyme Mania	54

-O-

Occupational Outlook Handbook	38
Official & Religious Mexican Holidays	50
Official Seed Starting Home Page, The	73
OneLook Dictionaries	11
On Line Te Reo Course	21
Oral Language Development Across the Curriculum, K-12	55
Origami Fun	3
Our Creative Diversity	86
Our Flag	34
Out on a Limb--A Guide to Getting Along	38
Overcrowding in Urban Schools	86
OWL Handouts	55
Owl Pellets	73
Oyez Baseball	34

-P-

Panic Button 3	61
Paper Bag Book Report	55
Paper Bag or Fabric Poncho	50
Paper Mache Masks--Maskmania	50
Parent Engagement as a School Reform Strategy	86
Parent Involvement in Elementary Language Arts: A Program Model	55
Parent Participation in Middle School Language Arts	55
Parts of a Whole	62
Passion for Change: Investigating the Evolution of Cultural Traditions	31
Peer Conflicts in the Classroom	86

102

TITLE INDEX

Performing Medieval Narrative Today: A Video Showcase	3
Philip and Alex's Guide to Web Publishing	8
Philosopher's Lighthouse, The--Shedding Light on Philosophy	17
Phonemic Awareness: An Important Early Step in Learning to Read	55
Photo Essay, A	55
Physical Science Activity Manual	73
PhysicsFront.org	73
Picasso	17
Pics4Learning	3
Pictures of Places.com	31
Pizza Family Reunion, A	62
Planet Pals	73
Planets or Not, Here We Come!	73
Planning for Parent Participation in Schools for Young Children	86
Planning for Success: Common Pitfalls \in the Planning of Early Foreign Language Programs	21
Plant Parts	73
Poetry for Kids	55
Poetry Screen Saver	55
Poison Prevention Game	14
Polar Postal History on the Web	47
Political Writings of George Orwell	55
Politics & Political Campaigns	34
POP Goes Antarctica?	73
Positive and Negative Integers: A Card Game	62
Poverty and Learning	86
Power Problem	62
Practical Do-Ables for Unlearning Racism	38
Preschool Coloring Book	14
Presidential Interview: A Panel of Presidents	34
Primer on Digital Literacy, A	8
Primer on Speaking and Writing Luganda, A	21
Prime Time Math	62
Privacy Pirates	8
Private See Dispute	34
Problem Solving and the Sports Page	62
Process of Sequencing--A Picture Card Game Activity	24
Programming in C	8
Project Appleseed	86
Promoting Diversity in Elementary School Curricula	86
Prongo.com	24
Proportionally Speaking	62
Prospects for Education Vouchers After the Supreme Court Ruling, The	87
Protocols	42
Punctuation: Less Is More?	55
Pygmalion Effect, The: A Dramatic Study in the Classroom	56

-Q-

Questioning Techniques	24
Que Tal in the Current Skies	73
Quick and Dirty Guide to Japanese, The	21
Quick Facts	38
Quiero Viajar a Espana!	31
Quikie Math: The Geometry Experience	62
Quiz Hub	24

-R-

Rainbow Raccoons, The	14
Random Acts of Kindness Activities	38
Random Acts of Kindness Lesson Plans	38
Reading and Writing in a Kindergarten Classroom	56
Recent Evidence on Preschool Programs	87
Recent Research on All-Day Kindergarten	87
Recess in Elementary School: What Does the Research Say?	87
Recycling Lesson Plan	74
Reinforcement Lesson in Place Value	62
Reinforcing Alphabet Names/Sounds	14
Relevant Approach to History, A	47
Reorganizing the Bill of Rights	34
Research Vessels	74
Resolving Conflicts and Making Peace: Basic Skills for Young Children	38

TITLE INDEX

Resource Rooms for Children: An Innovative Curricular Tool	87
Retaining Good Teachers in Urban Schools	87
Retaining Principals	87
Review of American History, A	47
RhymeZone Rhyming Dictionary, The	11
Right to Equal Opportunity	38
Rise and Fall of Jim Crow, The	47
Risk Behavior	39
RiskWatch	65
Rocks For Kids	74
Role of Metacognition in Second Language Teaching and Learning, The	21
Role of Online Communications in Schools, The: A National Study	87
Roll of Thunder: Hear My Cry Web Quest	39
Room 108	14
ROVer Ranch	74
RunStat 3	42

-S-

Safer Eggs: Laying the Groundwork	42
Safer Schools Through Environmental Design	87
SAFE: Safety Always for Everyone	65
Safety	65
Salmon Homing Instincts	74
Sammy Soil--A Downloadable Coloring Book	74
San Francisco Symphony Site for Kids	3
Save the Rainforest	74
Say Hello to the World	22
School-Based Budgeting	87
School Calendars	87
Schooling for Self-Determination: Research on the Effects of Including Native Language and Culture in the Schools	87
School Productivity	88
School Programs for African American Male Students	88
School Violence Prevention	88
Science Fair Home Page	74
Science is Fun	74
ScienceMaster	74
Science Role Plays	74
Search Hawaii! Cultural and Educational Pages	31
Sea Turtle Migration-Tracking Education Program	74
2nd Grade Treasure Trove	88
See What I Say: Connecting the Hearing with the Hearing Impaired	78
Self-Esteem Activity	39
Self-Esteem and Narcissism: Implications for Practice	88
September 11: What Our Children Need to Know	88
SET Toolkit	75
Seussville University	56
Seventy-First Came, The...To Gunskirchen Lager	47
Sexual Misconduct by School Employees	88
Shakespeare--His Life and Times	18
Shared Decision-Making	88
Sheep and Wolves	42
Shields, Knights and Heraldry	47
Shipwreck Island Adventure!	47
Should You Be the Boss?	88
SIGNhear	78
Sign Language	79
Simply Sharks!	75
Single-Use Foodservice Packaging--Facts and Fun Teacher's Kit	75
Sioux Indians, The	31
Six Corner Locomotion/Six Corner Roll	43
6th Grade Treasure Trove	88
SkillsDEN	8
SkyDEN	75
Small Schools and Teacher Professional Development	88
Smart Art	18
Smoking and Your Digestive System	43
Snakes of Massachusetts	75
Sociology Through Five Plays	3
Soda Play	75

TITLE INDEX

Solar System Bowl	75
Songs4Teachers	3
Songs for Teaching	3
SoundJunction	4
Sounds of Silence	79
Southeast Asian Adolescents: Identity and Adjustment	89
Spanish Christmas, A	50
Sparky the Fire Dog	65
Spartacus Encyclopedia of British History, The: British History	47
Spiro Mounds; Oklahoma's Past Indian History	47
Sports and Nutrition: The Winning Connection	43
SSSH--Successful, Simple Simulation, Hassle-Free	89
Stage Line/Time Line: A Musical Adventure	4
Stamps on Black History	18
StarChild	75
Star Politics	34
Starting Early: Environmental Education During the Early Childhood Years	89
States Mania	31
Stay Alive! Do You Know How?	65
Stepping Into the World of the American Musical Theatre: Dance Sets the Pace	4
Stories Behind the Songs	4
StoryPlace: The Children's Digital Library	14
Strategies for Teaching the Value \of Diversity	89
Student Diversity and Learning Needs	89
Student-Led Conferences at the Middle Level	89
Student Mobility and Academic Achievement	89
Student News Net	24
Students with Intellectual Disabilities: A Resource Guide for Teachers	79
Students with Visual Impairments	79
Student Truancy	89
Studying Watersheds: A Confluence of Important Ideas	75
StudyStack.com	24
Substance Abuse Policy	89
Substitute Teaching: An Insider's View	89
Success for All: A Summary of Evaluations	89
Successful Paragraphs	56
SunSmart	65
Sun, UV, and You	43
SupperTime	14
Surnames: What's in a Name?	11
Survival Kit	65
Swedish Language Course, A	22
Swiss Anthem	4
Swiss Ball Square Dance	43
Switch ZoO	75
Sworn to Serve	47
Synthesis of Scholarship in Multicultural Education, A	90

-T-

Talk About Trees	75
Talking to Your Child About Bias and Prejudice	39
Teacher Files	90
Teacher Preparation and Teacher-Child Interaction in Preschools	90
Teachers' Domain	75
Teacher's Guide for a Midsummer \Night's Dream	56
Teacher's Guide for Up From Slavery	56
Teacher's Guide to As You Like It	56
Teacher's Guide to the Holocaust, A	48
Teaching About Africa	31
Teaching America's Founding Documents	35
Teaching Creative Writing in the Elementary School	56
Teaching Democracy	35
Teaching History for Citizenship in the Elementary School	48
Teaching History with Technology	48
Teaching Ideas and Resources	14

TITLE INDEX

Teaching Poetry: Generating Genuine, Meaningful Responses	56
Teaching Resources Using Comics	4
Teaching Science in the Field	75
Teaching Tips to Use with the Signet Classic Shakespeare Series	56
Teaching Writing with Peer Response Groups Encouraging Revision	56
Teaching Young Children About Native Americans	90
Teach Me HTML	8
Team Approach to Oral History, A	48
TechEncyclopedia	11
Technology Tips for Classroom Teachers	8
Teen Central.Net	39
Teens Health, Food & Fitness	43
Temperature and Water Density	76
Ten C's for Evaluating Internet Sources	90
Test Anxiety	24
TestDEN	57
Test of Applied Creativity, Logic, and Reasoning	24
Thanksgiving on the Net	50
Theoretical Perspectives, Research Findings, and Classroom Implications of the Learning Styles of American Indian and Alaska Native Students	90
There Are Algae in Your House!	76
Thinking Fountain	76
Thinking of a Careers i Applied Mathematics	39
Thirteen Ed Online	90
This Is Mega-Mathematics!	62
This Dynamic Planet	31
ThisNation.com	35
Threads: Computers, Music, and a Little Theory	90
Three Dimensional Box Applet: Working with Volume	62
Time Traveller	48
Toilet Paper Solar System	76
Tox Town	76
Trial of Standing Bear, The	48
Turning It Around for All Youth: From Risk to Resilience	90
Turn on Inventiveness--Potato Possibilities	24
Tutorial on Using Perl and CGI to Enhance a Homepage, A	9
20 Field Day Activities Any Kid Can Do (And Do Well!)	43
Typing Bingo	9

-U-

Un-Birthday Present, The	4
Understanding Disabilities	79
Understanding Hispanic/Latino Culture and History Through the Use of Children's Literature	57
Under the Weather	76
United States Climate Page	31
U. S. States & Capitals Concentration Game	31
Universe in the Classroom, The	76
UpToTen	25
Urban Conservation Glossary, The	11
Urban Policies and Programs to Reduce Truancy	90
Urban School Finance: The Quest for Equal Educational Opportunity	90
Urban Youth in Community Service: Becoming Part of the Solution	91
Use of Substitution As a Creative Thinking Tool, The	39
Using Culturally and Linguistically Appropriate Assessments to Ensure that American Indian and Alaska Native Students Receive the Special Education Programs and Services They Need	91
Using Drama and Theatre to Promote Literacy Development: Some Basic Classroom Applications	4
Using Drama as a Resource for Giving Language More Meaning	4
Using Federal Funds to Improve Child Care	91

TITLE INDEX

Using Film, Video, and TV in the Classroom — 91
Using Primary Sources in the Primary Grades — 91

-V-

Verb Conjugation on line — 22
Very Bad Horrible No Good Day, The — 57
Video Games and Children — 91
Vietnam: A Children's Guide — 31
Virginia State Transportation Map — 31
Virtual Classroom, The — 91
Virtual Museum of Music Inventions, The — 4
Vocabulary Building — 57
Volcanoes of the United States — 76
Voting Simulation — 35

-W-

WASP on the Web — 48
Water Conservation Lesson Plan — 76
Waterford Press Free Games, Activities & More — 76
Weather Glossary — 11
Web Pages for Absolute Beginners — 9
We Can Talk: Cooperative Learning in the Elementary ESL Classroom — 22
Welcome to the Renaissance Art World — 4
We Shall Overcome: Historic Places of the Civil Rights Movement National Register Travel Itinerary — 48
Wetland Ecosystems II--Interactions and Ecosystems — 76
Whale Songs — 76
Whales on the Net — 76
What Causes Tooth Decay — 43
What Federal Statistics Reveal About Migrant Farmworkers: A Summary for Education — 91
What If? — 39
What the Blind Can See — 79
What They Left Behind--Early Multi-National Influences in the United States — 48

Where I Come From — 48
Where Oh Where — 25
Who Dunnit? — 77
Who I Am Poems — 91
Whole-School Reform — 91
Who's in the Bag? — 39
Why Files?, The — 91
WildFinder — 77
Will the Real Ben Franklin Please Stand Up? — 18
Wincalc — 62
Winfeed — 63
Winlab — 63
Women in Oceanography — 39
Woodwind Fingering Guide, The — 4
Word Central — 11
Working with Perfectionist Students — 92
Working with Shy or Withdrawn Students — 92
World-Class Standards and Local Pedagogies: Can We Do Both? — 92
World Factbook — 32
World on a String, The — 32
World War I: Trenches on the Web — 48
Writing Instruction: Changing Views Over the Years — 57

-X-Y-Z-

Yak's Corner — 32
Yarn Painting (Ofrendas) — 4
Year-Round Education: A Strategy for Overcrowded Schools — 92
YES I Can! Science — 77
You Can Control Your Weight As You Quit Smoking — 43
Young Children's Emotional Development and School Readiness — 92
Young Composers — 5
Your Own Classroom Court — 35
Your Voyage to Break the Language Barrier — 22
You've Got Spam: How to Can Unwanted E-Mail — 9

SUBJECT INDEX

ACCIDENT PREVENTION
Cartooning to Teach Safety 64
Disaster Strikes! 64
Electrical Safety World 64
Energy Safety 41
Farm Safety 4 Just Kids 64
Fire Safety & Education Factsheets 64
Fire Safety for Young Children 64
Indoor Electrical Safety Check 64
Natural Gas Safety World 65
RiskWatch 65
SAFE: Safety Always for Everyone 65
Safety 65
Sparky the Fire Dog 65

ACCOUNTING
Careers in Accounting 36

ACTION RESEARCH
Action Research in Early Childhood Education 80

ACTIVITIES
Aeronautics Educator Guide 66
Atom's Family, The 66
Children, Stress, and Natural Disasters: School Activities for Children 81
Chubbie Cubbie's Activity Ideas 12
Enchanted Learning Web Site 12
First-School 12
Funschool.com 12
Kids Heart, A 13
KinderArt Littles 13
Mouse Club, The 14
NFBkids 24
Nonindigenous Species: Activities for Youth 73
SET Toolkit 75
Seussville University 56
StoryPlace: The Children's Digital Library 14
Teacher Files 90
Thinking Fountain 76
This Is Mega-Mathematics! 62
Waterford Press Free Games, Activities & More 76

ACTIVITY BOOKS
Planet Pals 73
Single-Use Foodservice Packaging--Facts and Fun Teacher's Kit 75

ADMINISTRATION
Can Failing Schools Be Fixed? 81
Capitalizing on Small Class Size 81
Chapter I Schoolwide Projects: Advantages and Limitations 81
Children, Stress, and Natural Disasters: School Activities for Children 81
Dr. Mac's Amazing Behavior Management Advice Site 82

ADMINISTRATION (continued)
Education of Immigrant Children in New York City, The 83
Gangs in the Schools 83
Guidelines for Starting an Elementary School Foreign Language Program 20
History Textbook Controversies in Japan 46
Homeschooling 84
Implementing the Multiage Classroom 85
Implementing Whole-School Reform 85
Internet and Early Childhood Educators, The: Some Frequently Asked Questions 85
INTIME 85
Key Characteristics of Middle Level Schools 85
New Patterns of School Governance 86
Parent Engagement as a School Reform Strategy 86
Poverty and Learning 86
Recent Evidence on Preschool Programs 87
Recent Research on All-Day Kindergarten 87
Recess in Elementary School: What Does the Research Say? 87
Retaining Good Teachers in Urban Schools 87
Retaining Principals 87
Role of Online Communications in Schools, The: A National Study 87
Safer Schools Through Environmental Design 87
School-Based Budgeting 87
School Calendars 87
School Productivity 88
School Violence Prevention 88
Sexual Misconduct by School Employees 88
Shared Decision-Making 88
Should You Be the Boss? 88
Small Schools and Teacher Professional Development 88
Student Truancy 89
Substance Abuse Policy 89
Success for All: A Summary of Evaluations 89
Synthesis of Scholarship in Multicultural Education, A 90
Teacher Preparation and Teacher-Child Interaction in Preschools 90
Urban School Finance: The Quest for Equal Educational Opportunity 90
World-Class Standards and Local Pedagogies: Can We Do Both? 92
Year-Round Education: A Strategy for Overcrowded Schools 92

ADOLESCENCE
Adolescent & School Health 40
Alcohol, Peer Pressure and Underage Drinking Info for Young Teens 40
Gangs the Foster Family 84

SUBJECT INDEX

ADOLESCENCE (continued)
Motivating Low Performing Adolescent Readers 54
Teen Central.Net 39
Teens Health, Food & Fitness 43

AEROSPACE EDUCATION
Aeronautics Educator Guide 66
Amazing Space: Explorations 66
Astro-Venture 66
Birthday Moons 67
Changing Faces: A Study of Solar and Planetary Rotation Rates 68
Comets 68
Endeavour Views the Earth Electronic Picture Book 69
Making a Comet in the Classroom 72
Planets or Not, Here We Come! 73
Toilet Paper Solar System 76
Universe in the Classroom, The 76

AESOP
Aesop's Fables Online Collection 51

AFGHANISTAN
Afghanistan: The Harrison Forman Collection 26

AFRICA
Africa: Eating Senegal Style 26
AfriCam 26
African Art and Culture 26
African Flags Archive 26
African Folk Tales 26
Africa--South of the Sahara 26
Building an African Compound 27
Child's Daily Life in South Africa, A 27
Common African Food, A: Fou-Fou 27
Communicating Values and History Through Masks 27
Cuisine and Etiquette in Sierra Leone, Uganda, and Zambia 27
Everyday Life in Africa 28
Exploring African Music 28
Games and Toys Reflect Resources 28
Geographia 28
H-AfrTeach 29
Jambo Means Hello: An Introduction to Swahili 20
Kameshi Ne Mpuku: An African Game 29
Kamusi Project, The 20
Kwanzaa 50
Masai and I: A Cultural Comparison 30
Teaching About Africa 31

AFRICAN
Appreciating African Languages 19

AFRICAN AMERICANS
Address to the Negroes in the State of New York, An 44
African American Odyssey 44
Christmas Celebration in the Black Culture, A 49

AFRICAN AMERICANS (continued)
Ethnic Art: African, Mexican and Caribbean Perspectives 2
First Person Narratives of the American South, 1860-1920 45
Lift Every Voice and Sing 2
Literature and Art Through Our Eyes: The African American Children 54
Mop Top the Hip Hop Scientist 17
Mosaic America: Paths to the Present 46
Rise and Fall of Jim Crow, The 47
School Programs for African American Male Students 88
Stamps on Black History 18

AGING
Careers in Aging 36

AGRICULTURE
AgMag 26
Camp Silos 67
Farm Animals 69
Farm Safety 4 Just Kids 64
GardenWeb Glossary 10
Hello Dolly: A WebQuest 70
Kids Farm 13
Sammy Soil--A Downloadable Coloring Book 74

ALASKA
Alaska's Gold 44
Alaska Wildlife Notebook Series 66

ALCOHOL AND ALCOHOL ABUSE
Alcohol, Peer Pressure and Underage Drinking Info for Young Teens 40
Growing Up Drug Free 41

ALGEBRA
Algebra--One on One 58
Algebra Through Problem Solving 58
Awareness of Pre-Algebra Concepts 58
Design a Track 58
Math Function Mania 61
Three Dimensional Box Applet: Working with Volume 62

ALPHABET
ABC's of Snacking, The 12

AMPHIBIANS
Frogland 70

ANATOMY
Human Anatomy Online 71

ANCIENT HISTORY
Ancient Egypt 44
Ancient Mesopotamia: The History, Our History 44
Egyptian Mummies 45
Illustrated History of the Roman Empire 46

SUBJECT INDEX

ANIMALS
    Alaska Wildlife Notebook Series   66
    Animal Diversity Web   66
    ASPCA Kids   66
    Birds at the National Zoo   67
    Cetacean Fact Packs   68
    Farm Animals   69
    Florida Panther Net   70
    Honoring the Animal Spirits   29
    Snakes of Massachusetts   75
    Switch ZoO   75

ANTARCTICA
    POP Goes Antarctica?   73

ANTHONY, SUSAN B.
    Elizabeth Cady Stanton & Susan B. Anthony Papers Project Online, The   16

ANTHROPOLOGY
    Anthropology on the Internet for K-12   66

ARCHAEOLOGY
    Archeology Dig   66
    Dig--The Archaeology Magazine for Kids!   68

ARCHITECTURE
    Homes Around the World   29

ARTHRITIS
    Do I Have Arthritis?   41

ARTS AND CRAFTS
    African Art and Culture   26
    Artist Research Poster Lesson   1
    Artists of the Renaissance   15
    Artists: The Good, the Bad, and the Ugly   15
    ArtMagick   1
    Bird Cross Stitch Patterns   1
    Brush with Wildlife, A   1
    Chinese Dragon   27
    Coffee Can Drum   49
    Craftplace   1
    Do You Know Van Gogh?   15
    Draw and Color with Uncle Fred   1
    Early American Weaving   1
    Early Childhood Art Lessons   1
    Elementary Art Lesson Plans   1
    Idea Box   13
    Involving Community Members, Parents, and Community Agencies in Student Learning.   23
    Lesson #29: Textured Pottery Using Self-Hardening Clay and Multicultural Designs   2
    Lesson Plans   2
    Literature and Art Through Our Eyes: The African American Children   54
    Make a Papier Mache Bowl   2
    Making a Pinata   2
    Native American Technology and Art   3

ARTS AND CRAFTS   (continued)
    Origami Fun   3
    Paper Bag or Fabric Poncho   50
    Paper Mache Masks--Maskmania   50
    Picasso   17
    Smart Art   18
    Teaching Resources Using Comics   4
    Un-Birthday Present, The   4
    Welcome to the Renaissance Art World   4
    Yarn Painting (Ofrendas)   4

ASIA
    Chinese Dragon   27
    Geographia   28
    Vietnam: A Children's Guide   31

ASTRONAUTS
    Astronaut Biographies   15

ASTRONOMY
    Amazing Space: Explorations   66
    Astronomy Picture of the Day   66
    Birthday Moons   67
    Birthday Moons: It's Just a Phase You're Going Through   67
    Changing Faces: A Study of Solar and Planetary Rotation Rates   68
    Comets   68
    Constellations, The   68
    Eyes on the Sky, Feet on the Ground   69
    How to View an Eclipse   71
    Journey Through the Galaxy   71
    Modeling Eclipses   72
    Nine Planets, The: A Multimedia Tour of the Solar System   72
    North American Skies   73
    Planets or Not, Here We Come!   73
    Que Tal in the Current Skies   73
    SkyDEN   75
    Solar System Bowl   75
    StarChild   75
    Toilet Paper Solar System   76
    Universe in the Classroom, The   76

AT-RISK YOUTH
    Turning It Around for All Youth: From Risk to Resilience   90

ATTENTION DEFICIT DISORDER
    ADHD eBook   78

AUSTRALIA
    Aboriginal English   19
    Australian Folk Songs   1
    On Line Te Reo Course   21

AUTISM
    Alternatives to Behaviorism   78
    Understanding Disabilities   79

SUBJECT INDEX

AUTOMOBILES
Automobile Safety Articles 64

BATTLESHIPS
All Hands on Deck 44

BEHAVIOR
Dr. Mac's Amazing Behavior Management Advice Site 82

BIAS
Determining the Existence of Gender Bias in Daily Tasks 82
Gender Stereotypes and Advertisements 37
Language in Classroom Texts 37
Right to Equal Opportunity 38

BIOGRAPHIES
Abraham Lincoln Online 15
Artist Research Poster Lesson 1
Artists of the Renaissance 15
Astronaut Biographies 15
Biographical Dictionary 10
Biographies of Explorers and Associated People 15
Biography-Center 15
Biography.com 15
Colonial Hall 15
Confucius--His Life and Times 15
Do You Know Van Gogh? 15
Dr. Martin Luther King, Jr. 16
Einstein: Man in Spacetime 16
Elizabeth Cady Stanton & Susan B. Anthony Papers Project Online, The 16
Famous Canadians 16
Famous Hispanics in the World and History 16
Famous People with Perfect Pitch 16
Famous Person--Who Am I? 16
4000 Years of Women in Science 16
Gallery of Achievers 16
Helen Keller Biography 16
Heroism in Action 16
Hitler & Stalin 17
Indexes of Biographies 17
Invention Dimension 17
Laura Ingalls Wilder 17
Leonardo Da Vinci: A Man of Both Worlds 17
Life of Abraham Lincoln, The: An Illustrated Timeline for Young Readers 17
Meet Amazing Americans 17
Mop Top the Hip Hop Scientist 17
National Women's Hall of Fame 17
Philosopher's Lighthouse, The--Shedding Light on Philosophy 17
Picasso 17
Smart Art 18
Star Politics 34
Un-Birthday Present, The 4

BIOGRAPHIES (continued)
Welcome to the Renaissance Art World 4
Will the Real Ben Franklin Please Stand Up? 18

BIOLOGY
BioInteractive 67
Genetic Science Learning Center 70
Human Anatomy Online 71
Make a Splash with Color 2
Mutualism and Co-evolution 72
Teachers' Domain 75

BIRDS
Birds at the National Zoo 67
Bluebird Quest, A 67

BLINDNESS
American Sign Language as a Foreign Language 19
General Information About Blindness 78
Understanding Disabilities 79
What the Blind Can See 79

BLOGS
Creating a Blog: A Workshop for Teens 7

BOTANY
GardenWeb Glossary 10
Great Plant Escape, The 70
Investigating Plants 71
Lewis and Clark as Naturalists 72
Mutualism and Co-evolution 72
Plant Parts 73

CALCULATORS
Abacus, The--The Art of Calculating with Beads 58
Calculators On-Line Center 58
Wincalc 62

CALENDARS
Make a Multi-Cultural Calendar 50

CANADA
Canada on Postcards 27
Famous Canadians 16

CANCER
Health Fact Sheets 41
Health Fact Sheets 41
Health Fact Sheets 42

CAREERS
America's Career InfoNet 36
Career Development for All Students 36
Career Guide for the Atmospheric Sciences, A 36
Careers and Industries Overview 36
Careers in Accounting 36
Careers in Aging 36
Careers in Psychology 36
Careers in the Genetics Field 36
Career WebQuest 36

112

SUBJECT INDEX

CAREERS (continued)
  Challenges of Our Changing Atmosphere: Careers in Atmospheric Research and Applied Meteorology 36
  Communication Strategies for Employment Interviews 37
  Entertainment Careers 37
  Exploring Occupations: Getting You Started on Your Career Path! 37
  50 Careers in Trees 37
  Handouts and Information Guides 37
  Job Genie 37
  LifeWorks 38
  Marinecareers 38
  Matching Yourself with the World of Work 38
  Military Careers 38
  Occupational Outlook Handbook 38
  Quick Facts 38
  Student News Net 24
  Thinking of a Careers i Applied Mathematics 39
  Women in Oceanography 39

CARIBBEAN
  Ethnic Art: African, Mexican and Caribbean Perspectives 2

CARTOGRAPHY
  Exploring Caves 28
  Learning the Compass 29
  Mathematics of Cartography 30

CEREMONIES
  Coffee Can Drum 49

CGI
  CGI Resource Index, The 6

CHAPTER ONE PROGRAMS
  Chapter I Schoolwide Projects: Advantages and Limitations 81

CHARACTER EDUCATION
  Character Education Through Children's Literature 51

CHARTER SCHOOLS
  Charter Schools: An Approach for Rural Education? 81

CHILD CARE
  Babysitter Handbook, The 64
  Using Federal Funds to Improve Child Care 91

CHILD SAFETY
  GetNetWise 7

CHINA
  Chinese Dragon 27

CHINESE
  Working with Perfectionist Students 92

CHRISTIANITY
  Easter 49

CHRISTMAS
  Christmas at the Cottage 49
  Christmas in Poland 49
  Christmas Traditions 49
  Christmas--Where Did It Come From? Where Is It Going? 49
  Hawaiian Christmas Trees 49
  Holiday Traditions 50
  Spanish Christmas, A 50

CIGARETTES
  Smoking and Your Digestive System 43

CITIZENSHIP
  Catch the Spirit: A Student's Guide to Community Service 81
  Citizenship and the Constitution 33
  Hunger Site, The 84
  Issue-Centered Civic Education in Middle Schools 33
  Kids Next Door 34
  Random Acts of Kindness Activities 38
  Random Acts of Kindness Lesson Plans 38
  Teaching History for Citizenship in the Elementary School 48

CIVICS
  Issue-Centered Civic Education in Middle Schools 33
  Star Politics 34

CIVIL RIGHTS
  Actions and Reactions 44

CIVIL RIGHTS MOVEMENT
  We Shall Overcome: Historic Places of the Civil Rights Movement National Register Travel Itinerary 48

CIVIL WAR
  American Civil War Webquest, The 44
  Civil War Through a Child's Eye, The 45
  Rise and Fall of Jim Crow, The 47

C LANGUAGE
  C-Language Course 6
  Programming in C 8

CLIMATE
  Dan's Wild, Wild Weather Page 68
  Under the Weather 76
  United States Climate Page 31

CLONING
  Hello Dolly: A WebQuest 70
  I Can Do That! 71

COACHING
  Building Leadership Skills in Middle School Girls Through Interscholastic Athletics 40

COAL
  Coal Science Fair Ideas 68

SUBJECT INDEX

COLOR
Make a Splash with Color 2

COLORING BOOKS
Ivy's Coloring Page Search Engine 13
Preschool Coloring Book 14
Sammy Soil--A Downloadable Coloring Book 74

COMMUNITY PROGRAMS
Urban Youth in Community Service: Becoming Part of the Solution 91

COMMUNITY SERVICE
Catch the Spirit: A Student's Guide to Community Service 81

COMPUTERS AND COMPUTER EDUCATION
Ainsworth Computer Seminar 6
bNetS@vvy 6
CGI Resource Index, The 6
C-Language Course 6
Classroom Learning 2.0 6
Computer Almanac 6
Computer and Internet Use by Children and Adolescents in 2001: Statistical Analysis Report 6
Computer Assisted Writing Instruction 52
Computers and How They Work 6
Computers: History and Development 6
Digital Divide and Its Implications for the Language Arts, The 52
Few Scanning Tips, A 7
FILExt 7
Find Lost Files and Folders 7
Goetz's Programming Kit 7
How Do They Do That with HTML? 7
HTML Goodies 7
Jan's Illustrated Computer Literacy 101 8
Karbosguide.com 8
Mouse Club, The 14
Philip and Alex's Guide to Web Publishing 8
Programming in C 8
SkillsDEN 8
Teach Me HTML 8
TechEncyclopedia 11
Ten C's for Evaluating Internet Sources 90
Typing Bingo 9

CONFLICT RESOLUTION
Conflict Resolution Programs in Schools 81
Out on a Limb--A Guide to Getting Along 38
Peer Conflicts in the Classroom 86
SSSH--Successful, Simple Simulation, Hassle-Free 89

CONFUCIUS
Confucius--His Life and Times 15

CONSERVATION
Conserving America's Fisheries 68
Educational Poster on Water Pollution 69
Sea Turtle Migration-Tracking Education Program 74
Water Conservation Lesson Plan 76
Wetland Ecosystems II--Interactions and Ecosystems 76

CONSTITUTION OF THE UNITED STATES
Citizenship and the Constitution 33
Constitution of the United States and the Declaration of Independence 33
Constitution, The: Our Plan for Government 33
Interactive Constitution 33
Reorganizing the Bill of Rights 34
Teaching America's Founding Documents 35

COSTUMES
Dramatic Education, A 1

CRIME PREVENTION
School Violence Prevention 88

CULTURE
Cultural Spaces 27
Culture of the Frisians 27
Cultures of the Andes 27
Everyone Has a Culture--Everyone Is Different 28
Exploring the Function of Heroes and Heroines in Children's Literature from Around the World 52
Iceberg, The 84
In My Other Life 37
Native American Technology and Art 3
Our Creative Diversity 86
Passion for Change: Investigating the Evolution of Cultural Traditions 31
Understanding Hispanic/Latino Culture and History Through the Use of Children's Literature 57
Where I Come From 48

CURRENT EVENTS
NewsDEN 24
Student News Net 24
Why Files?, The 91
Yak's Corner 32

CURRICULUM GUIDES
Kentucky Bug Connection Teaching Resources 71

CZECH REPUBLIC
Little Czech Primer in Pictures 21

DANCES AND FESTIVALS
Festivals Around the World 49
Stepping Into the World of the American Musical Theatre: Dance Sets the Pace 4
Swiss Ball Square Dance 43

SUBJECT INDEX

DATABASE PROGRAMS
  Custom Addressbook 0.7.2 82
  Database of Award-Winning Children's Literature 52
DA VINCI, LEONARDO
  Leonardo Da Vinci: A Man of Both Worlds 17
DEAFNESS
  Hard of Hearing and Deaf Students: A Resource Guide to Support Classroom Teachers 78
  See What I Say: Connecting the Hearing with the Hearing Impaired 78
  Sign Language 79
  Sounds of Silence 79
  Understanding Disabilities 79
DEATH AND DYING
  Coping with Death and Dying 37
DECISION MAKING
  What If? 39
DECLARATION OF INDEPENDENCE
  Constitution of the United States and the Declaration of Independence 33
  Declare the Causes: The Declaration of Independence 33
DEMOCRACY
  Teaching Democracy 35
DEPRESSION
  Health Fact Sheets 41
  Health Fact Sheets 41
  Health Fact Sheets 42
DESEGREGATION
  Changing Face of Racial Isolation and Desegregation in Urban Schools 81
DEWEY DECIMAL SYSTEM
  Decimal Search 52
DIABETES
  Health Fact Sheets 41
  Health Fact Sheets 41
  Health Fact Sheets 42
DICTIONARIES
  ABC's of Legal Terms 10
  Acronym Finder 10
  Alan Cooper's Homonym List 10
  Biographical Dictionary 10
  Encyclopedia.com 10
  Glossary of Internet & Web Terms 10
  Internet Acronym Server 10
  Internet Glossary of Soil Science Terms 10
  LOGOS Multilingual Portal 11
  OneLook Dictionaries 11
  RhymeZone Rhyming Dictionary, The 11
  Surnames: What's in a Name? 11
  TechEncyclopedia 11

DIETS AND DIETING
  Do You Know the Health Risks of Being Overweight? 41
DIGESTIVE SYSTEM
  Smoking and Your Digestive System 43
DISABILITIES
  Issues in the Education of American Indian and Alaska Native Students with Disabilities 85
DISABLED
  Americans with Disabilities Act: Questions and Answers 80
DISASTER PREPAREDNESS
  Children, Stress, and Natural Disasters: School Activities for Children 81
DISCIPLINE
  Are You With It? 80
DISCRIMINATION
  Practical Do-Ables for Unlearning Racism 38
DISEASE PREVENTION
  Communicable Disease Fact Sheets 40
  Health Fact Sheets 41
  Health Fact Sheets 41
  Health Fact Sheets 42
DISEASES
  Ah Choo! 40
  Colds & Flu: Time Only Sure Cure 40
  Communicable Disease Fact Sheets 40
  Do I Have Arthritis? 41
  Infection, Detection, Protection 71
DIVERSITY
  Diversity Within Unity: Essential Principles for Teaching and Learning in a Multicultural Society 82
  ePALS Classroom Exchange 28
  Our Creative Diversity 86
  Promoting Diversity in Elementary School Curricula 86
  Strategies for Teaching the Value of Diversity 89
DNA
  DNA for Dinner? 68
DRAMA
  Ask the Presidents 33
  Creative Dramatics in the Language Arts Classroom 52
  Dramatic Education, A 1
  Grand Pantheon, The 2
  Performing Medieval Narrative Today: A Video Showcase 3
  Sociology Through Five Plays 3
  Stage Line/Time Line: A Musical Adventure 4
  Stepping Into the World of the American Musical Theatre: Dance Sets the Pace 4

SUBJECT INDEX

DRAMA (continued)
 Using Drama and Theatre to Promote Literacy Development: Some Basic Classroom Applications 4
 Using Drama as a Resource for Giving Language More Meaning 4
DRAWING
 Draw and Color with Uncle Fred 1
DRUGS AND DRUG ABUSE
 Growing Up Drug Free 41
 Substance Abuse Policy 89
DUTCH
 AllWords.com 10
 UpToTen 25
DYSLEXIA
 Everything You Always Wanted to Know About Dyslexia 78
EARLY LEARNING
 ABC's of Snacking, The 12
 ABCteach 23
 Action Research in Early Childhood Education 80
 ALFY: The Web Portal for Kids 12
 Alphabet Soup 12
 Child-Initiated Learning Activities for Young Children Living in Poverty 81
 Chubbie Cubbie's Activity Ideas 12
 Drawing for Children 12
 Early Childhood Art Lessons 1
 Enchanted Learning Web Site 12
 Encouraging Creativity in Early Childhood Classrooms 83
 Everything Preschool 12
 First-School 12
 4Kids2Play 12
 Funschool.com 12
 Game Goo 12
 Green Bean's Treehouse 12
 ICT Games 13
 Idea Box 13
 Instructional Models for Early Childhood Education 85
 Integrating Children with Disabilities Into Preschool 78
 Internet and Early Childhood Educators, The: Some Frequently Asked Questions 85
 Kids Heart, A 13
 KidsKonnect 23
 KidsPsych 13
 KinderArt Littles 13
 Language Development in the Early Years 54
 Larry's Animals-n-Things 13
 Larry's Count 13
 Larry's Songs 13
 Lasting Benefits of Preschool Programs 85
 Learn Letters 13

EARLY LEARNING (continued)
 Letter Sounds 13
 Literacy Center 13
 Little Red House, The 14
 Mouse Club, The 14
 Mystery Pictures 14
 Planning for Success: Common Pitfalls in the Planning of Early Foreign Language Programs 21
 Poison Prevention Game 14
 Preschool Coloring Book 14
 Prongo.com 24
 Rainbow Raccoons, The 14
 Recent Evidence on Preschool Programs 87
 Reinforcing Alphabet Names/Sounds 14
 Resolving Conflicts and Making Peace: Basic Skills for Young Children 38
 Resource Rooms for Children: An Innovative Curricular Tool 87
 Room 108 14
 Starting Early: Environmental Education During the Early Childhood Years 89
 StoryPlace: The Children's Digital Library 14
 SupperTime 14
 Teacher Preparation and Teacher-Child Interaction in Preschools 90
 UpToTen 25
 Young Children's Emotional Development and School Readiness 92
EARTH DAY
 Planet Pals 73
EARTH SCIENCE
 Dig--The Archaeology Magazine for Kids! 68
 Internet Glossary of Soil Science Terms 10
 Rocks For Kids 74
EATING DISORDERS
 Health Fact Sheets 41
 Health Fact Sheets 41
 Health Fact Sheets 42
ECOLOGY
 Carolina Coastal Science 68
 Ecology Data Tip Archives 69
ECOSYSTEMS
 Ecosystems 69
EGYPT
 Ancient Egypt 44
 Coptic Language, The 19
 Egyptian Mummies 45
 Nile Adventure 30
EINSTEIN, ALBERT
 Einstein: Man in Spacetime 16
ELECTRICITY
 Electrical Safety World 64

SUBJECT INDEX

ELECTRICITY (continued)
Electrical Safety World 64
Electric Universe, The 69

ELECTRONIC MAILING LISTS
ePALS Classroom Exchange 28

EMAIL
Chatback Trust, The 78
You've Got Spam: How to Can Unwanted E-Mail 9

ENDANGERED SPECIES
Animal Info--Endangered Animals 66
Conserving America's Fisheries 68
Endangered/Threatened Species 69
Florida Panther Net 70

ENERGY
Atom's Family, The 66
Classroom Energy! 68
Coal Science Fair Ideas 68
Electrical Safety World 64
Energy Safety 41
FT Exploring 70
Geothermal Energy 70

ENGINEERING
Keep the Traffic Moving! 60
ROVer Ranch 74
Why Files?, The 91

ENGLAND
Guide to British Life, Culture and Customs 29

ENGLISH
English-Only Movement: Its Consequences for the Education of Language Minority Children 52
TestDEN 57

ENGLISH AS A SECOND LANGUAGE
EverythingESL.net 52
We Can Talk: Cooperative Learning in the Elementary ESL Classroom 22

ENTOMOLOGY
Amateur Entomologist 66
Kentucky Bug Connection Teaching Resources 71

ENVIRONMENTAL EDUCATION
Aluminum Beverage Cans: The ABCs of Environmental Education 66
Build-a-Prairie 67
Choosing Instructional Materials for Environmental Education 81
Earth Force 69
Ecology Data Tip Archives 69
Finding Funding for Environmental Education Efforts 69
Global Issues and Environmental Education 70
Planet Pals 73
Sea Turtle Migration-Tracking Education Program 74

ENVIRONMENTAL EDUCATION (continued)
Single-Use Foodservice Packaging--Facts and FunTeacher's Kit 75
Starting Early: Environmental Education During the Early Childhood Years 89
Studying Watersheds: A Confluence of Important Ideas 75
Tox Town 76
Urban Conservation Glossary, The 11

EQUALITY
Girlstart 23

ETHNIC CUISINE
Africa: Eating Senegal Style 26
Common African Food, A: Fou-Fou 27
Cuisine and Etiquette in Sierra Leone, Uganda, and Zambia 27

EUROPE
Culture of the Frisians 27
Geographia 28
Guide to British Life, Culture and Customs 29
Little Czech Primer in Pictures 21
Spanish Christmas, A 50
Swiss Anthem 4

EVOLUTION
Becoming Human 67

EXERCISE
Ball Monster 40
Beanbag Freeze Tag 40
Best Bones Forever! 40
Fitness Partner 41
KidsRunning.Com 42
Lacrosse Tag 42

EXPLORERS AND EXPLORATION
Biographies of Explorers and Associated People 15

FABRICS AND TEXTILES
Anglo-Saxon and Viking Crafts--Textiles 44

FAIRY TALES
Fairy Tales Around the World 53
Gender Equity in Fairy Tales 53

FAMILY LIFE
Video Games and Children 91

FAMOUS PEOPLE
Artist Research Poster Lesson 1
Artists of the Renaissance 15
ArtMagick 1
Astronaut Biographies 15
Biographies of Explorers and Associated People 15
Biography-Center 15
Biography.com 15
Colonial Hall 15
Confucius--His Life and Times 15

SUBJECT INDEX

FAMOUS PEOPLE (continued)
Contemporary Art Experience, The 15
Do You Know Van Gogh? 15
Dr. Martin Luther King, Jr. 16
Einstein: Man in Spacetime 16
Erwin E. Smith: Teaching Guide 45
Famous Canadians 16
Famous Hispanics in the World and History 16
Famous People with Perfect Pitch 16
Famous Person--Who Am I? 16
4000 Years of Women in Science 16
Great Thinkers: A Study in Philosophy 16
Helen Keller Biography 16
Heroism in Action 16
Hitler & Stalin 17
Indexes of Biographies 17
Invention Dimension 17
Laura Ingalls Wilder 17
Leonardo Da Vinci: A Man of Both Worlds 17
Life of Abraham Lincoln, The: An Illustrated Timeline for Young Readers 17
Meet Amazing Americans 17
Mop Top the Hip Hop Scientist 17
National Women's Hall of Fame 17
Philosopher's Lighthouse, The--Shedding Light on Philosophy 17
Picasso 17
Political Writings of George Orwell 55
Presidential Interview: A Panel of Presidents 34
Smart Art 18
Star Politics 34
Un-Birthday Present, The 4
Welcome to the Renaissance Art World 4
Will the Real Ben Franklin Please Stand Up? 18

FIELD TRIPS
Teaching Science in the Field 75

FIRE AND FIRE PREVENTION
Fire Safety & Education Factsheets 64
Fire Safety WebQuest 64
Making Your Home Safe from Fire and Carbon Monoxide 65
Sparky the Fire Dog 65

FIRE SAFETY
Fire Safety & Education Factsheets 64
Fire Safety for Young Children 64
Making Your Home Safe from Fire and Carbon Monoxide 65
Sparky the Fire Dog 65

FIRST AID
Survival Kit 65

FISH AND FISHING
Conserving America's Fisheries 68
Salmon Homing Instincts 74

FLAGS
African Flags Archive 26
Our Flag 34

FLORIDA
Florida Panther Net 70

FOLK SONGS
Australian Folk Songs 1

FOLK TALES
African Folk Tales 26

FOOD GUIDE PYRAMID
Kid's World - Nutrition 42

FOODS
Are Bioengineered Foods Safe? 40
Bulking Up Fiber's Healthful Reputation 40
Dietary Guidelines for Americans 41
Eating for Life 41
Fight BAC!: Four Simple Steps to Food Safety 41
Making Healthy Food Choices 42
Safer Eggs: Laying the Groundwork 42

FOREIGN LANGUAGES
Aboriginal English 19
African Languages at the K-12 Level 19
Alien Language 19
AllWords.com 10
American Sign Language as a Foreign Language 19
Appreciating African Languages 19
Assessing Young Children's Social Competence 80
Brain Research: Implications for Second Language Learning 19
CGI Made Really Easy 6
Civilisation Francaise 19
Coptic Language, The 19
Cultures of the Andes 27
Developing Language Proficiency and Connecting School to Students's Lives: Two Standards for Effective Teaching 82
Dictionary.com 10
EspanOle! 19
First-School 12
Free Online Pronunciation Guide 19
French Language Course 19
French Online Grammar Quiz 20
German American Contributions to Mainstream Culture 20
German for Music Lovers 20
Guidelines for Starting an Elementary School Foreign Language Program 20
Hausa Online Grammar 20
Instructional Models for Early Childhood Education 85
Interactive On-Line Reference Grammar, An 20
Irish Lessons 20
Italian Electronic Classroom, The 20

SUBJECT INDEX

FOREIGN LANGUAGES (continued)
Jambo Means Hello: An Introduction to Swahili 20
Jan's Illustrated Computer Literacy 101 8
Kamusi Project, The 20
Kanienkehaka Language Homepage 20
Language and Literacy Environments in Preschools 85
Languages Across the Curriculum 20
Learn to Read Bengali 21
Learn to Read Punjabi 21
Learn to Read Sanskrit 21
Learn to Read Spanish 21
Learn to Read Tamil 21
Learn to Read Urdu 21
Little Czech Primer in Pictures 21
LOGOS Multilingual Portal 11
Mathematics Standards for Pre-Kindergarten Through Grade 2 61
Middle Schools and Foreign Languages: A View for the Future 21
On Line Te Reo Course 21
Primer on Speaking and Writing Luganda, A 21
Quick and Dirty Guide to Japanese, The 21
Quiero Viajar a Espana! 31
Recent Evidence on Preschool Programs 87
Recent Research on All-Day Kindergarten 87
Recess in Elementary School: What Does the Research Say? 87
Role of Metacognition in Second Language Teaching and Learning, The 21
Say Hello to the World 22
Schooling for Self-Determination: Research on the Effects of Including Native Language and Culture in the Schools 87
Student Mobility and Academic Achievement 89
Swedish Language Course, A 22
Teacher Preparation and Teacher-Child Interaction in Preschools 90
UpToTen 25
Verb Conjugation on line 22
We Can Talk: Cooperative Learning in the Elementary ESL Classroom 22
Working with Perfectionist Students 92
YES I Can! Science 77
Your Voyage to Break the Language Barrier 22

FORESTS AND FORESTRY
50 Careers in Trees 37
Forest Stewardship 70
Healthy Forests 70
Leaf ID and Leaf Bingo 72
Save the Rainforest 74
Talk About Trees 75

FRACTALS
Winfeed 63

FRANK, ANNE
Anne Frank in the World Teacher Workbook 15

FRANKLIN, BEN
Will the Real Ben Franklin Please Stand Up? 18

FRENCH
Alien Language 19
AllWords.com 10
Civilisation Francaise 19
French Language Course 19
French Online Grammar Quiz 20
UpToTen 25
YES I Can! Science 77
Your Voyage to Break the Language Barrier 22

FROGS
Frogland 70

GAMES
Build-a-Prairie 67
4Kids2Play 12
Games and Toys Reflect Resources 28
Kameshi Ne Mpuku: An African Game 29
Logical Games and Puzzles 1 60
Logical Games and Puzzles 2 60
Logical Games and Puzzles 3 60
Math Function Mania 61
Poison Prevention Game 14
Privacy Pirates 8
Prongo.com 24
States Mania 31
Waterford Press Free Games, Activities & More 76

GANGS
Gangs in the Schools 83

GARDENS AND GARDENING
Official Seed Starting Home Page, The 73

GENDER
Determining the Existence of Gender Bias in Daily Tasks 82
Gender Differences in Educational Achievement within Racial and Ethnic Groups 84
Gender Equity in Fairy Tales 53
Gender Stereotypes and Advertisements 37
Language in Classroom Texts 37
Right to Equal Opportunity 38

GENERAL EDUCATION
EducatingJane.com 23
Knowledge Master 23

GENETICS
Careers in the Genetics Field 36
Genetic Science Learning Center 70
I Can Do That! 71

GEOGRAPHY
AfriCam 26
Baltimore Curriculum Project Lesson Plans 23

119

SUBJECT INDEX

GEOGRAPHY (continued)
Fact Monster 10
Geographia 28
Geo-Images Project 84
Global Online Adventure Learning Site 28
Helping Your Child Learn Geography 29
Homes Around the World 29
Hoover Dam Learning Packet 29
Ideas for Exploring Our City and State 29
Learning the Compass 29
Let Me Tell You About My State! 29
Make a Village 30
Making an Illustrated Dictionary with Geographic Terms 30
Math of Geography, The 61
MegaMaps--Walk Through the Continents 30
Minnesota State Highway Map 30
Mr. Dowling's Electronic Passport 30
National Geographic GeoBee Challenge 30
Pictures of Places.com 31
States Mania 31
Virginia State Transportation Map 31
Where Oh Where 25
World Factbook 32
World on a String, The 32

GEOLOGY
Exploring Caves 28
Minerals by Name 72
This Dynamic Planet 31
Volcanoes of the United States 76

GEOMETRY
Geo-Critters 59
Lighting the Perimeter 60
Math Cove 60
Native American Geometry 61
Quikie Math: The Geometry Experience 62

GERMAN
Alien Language 19
AllWords.com 10
CGI Made Really Easy 6
Deutsch Plus 19
German American Contributions to Mainstream Culture 20
German for Music Lovers 20
Your Voyage to Break the Language Barrier 22

GIFTED STUDENTS
Creative Strategies for Teaching Language Arts to Gifted Students 52
Gifted Readers and Reading Instruction 53
Hoagies' Gifted Education Page 23

GLOSSARIES
AllWords.com 10
Baroque Reference, The 10

GLOSSARIES (continued)
Dictionary.com 10
Fact Monster 10
FILExt 7
GardenWeb Glossary 10
Kamusi Project, The 20
Making an Illustrated Dictionary with Geographic Terms 30
OneLook Dictionaries 11
Urban Conservation Glossary, The 11
Weather Glossary 11
Word Central 11

GOVERNMENT
American Revolution Simulation 44
Annenberg Classroom 33
Ask the Presidents 33
Ben's Guide to U. S. Government for Kids 33
Citizenship and the Constitution 33
Constitution of the United States and the Declaration of Independence 33
Constitution, The: Our Plan for Government 33
Declare the Causes: The Declaration of Independence 33
Great Depression and the 1990s, The 45
How a Bill Becomes a Law 33
How Our Laws Are Made 33
Justice 34
Justice for Kids and Youth 34
Kids Next Door 34
Know Your Local Government 34
Laws--Who Needs Them? 34
Politics & Political Campaigns 34
Presidential Interview: A Panel of Presidents 34
Reorganizing the Bill of Rights 34
Star Politics 34
Teaching America's Founding Documents 35
Teaching Democracy 35
ThisNation.com 35
Using Federal Funds to Improve Child Care 91
Voting Simulation 35
Your Own Classroom Court 35

GRAMMAR
Basic Grammar Review Using Jabberwocky 51

GRAPHICS
Banner Generator, The 6
Geo-Images Project 84
Pics4Learning 3

GRAPHS AND GRAPHING
Graphing from a 5th Grader's Point of View 59

GREAT BRITAIN
Guide to British Life, Culture and Customs 29
Spartacus Encyclopedia of British History, The: British History 47

SUBJECT INDEX

GUIDANCE
America's Career InfoNet 36
Assessing Young Children's Social Competence 80
Coping with Death and Dying 37
Exploring Occupations: Getting You Started on Your Career Path! 37
Let's Get Along 37
Risk Behavior 39
Self-Esteem Activity 39
Teen Central.Net 39
Test Anxiety 24
Who's in the Bag? 39

GULF OF MEXICO
Living Gulf, The: A Place to Treasure 29

HANDICAPPED
See What I Say: Connecting the Hearing with the Hearing Impaired 78
Sign Language 79
Sounds of Silence 79

HANUKKAH
How to Celebrate Chanukah 50

HAWAII
Hawaiian Christmas Trees 49
Search Hawaii! Cultural and Educational Pages 31

HEALTH AND HEALTH EDUCATION
Adolescent & School Health 40
Careers in Aging 36
Colds & Flu: Time Only Sure Cure 40
Health Finder 42
Rainbow Raccoons, The 14
Risk Behavior 39

HEALTH HABITS
Ah Choo! 40
Infection, Detection, Protection 71
Kids World 42
Kid's World - Nutrition 42
Smoking and Your Digestive System 43
Sun, UV, and You 43
What Causes Tooth Decay 43
You Can Control Your Weight As You Quit Smoking 43

HIGH BLOOD PRESSURE
Health Fact Sheets 41
Health Fact Sheets 42

HISPANICS
Expanding Fifth Grade Ethnic Awareness (Latino and Native American) Through Literature 28
Health Fact Sheets 41
Latinos in School: Some Facts and Findings 86
Mosaic America: Paths to the Present 46
Understanding Hispanic/Latino Culture and History Through the Use of Children's Literature 57

HISTORY
Abraham Lincoln Online 15
Actions and Reactions 44
African American Odyssey 44
Alaska's Gold 44
All Hands on Deck 44
American Journeys 44
American Revolution at a Glance 44
American Revolution Simulation 44
Anglo-Saxon and Viking Crafts--Textiles 44
Anne Frank in the World Teacher Workbook 15
Archeology Dig 66
Around the World in 1896 45
Baltimore Curriculum Project Lesson Plans 23
Biographical Dictionary 10
Build Your Own Medieval Castle 45
Colonial Hall 15
Computers: History and Development 6
Coptic Language, The 19
18th Century History 45
Erwin E. Smith: Teaching Guide 45
European Voyages of Exploration 45
Experience the Life 45
Face to Face--Stories from the Aftermath of Infamy 45
Famous Canadians 16
Famous Person--Who Am I? 16
First Person Narratives of the American South, 1860-1920 45
Gallery of Achievers 16
Grand Pantheon, The 2
Great Depression and the 1990s, The 45
Gunfighters of the Old West 46
Handbook of Texas Online 29
Hello, I Am Deborah Sampson 46
History Happens 46
History Textbook Controversies in Japan 46
History Wired 46
How a Bill Becomes a Law 33
How the Internet Came to Be 7
Hunger Site, The 84
Illustrated History of the Roman Empire 46
Lewis and Clark as Naturalists 72
Light in the Forest, The 54
Making of America 46
Mr. Dowling's Electronic Passport 30
Native Americans--Searching for Knowledge and Understanding 46
1900s, The 47
Number the Stars: A WebQuest About the Holocaust 47
Polar Postal History on the Web 47
Presidential Interview: A Panel of Presidents 34
Rainbow Raccoons, The 14
Relevant Approach to History, A 47
Review of American History, A 47

121

SUBJECT INDEX

HISTORY (continued)
  Rise and Fall of Jim Crow, The 47
  Shields, Knights and Heraldry 47
  Shipwreck Island Adventure! 47
  Spartacus Encyclopedia of British History, The: British History 47
  Spiro Mounds; Oklahoma's Past Indian History 47
  Stamps on Black History 18
  Stories Behind the Songs 4
  Sworn to Serve 47
  Teacher's Guide to the Holocaust, A 48
  Teaching History for Citizenship in the Elementary School 48
  Team Approach to Oral History, A 48
  Time Traveller 48
  WASP on the Web 48
  We Shall Overcome: Historic Places of the Civil Rights Movement National Register Travel Itinerary 48
  Where Oh Where 25
  World War I: Trenches on the Web 48

HOBBIES
  Bird Cross Stitch Patterns 1
  Early American Weaving 1
  Polar Postal History on the Web 47

HOLIDAYS
  Christmas at the Cottage 49
  Christmas Celebration in the Black Culture, A 49
  Christmas in Poland 49
  Christmas Traditions 49
  Christmas--Where Did It Come From? Where Is It Going? 49
  Easter 49
  Easter on the Net 49
  For Whom the Clock Strikes 49
  Hawaiian Christmas Trees 49
  Holiday Traditions 50
  How to Celebrate Chanukah 50
  Kwanzaa 50
  Making a Pinata 2
  Official & Religious Mexican Holidays 50
  Spanish Christmas, A 50
  Thanksgiving on the Net 50

HOLOCAUST
  Jacques Lipetz 46
  Number the Stars: A WebQuest About the Holocaust 47
  Seventy-First Came, The...To Gunskirchen Lager 47
  Teacher's Guide to the Holocaust, A 48

HOMESCHOOLING
  Homeschooling 84

HOMEWORK HELPERS
  KidsKonnect 23
  ScienceMaster 74
  StudyStack.com 24

HORTICULTURE
  GardenWeb Glossary 10

HTML
  How Do They Do That with HTML? 7
  HTML Goodies 7
  HTML Imager Version 1.2a 7
  Lissa Explains It All 8
  Teach Me HTML 8
  Tutorial on Using Perl and CGI to Enhance a Homepage, A 9
  Web Pages for Absolute Beginners 9

HUBBLE TELESCOPE
  Amazing Space: Explorations 66

HUMANE EDUCATION
  ASPCA Kids 66

HUMANITIES EDUCATION
  Light in the Forest, The 54

HUMAN RIGHTS
  Country Reports on Human Rights Practices 27

HURRICANES
  Hurricane Hunters, The 71
  Hurricanes and Tropical Storms 71

HYPERCARD
  Endeavour Views the Earth Electronic Picture Book 69

IMMIGRANTS
  Education of Immigrant Children in New York City, The 83

INDIA
  Blind Men and the Elephant, The 80
  Learn to Read Punjabi 21

INSECTS
  Amateur Entomologist 66
  ButterflySite.com 67

INVASIVE SPECIES
  Nonindigenous Species: Activities for Youth 73

INVENTORS AND INVENTIONS
  Invention Dimension 17

IRAQ
  Ancient Mesopotamia: The History, Our History 44

IRISH
  Irish Lessons 20

ITALIAN
  AllWords.com 10
  Italian Electronic Classroom, The 20
  UpToTen 25

SUBJECT INDEX

JAPAN
   History Textbook Controversies in Japan   46
   Japanese Education in Grades K-12   29

JAPANESE
   Quick and Dirty Guide to Japanese, The   21

JOURNALISM
   Behind the Scenes Look at the Landrum News Network, A   80

JUDAISM
   How to Celebrate Chanukah   50

JUSTICE SYSTEM
   Justice   34
   Justice for Kids and Youth   34

KELLER, HELEN
   Helen Keller Biography   16

KEYBOARDING
   Learn 2 Type   8
   Typing Bingo   9

KINDERGARTEN PROGRAMS
   Full-Day Kindergarten Programs   83

KING, DR. MARTIN LUTHER
   Dr. Martin Luther King, Jr.   16

KOREAN
   UpToTen   25

KWANZA
   Christmas Celebration in the Black Culture, A   49
   Kwanzaa   50

LANGUAGE ARTS
   Adverbily   51
   Alan Cooper's Homonym List   10
   Alex Catalogue of Electronic Texts   51
   ArtMagick   1
   Basic Grammar Review Using Jabberwocky   51
   Brain Food   23
   Busy as a Bee   51
   Carol Hurst's Children's Literature Site   51
   Children's Literacy Development: Suggestions for Parent Involvement   51
   Children's Storybooks Online--Older Children   51
   Children's Storybooks Online--Young Children   51
   Collaborating on a Newspaper in the Elementary Classroom   51
   Computer Assisted Writing Instruction   52
   Creative Dramatics in the Language Arts Classroom   52
   Creative Strategies for Teaching Language Arts to Gifted Students   52
   Decimal Search   52
   Effective Use of Student Journal Writing   52
   Einstein Club   52
   FableVision Place   53
   Fairy Tales Around the World   53

LANGUAGE ARTS (continued)
   Familiar Quotations--Passages, Phrases and Proverbs Traced to Their Sources   10
   Famous Quotes by Categories and Subjects   53
   Funbrain.com   12
   Game Goo   12
   Gifted Readers and Reading Instruction   53
   Giggle Poetry   53
   Grand Pantheon, The   2
   Helping Children Overcome Reading Difficulties   53
   Helping Children Understand Literary Genres   53
   Helping the Underachiever in Reading   53
   Horrid Homonyms   53
   Integrating Literature into Middle School Reading Classrooms   53
   Jeff's Poems for Kids   54
   Kids@Random   54
   KidsReads   54
   Kim's Korner for Teacher Talk   54
   Language Development in the Early Years   54
   Let's Get Along   37
   Literature as Lessons on the Diversity of Culture   54
   Little Red House, The   14
   LOGOS Multilingual Portal   11
   Mathematics and Reading Connection, The   54
   Motivating Low Performing Adolescent Readers   54
   New Look at Literature Instruction, A   54
   Number the Stars: A WebQuest About the Holocaust   47
   Nursery Rhyme Mania   54
   Oral Language Development Across the Curriculum, K-12   55
   OWL Handouts   55
   Paper Bag Book Report   55
   Parent Involvement in Elementary Language Arts: A Program Model   55
   Parent Participation in Middle School Language Arts   55
   Phonemic Awareness: An Important Early Step in Learning to Read   55
   Poetry for Kids   55
   Poetry Screen Saver   55
   Political Writings of George Orwell   55
   Punctuation: Less Is More?   55
   Pygmalion Effect, The: A Dramatic Study in the Classroom   56
   Quiz Hub   24
   Reading and Writing in a Kindergarten Classroom   56
   Reinforcing Alphabet Names/Sounds   14
   RhymeZone Rhyming Dictionary, The   11
   Seussville University   56
   Shakespeare--His Life and Times   18
   Sociology Through Five Plays   3
   Stage Line/Time Line: A Musical Adventure   4
   Star Politics   34
   Successful Paragraphs   56

SUBJECT INDEX

LANGUAGE ARTS (continued)
Switch ZoO 75
Teaching Creative Writing in the Elementary School 56
Teaching Poetry: Generating Genuine, Meaningful Responses 56
Teaching Writing with Peer Response Groups Encouraging Revision 56
TestDEN 57
Using Film, Video, and TV in the Classroom 91
Very Bad Horrible No Good Day, The 57
Vocabulary Building 57
Word Central 11

LANGUAGE IMMERSION
Integrating Language and Content: Lessons from Immersion 20

LATIN AMERICA
Geographia 28

LAWS AND LAWMAKING
ABC's of Legal Terms 10
How Our Laws Are Made 33
Laws--Who Needs Them? 34
Your Own Classroom Court 35

LEARNING STYLES
Attending to Learning Styles in Mathematics and Science Classrooms 80
Student Diversity and Learning Needs 89
Theoretical Perspectives, Research Findings, and Classroom Implications of the Learning Styles of American Indian and Alaska Native Students 90

LESSON PLANS
Accentuate the Positive 58
Achievements and Challenges of Peru, The 26
Addition and Subtraction Game 58
Adverbily 51
Africa: Eating Senegal Style 26
African Art and Culture 26
Ah Choo! 40
Alcohol, Peer Pressure and Underage Drinking Info for Young Teens 40
All Hands on Deck 44
American Revolution Simulation 44
Anne Frank in the World Teacher Workbook 15
Annenberg Classroom 33
Appreciating African Languages 19
Archeology Dig 66
Artist Research Poster Lesson 1
Atom's Family, The 66
Awareness of Pre-Algebra Concepts 58
Ball Monster 40
Baltimore Curriculum Project Lesson Plans 23
Basic Grammar Review Using Jabberwocky 51
Beanbag Freeze Tag 40

LESSON PLANS (continued)
Bean Toss 58
Become a Logophile 51
Birthday Moons: It's Just a Phase You're Going Through 67
Blind Men and the Elephant, The 80
Box of Crayons, A 36
Boy/Girl Pieces 80
Building an African Compound 27
Busy as a Bee 51
Canada on Postcards 27
Child's Daily Life in South Africa, A 27
Chinese Dragon 27
Christmas Celebration in the Black Culture, A 49
Citizenship and the Constitution 33
Coffee Can Drum 49
Color Code Writing 12
Common African Food, A: Fou-Fou 27
Communicating Values and History Through Masks 27
Constitution, The: Our Plan for Government 33
Create-a-Composition 1
Cuisine and Etiquette in Sierra Leone, Uganda, and Zambia 27
Cultural Spaces 27
Decimal Search 52
Derivation of Pi, The 58
Design a Track 58
Determining the Existence of Gender Bias in Daily Tasks 82
Early American Weaving 1
Early Childhood Art Lessons 1
Ecology Data Tip Archives 69
Ecosystems 69
Edible State Map 28
Einstein Club 52
Electronic Mapping 28
Elementary Art Lesson Plans 1
Ethnic Art: African, Mexican and Caribbean Perspectives 2
Everyday Life in Africa 28
Everyone Has a Culture--Everyone Is Different 28
Expanding Fifth Grade Ethnic Awareness (Latino and Native American) Through Literature 28
Exploring African Music 28
Exploring Language: Definitions Activity 83
Factoring Large Numbers 59
Family Finding: Exploring Multicultural Families Using Film 83
15 Fantastic Id 41
First Impressions 83
Florida Panther Net 70
Football Review 23
Forest Stewardship 70
For Whom the Clock Strikes 49

124

SUBJECT INDEX

LESSON PLANS (continued)

Fraction Conversion Bingo 59
Friction, Forces and Motion 70
Fun With Estimation 59
Games and Toys Reflect Resources 28
Gender Equity in Fairy Tales 53
Gender Stereotypes and Advertisements 37
General Information About Blindness 78
Geo-Critters 59
German American Contributions to Mainstream Culture 20
Getting Started--Respect Activity 84
Gunfighters of the Old West 46
Harmonica Lessons 2
Healthy Forests 70
Hello, I Am Deborah Sampson 46
Horrid Homonyms 53
How a Bill Becomes a Law 33
How to Earn Commendable Marks in Fourth Grade 23
Iceberg, The 84
Ideas for Exploring Our City and State 29
In My Other Life 37
Involving Community Members, Parents, and Community Agencies in Student Learning. 23
It's So Simple 71
Jambo Means Hello: An Introduction to Swahili 20
Justice 34
Kameshi Ne Mpuku: An African Game 29
Kentucky Bug Connection Teaching Resources 71
Know Your Local Government 34
Kwanzaa 50
Lacrosse Tag 42
Landing 42
Language in Classroom Texts 37
Laws--Who Needs Them? 34
Leaf ID and Leaf Bingo 72
Lesson #29: Textured Pottery Using Self-Hardening Clay and Multicultural Designs 2
Lesson Plans 2
Let Me Tell You About My State! 29
Let's Get Along 37
Literature and Art Through Our Eyes: The African American Children 54
Little Red House, The 14
Magnets 72
Make a Papier Mache Bowl 2
Making an Illustrated Dictionary with Geographic Terms 30
M&M Math 60
Mars Fraction Hunt 60
Masai and I: A Cultural Comparison 30
Math Jeopardy 61
Mini-Unit Topic: Native Americans 30
Mix 'n Match 3

LESSON PLANS (continued)

Mosaic America: Paths to the Present 46
Mr. Dowling's Electronic Passport 30
Multicultural Person, The 86
Mutualism and Co-evolution 72
Mystery Pictures 14
Native Americans--Searching for Knowledge and Understanding 46
Owl Pellets 73
Panic Button 3 61
Paper Bag Book Report 55
Paper Bag or Fabric Poncho 50
Paper Mache Masks--Maskmania 50
Parts of a Whole 62
Passion for Change: Investigating the Evolution of Cultural Traditions 31
Photo Essay, A 55
PhysicsFront.org 73
Positive and Negative Integers: A Card Game 62
Power Problem 62
Presidential Interview: A Panel of Presidents 34
Private See Dispute 34
Problem Solving and the Sports Page 62
Process of Sequencing--A Picture Card Game Activity 24
Promoting Diversity in Elementary School Curricula 86
Proportionally Speaking 62
Protocols 42
Pygmalion Effect, The: A Dramatic Study in the Classroom 56
Random Acts of Kindness Lesson Plans 38
Recycling Lesson Plan 74
Reinforcement Lesson in Place Value 62
Reinforcing Alphabet Names/Sounds 14
Relevant Approach to History, A 47
Reorganizing the Bill of Rights 34
Review of American History, A 47
Right to Equal Opportunity 38
Risk Behavior 39
Safety 65
Salmon Homing Instincts 74
Science Role Plays 74
Self-Esteem Activity 39
SET Toolkit 75
Sheep and Wolves 42
Single-Use Foodservice Packaging--Facts and Fun Teacher's Kit 75
Sioux Indians, The 31
Six Corner Locomotion/Six Corner Roll 43
Solar System Bowl 75
Songs for Teaching 3
Stage Line/Time Line: A Musical Adventure 4
Stepping Into the World of the American Musical Theatre: Dance Sets the Pace 4

125

SUBJECT INDEX

LESSON PLANS (continued)
   Strategies for Teaching the Value of Diversity 89
   Successful Paragraphs 56
   SunSmart 65
   Survival Kit 65
   Swiss Ball Square Dance 43
   Talk About Trees 75
   Teacher Files 90
   Teaching Ideas and Resources 14
   Teaching Resources Using Comics 4
   Team Approach to Oral History, A 48
   Temperature and Water Density 76
   Test of Applied Creativity, Logic, and Reasoning 24
   There Are Algae in Your House! 76
   Thinking Fountain 76
   Toilet Paper Solar System 76
   Turn on Inventiveness--Potato Possibilities 24
   20 Field Day Activities Any Kid Can Do (And Do
      Well!) 43
   Typing Bingo 9
   Un-Birthday Present, The 4
   Understanding Hispanic/Latino Culture and History
      Through the Use of Children's Literature 57
   Under the Weather 76
   Use of Substitution As a Creative Thinking Tool, The 39
   Using Drama as a Resource for Giving Language
      More Meaning 4
   Vocabulary Building 57
   Water Conservation Lesson Plan 76
   Wetland Ecosystems II--Interactions and Ecosystems 76
   What Causes Tooth Decay 43
   Where I Come From 48
   Where Oh Where 25
   Who I Am Poems 91
   Who's in the Bag? 39
   Will the Real Ben Franklin Please Stand Up? 18
   World on a String, The 32
   Yarn Painting (Ofrendas) 4
   Your Own Classroom Court 35

LEWIS AND CLARK
   Lewis and Clark as Naturalists 72

LIBRARIES
   Creating an A+++ Classroom Library 82

LINCOLN, PRESIDENT ABRAHAM
   Abraham Lincoln Online 15
   Life of Abraham Lincoln, The: An Illustrated
      Timeline for Young Readers 17

LITERACY
   Let's Get Along 37

LITERATURE
   Aesop's Fables Online Collection 51
   Alex Catalogue of Electronic Texts 51
   Baltimore Curriculum Project Lesson Plans 23

LITERATURE (continued)
   Bookhive 51
   Carol Hurst's Children's Literature Site 51
   Children's Literacy Development: Suggestions for
      Parent Involvement 51
   Children's Storybooks Online--Older Children 51
   Children's Storybooks Online--Young Children 51
   Database of Award-Winning Children's Literature 52
   Exploring the Function of Heroes and Heroines in
      Children's Literature from Around the
      World 52
   Fairy Tales Around the World 53
   Familiar Quotations--Passages, Phrases and
      Proverbs Traced to Their Sources 10
   Geo-Critters 59
   Grand Pantheon, The 2
   Helping Children Understand Literary Genres 53
   Integrating Literature into Middle School Reading
      Classrooms 53
   KidsReads 54
   Laura Ingalls Wilder 17
   Light in the Forest, The 54
   Literature and Art Through Our Eyes: The African
      American Children 54
   Literature as Lessons on the Diversity of Culture 54
   New Look at Literature Instruction, A 54
   Number the Stars: A WebQuest About the Holocaust 47
   OWL Handouts 55
   Paper Bag Book Report 55
   Performing Medieval Narrative Today: A Video
      Showcase 3
   Political Writings of George Orwell 55
   Pygmalion Effect, The: A Dramatic Study in
      the Classroom 56
   RhymeZone Rhyming Dictionary, The 11
   Seussville University 56
   Shakespeare--His Life and Times 18
   Sociology Through Five Plays 3
   Stage Line/Time Line: A Musical Adventure 4
   Teacher's Guide for a Midsummer Night's Dream 56
   Teacher's Guide for Up From Slavery 56
   Teacher's Guide to As You Like It 56
   Teaching Tips to Use with the Signet Classic
      Shakespeare Series 56
   Team Approach to Oral History, A 48

LYRICS
   Stories Behind the Songs 4

MACINTOSH
   Addition & Subtraction Concentration Game 58
   U. S. States & Capitals Concentration Game 31

MAGAZINES
   Karbosguide.com 8

SUBJECT INDEX

MAILING LISTS
   H-AfrTeach 29
MAMMALS
   Animal Info--Endangered Animals 66
   Mammals of Texas, The 72
   Whale Songs 76
MAORI
   On Line Te Reo Course 21
MAPS AND MAPMAKING
   Edible State Map 28
   Electronic Mapping 28
   Exploring Caves 28
   Mathematics of Cartography 30
   MegaMaps--Walk Through the Continents 30
   Minnesota State Highway Map 30
   This Dynamic Planet 31
   Virginia State Transportation Map 31
MARINE LIFE
   Cetacean Fact Packs 68
   Whale Songs 76
MASKS AND MASKMAKING
   Another Face--Masks Around the World 26
   Communicating Values and History Through Masks 27
   Paper Mache Masks--Maskmania 50
MATHEMATICS
   Abacus, The--The Art of Calculating with Beads 58
   Accentuate the Positive 58
   Addition & Subtraction Concentration Game 58
   Addition and Subtraction Game 58
   ALFY: The Web Portal for Kids 12
   Algebra--One on One 58
   Algebra Through Problem Solving 58
   Ask Dr. Math 58
   Attending to Learning Styles in Mathematics and Science Classrooms 80
   Aunty Math 58
   Awareness of Pre-Algebra Concepts 58
   Bean Toss 58
   Brain Food 23
   Calculators On-Line Center 58
   Derivation of Pi, The 58
   Equal Mathematics Education for Female Students 59
   Fact Monster 10
   Factoring Large Numbers 59
   Fraction Conversion Bingo 59
   Fraction Fun 59
   Funbrain.com 12
   Fun With Estimation 59
   Geo-Critters 59
   Girlstart 23
   Green Bean's Treehouse 12
   Helping Your Child Learn Math 59

MATHEMATICS (continued)
   Hungry for Math 59
   Indexes of Biographies 17
   Interactive Demos 1 59
   Interactive Demos 2 59
   Investigating Patterns: Symmetry and Tessellations 60
   Involving Community Members, Parents, and Community Agencies in Student Learning. 23
   Jefferson Lab--Science Education 71
   Keep the Traffic Moving! 60
   Lighting the Perimeter 60
   Logical Games and Puzzles 1 60
   Logical Games and Puzzles 2 60
   Logical Games and Puzzles 3 60
   Making Mathematical Connections in Middle School 60
   M&M Math 60
   Mars Fraction Hunt 60
   Math Cats 60
   Math Cove 60
   MathDEN 60
   Mathematical Quotations Server 61
   Mathematics and Reading Connection, The 54
   Mathematics Standards for Pre-Kindergarten Through Grade 2 61
   Math Function Mania 61
   Math Jeopardy 61
   Math League Help Topics 61
   Math of Geography, The 61
   Metrics Matter 61
   Mr. Pitonyak's Pyramid Puzzle 61
   Mrs. Glosser's Math Goodies 61
   Native American Geometry 61
   NCTM Illuminations 61
   Panic Button 3 61
   Parts of a Whole 62
   Pizza Family Reunion, A 62
   Positive and Negative Integers: A Card Game 62
   Power Problem 62
   Prime Time Math 62
   Problem Solving and the Sports Page 62
   Proportionally Speaking 62
   Quikie Math: The Geometry Experience 62
   Quiz Hub 24
   Reinforcement Lesson in Place Value 62
   Thinking of a Careers i Applied Mathematics 39
   This Is Mega-Mathematics! 62
   Why Files?, The 91
   Winlab 63
MEDICINE
   LifeWorks 38
   Quick Facts 38

SUBJECT INDEX

MENTAL HEALTH
Anxiety Disorders 40

METEOROLOGY
Career Guide for the Atmospheric Sciences, A 36
Challenges of Our Changing Atmosphere: Careers in Atmospheric Research and Applied Meteorology 36
Dan's Wild, Wild Weather Page 68

METRIC SYSTEM
Metrics Matter 61
Reinforcement Lesson in Place Value 62

MEXICO
Ethnic Art: African, Mexican and Caribbean Perspectives 2
Making a Pinata 2
Mexican WebQuest 30
Official & Religious Mexican Holidays 50
Paper Bag or Fabric Poncho 50
Yarn Painting (Ofrendas) 4

MIDI FILES
HymnSite.Com 2

MIGRANTS
Identification and Recruitment of Migrant Students: Strategies and Resources 84
Involving Migrant Families in Education 85
What Federal Statistics Reveal About Migrant Farmworkers: A Summary for Education 91

MINES AND MINERAL RESOURCES
Coal Science Fair Ideas 68
Minerals by Name 72
Rocks For Kids 74

MINNESOTA
AgMag 26
Minnesota State Highway Map 30

MINORITIES
Assessing Bilingual Students for Placement and Instruction 80
English-Only Movement: Its Consequences for the Education of Language Minority Children 52

MULTIAGE EDUCATION
Multiage-Educators Home Page, The 23

MULTICULTURAL EDUCATION
Diversity Within Unity: Essential Principles for Teaching and Learning in a Multicultural Society 82
ePALS Classroom Exchange 28
Family Involvement in Early Multicultural Learning 83
Four Directions 83
Literature as Lessons on the Diversity of Culture 54

MUMMIES
Egyptian Mummies 45

MUSIC
Australian Folk Songs 1
Baltimore Curriculum Project Lesson Plans 23
Baroque Reference, The 10
Colomusic 1
Create-a-Composition 1
Creating Music 1
Exploring African Music 28
Famous People with Perfect Pitch 16
FastMIDI Player 2
German for Music Lovers 20
Harmonica Lessons 2
HymnSite.Com 2
Jack's Harmonica Page 2
JazClass 2
Larry's Songs 13
Lift Every Voice and Sing 2
Mix 'n Match 3
Museum of Musical Instruments, The 3
Music from Across America 3
Music of Yesterday and Today 3
Quiz Hub 24
San Francisco Symphony Site for Kids 3
Songs4Teachers 3
Songs for Teaching 3
SoundJunction 4
Stories Behind the Songs 4
Swiss Anthem 4
Threads: Computers, Music, and a Little Theory 90
Virtual Museum of Music Inventions, The 4
Woodwind Fingering Guide, The 4
Young Composers 5

MUSICAL INSTRUMENTS
Museum of Musical Instruments, The 3

NATIONAL ANTHEMS
Swiss Anthem 4

NATIONAL PARKS
Appomattox Court House Teacher's Packet 26

NATIVE AMERICANS
Cherokee Indians 49
Expanding Fifth Grade Ethnic Awareness (Latino and Native American) Through Literature 28
First Americans 45
Four Directions 83
Honoring the Animal Spirits 29
Images of Native Americans 46
Issues in the Education of American Indian and Alaska Native Students with Disabilities 85
Kanienkehaka Language Homepage 20
Make a Papier Mache Bowl 2
Mini-Unit Topic: Native Americans 30

SUBJECT INDEX

NATIVE AMERICANS (continued)
- Mosaic America: Paths to the Present 46
- Native American Geometry 61
- Native Americans--Searching for Knowledge and Understanding 46
- Native American Technology and Art 3
- Not Indians Many Tribes: Native American Diversity 30
- Schooling for Self-Determination: Research on the Effects of Including Native Language and Culture in the Schools 87
- Sioux Indians, The 31
- Spiro Mounds; Oklahoma's Past Indian History 47
- Teaching Young Children About Native Americans 90
- Theoretical Perspectives, Research Findings, and Classroom Implications of the Learning Styles of American Indian and Alaska Native Students 90
- Trial of Standing Bear, The 48
- Using Culturally and Linguistically Appropriate Assessments to Ensure that American Indian and Alaska Native Students Receive the Special Education Programs and Services They Need 91

NATURAL DISASTERS
- Disaster Strikes! 64

NATURAL RESOURCES
- Natural Gas Safety World 65

NATURE STUDY
- Backyard Nature 67
- Kentucky Bug Connection Teaching Resources 71
- Nonindigenous Species: Activities for Youth 73
- Official Seed Starting Home Page, The 73
- Whales on the Net 76
- WildFinder 77

NETHERLANDS
- Culture of the Frisians 27

NEWSLETTERS
- Que Tal in the Current Skies 73
- Universe in the Classroom, The 76

NEWSPAPERS
- Collaborating on a Newspaper in the Elementary Classroom 51

NILE RIVER
- Nile Adventure 30

NUTRITION
- Are Bioengineered Foods Safe? 40
- Best Bones Forever! 40
- Bulking Up Fiber's Healthful Reputation 40
- Dietary Guidelines for Americans 41
- Do You Know the Health Risks of Being Overweight? 41

NUTRITION (continued)
- Eating for Life 41
- Fight BAC!: Four Simple Steps to Food Safety 41
- Kid's World - Nutrition 42
- Making Healthy Food Choices 42
- Safer Eggs: Laying the Groundwork 42
- Sports and Nutrition: The Winning Connection 43
- Teens Health, Food & Fitness 43
- There Are Algae in Your House! 76

OBESITY
- Do You Know the Health Risks of Being Overweight? 41

OCEAN LIFE
- Simply Sharks! 75
- Whales on the Net 76

OCEANOGRAPHY
- Marinecareers 38
- Research Vessels 74
- Women in Oceanography 39

OCEANS
- Carolina Coastal Science 68
- Living Gulf, The: A Place to Treasure 29

OKLAHOMA
- Spiro Mounds; Oklahoma's Past Indian History 47

ONLINE COURSES
- Becoming Webwise 6
- Deutsch Plus 19

ORIGAMI
- Origami Fun 3

ORWELL, GEORGE
- Political Writings of George Orwell 55

PAINTING
- Brush with Wildlife, A 1

PALEONTOLOGY
- Dig--The Archaeology Magazine for Kids! 68

PARENTS AND PARENTING
- Adopted Children in the Early Childhood Classroom 80
- bNetS@vvy 6
- Children's Literacy Development: Suggestions for Parent Involvement 51
- Family Diversity in Urban Schools 83
- Family Involvement in Early Multicultural Learning 83
- Full-Day Kindergarten Programs 83
- Growing Up Drug Free 41
- Helping Your Child Learn Geography 29
- Helping Your Child Learn Math 59
- Hoagies' Gifted Education Page 23
- Involving Migrant Families in Education 85
- Parent Engagement as a School Reform Strategy 86
- Parent Involvement in Elementary Language Arts: A Program Model 55
- Parent Participation in Middle School Language Arts 55

SUBJECT INDEX

PARENTS AND PARENTING (continued)
  Project Appleseed 8
  Recent Research on All-Day Kindergarten 87
  Student-Led Conferences at the Middle Level 89
PARENT TEACHER CONFERENCES
  Planning for Parent Participation in Schools for Young Children 86
PATHOLOGY
  Who Dunnit? 77
PEACE
  Resolving Conflicts and Making Peace: Basic Skills for Young Children 38
PEARL HARBOR
  Face to Face--Stories from the Aftermath of Infamy 45
PERIPHERALS
  Few Scanning Tips, A 7
PERL
  Tutorial on Using Perl and CGI to Enhance a Homepage, A 9
PERU
  Achievements and Challenges of Peru, The 26
PHILATELY
  Polar Postal History on the Web 47
  Stamps on Black History 18
PHILOSOPHY
  Alex Catalogue of Electronic Texts 51
  Confucius--His Life and Times 15
  Great Thinkers: A Study in Philosophy 16
  Philosopher's Lighthouse, The--Shedding Light on Philosophy 17
PHOTOGRAPHY
  Images of Native Americans 46
PHYSICAL EDUCATION
  Are You With It? 80
PHYSICAL EDUCATION
  Ball Monster 40
  Beanbag Freeze Tag 40
  Best Bones Forever! 40
  15 Fantastic Id 41
  KidsRunning.Com 42
  Lacrosse Tag 42
  Landing 42
  Protocols 42
  Sheep and Wolves 42
  Six Corner Locomotion/Six Corner Roll 43
  Sports and Nutrition: The Winning Connection 43
  20 Field Day Activities Any Kid Can Do (And Do Well!) 43
PHYSICAL FITNESS
  Fitness Partner 41
  Teens Health, Food & Fitness 43

PHYSICS
  Center for History of Physics, The 68
  Fear of Physics 69
  Friction, Forces and Motion 70
  How Fast Are You Going? 70
  It's So Simple 71
  Magnets 72
  Mousetrap Racer!!! 72
  PhysicsFront.org 73
  Soda Play 75
PICASSO, PABLO
  Picasso 17
PLAYS
  Grand Pantheon, The 2
POETRY
  ArtMagick 1
  Giggle Poetry 53
  Jeff's Poems for Kids 54
  Teaching Poetry: Generating Genuine, Meaningful Responses 56
  Very Bad Horrible No Good Day, The 57
POISON PREVENTION
  Poison Prevention Game 14
POLAND
  Christmas in Poland 49
POLITICS
  Star Politics 34
POLLUTION
  POP Goes Antarctica? 73
  Tox Town 76
PORTUGAL
  European Voyages of Exploration 45
PORTUGUESE
  Your Voyage to Break the Language Barrier 22
POVERTY
  Child-Initiated Learning Activities for Young Children Living in Poverty 81
  Poverty and Learning 86
POWER
  Electric Universe, The 69
PRESIDENTS OF THE UNITED STATES
  Abraham Lincoln Online 15
  Ask the Presidents 33
  Life of Abraham Lincoln, The: An Illustrated Timeline for Young Readers 17
  Presidential Interview: A Panel of Presidents 34
PRIVACY
  Privacy Pirates 8
  Private See Dispute 34

SUBJECT INDEX

PROGRAMMING
Banner Generator, The 6
CGI Made Really Easy 6
CGI Resource Index, The 6
C-Language Course 6
First Guide to PostScript, A 7
Goetz's Programming Kit 7
HJ-Install 2.9 7
HTML Goodies 7
Lissa Explains It All 8
Menuz 8
Programming in C 8
Tutorial on Using Perl and CGI to Enhance a Homepage, A 9
Web Pages for Absolute Beginners 9

PROGRAMS
Addition & Subtraction Concentration Game 58
Ainsworth Computer Seminar 6
Algebra--One on One 58
Build-a-Prairie 67
Build Your Own Medieval Castle 45
Custom Addressbook 0.7.2 82
FastMIDI Player 2
Free Animated GIFs 7
Goetz's Programming Kit 7
HJ-Install 2.9 7
HTML Imager Version 1.2a 7
Interactive Demos 1 59
Interactive Demos 2 59
Larry's Animals-n-Things 13
Larry's Count 13
Larry's Songs 13
Learn Letters 13
Letter Sounds 13
Logical Games and Puzzles 1 60
Logical Games and Puzzles 2 60
Logical Games and Puzzles 3 60
Make a Village 30
Math Function Mania 61
MegaMaps--Walk Through the Continents 30
Poetry Screen Saver 55
Prime Time Math 62
RunStat 3 42
Shields, Knights and Heraldry 47
States Mania 31
SupperTime 14
U. S. States & Capitals Concentration Game 31
Verb Conjugation on line 22
Wincalc 62
Winfeed 63
Winlab 63

QUOTATIONS
Familiar Quotations--Passages, Phrases and Proverbs Traced to Their Sources 10
Famous Quotes by Categories and Subjects 53
Mathematical Quotations Server 61

RACISM AND PREJUDICE
Actions and Reactions 44
Anne Frank in the World Teacher Workbook 15
Box of Crayons, A 36
Boy/Girl Pieces 80
Changing Attitudes in America 36
Exploring Language: Definitions Activity 83
Jacques Lipetz 46
Number the Stars: A WebQuest About the Holocaust 47
Practical Do-Ables for Unlearning Racism 38
Promoting Diversity in Elementary School Curricula 86
Roll of Thunder: Hear My Cry Web Quest 39
Seventy-First Came, The...To Gunskirchen Lager 47
Talking to Your Child About Bias and Prejudice 39

RAINFORESTS
Me? Live in a Rainforest? 72
Save the Rainforest 74

READING
Database of Award-Winning Children's Literature 52
Game Goo 12
Helping Children Overcome Reading Difficulties 53
Helping the Underachiever in Reading 53
Helping Underachieving Boys Read Well and Often 53
Mathematics and Reading Connection, The 54
Phonemic Awareness: An Important Early Step in Learning to Read 55
Reading and Writing in a Kindergarten Classroom 56

REASONING
ALFY: The Web Portal for Kids 12
Questioning Techniques 24

RECESS
Recess in Elementary School: What Does the Research Say? 87

RECIPES
ABC's of Snacking, The 12
Cuisine and Etiquette in Sierra Leone, Uganda, and Zambia 27

RECYCLING
Aluminum Beverage Cans: The ABCs of Environmental Education 66
Recycling Lesson Plan 74
Single-Use Foodservice Packaging--Facts and Fun Teacher's Kit 75

REFERENCE
Noodle Tools 24

RELATIONSHIPS
Let's Get Along 37

SUBJECT INDEX

RELIGION
   Boy/Girl Pieces 80
   Easter 49
   Easter on the Net 49
   HymnSite.Com 2

RESEARCH
   Noodle Tools 24

REVOLUTIONARY WAR
   Hello, I Am Deborah Sampson 46

RIVERS
   Nile Adventure 30

ROBOTS
   ROVer Ranch 74

ROME
   Illustrated History of the Roman Empire 46

RUNNING
   KidsRunning.Com 42

RURAL EDUCATION
   Charter Schools: An Approach for Rural Education? 81

RUSSIAN
   Interactive On-Line Reference Grammar, An 20

SAFETY
   Automobile Safety Articles 64
   Cartooning to Teach Safety 64
   Crool Zone? 64
   Disaster Strikes! 64
   Electrical Safety World 64
   Electrical Safety World 64
   Energy Safety 41
   Farm Safety 4 Just Kids 64
   Fire Safety & Education Factsheets 64
   Fire Safety WebQuest 64
   Indoor Electrical Safety Check 64
   Natural Gas Safety World 65
   RiskWatch 65
   SAFE: Safety Always for Everyone 65
   Safety 65
   Sparky the Fire Dog 65
   Stay Alive! Do You Know How? 65
   SunSmart 65

SCANNERS
   Few Scanning Tips, A 7

SCHOOL REFORM
   Data Inquiry and Analysis for Educational Reform 82
   Parent Engagement as a School Reform Strategy 86
   Success for All: A Summary of Evaluations 89
   Whole-School Reform 91

SCIENCE
   Atom's Family, The 66
   Attending to Learning Styles in Mathematics and
      Science Classrooms 80

SCIENCE (continued)
   Bizarre Stuff You Can Make in Your Kitchen 67
   Career Guide for the Atmospheric Sciences, A 36
   Challenges of Our Changing Atmosphere: Careers
      in Atmospheric Research and
      Applied Meteorology 36
   Constellations, The 68
   Cool Science for Curious Kids 68
   Dan's Wild, Wild Weather Page 68
   DNA for Dinner? 68
   Edible/Inedible Experiments Archive 69
   Electric Universe, The 69
   Exploring Caves 28
   Fact Monster 10
   Fear of Physics 69
   Five Senses 70
   4000 Years of Women in Science 16
   FT Exploring 70
   Girlstart 23
   Great Plant Escape, The 70
   How Stuff Works 71
   Involving Community Members, Parents, and
      Community Agencies in Student Learning. 23
   Jefferson Lab--Science Education 71
   Journey North, The 71
   MathMol Hypermedia Textbook 61
   Mop Top the Hip Hop Scientist 17
   My Day As an Insect 72
   Nine Planets, The: A Multimedia Tour of the Solar
      System 72
   North American Skies 73
   Nova--Science in the News 73
   Physical Science Activity Manual 73
   Quiz Hub 24
   Rainbow Raccoons, The 14
   Research Vessels 74
   Science Fair Home Page 74
   Science is Fun 74
   ScienceMaster 74
   Science Role Plays 74
   Sea Turtle Migration-Tracking Education Program 74
   SET Toolkit 75
   There Are Algae in Your House! 76
   Thinking Fountain 76
   Waterford Press Free Games, Activities & More 76
   Who Dunnit? 77
   Why Files?, The 91
   YES I Can! Science 77

SCIENCE EXPERIMENTS
   Edible/Inedible Experiments Archive 69
   Physical Science Activity Manual 73
   Science is Fun 74

SUBJECT INDEX

SCIENCE FAIR PROJECTS
    Bizarre Stuff You Can Make in Your Kitchen 67
    Science Fair Home Page 74
SCIENCE PROJECTS
    Making a Comet in the Classroom 72
SCREENSAVERS
    Poetry Screen Saver 55
SEARCH ENGINES
    Ivy's Coloring Page Search Engine 13
SECURITY
    Safer Schools Through Environmental Design 87
SEGREGATION
    Rise and Fall of Jim Crow, The 47
    Roll of Thunder: Hear My Cry Web Quest 39
SELF ESTEEM
    Self-Esteem Activity 39
    Self-Esteem and Narcissism: Implications for Practice 88
SENSES
    Five Senses 70
SEPTEMBER 11
    September 11: What Our Children Need to Know 88
SEXISM
    Boy/Girl Pieces 80
    Exploring Language: Definitions Activity 83
SEXUAL ABUSE
    Sexual Misconduct by School Employees 88
SEXUAL ORIENTATION
    Boy/Girl Pieces 80
SHAKESPEARE, WILLIAM
    Shakespeare--His Life and Times 18
    Teacher's Guide for a Midsummer Night's Dream 56
    Teacher's Guide to As You Like It 56
    Teaching Tips to Use with the Signet Classic Shakespeare Series 56
SHARKS
    Simply Sharks! 75
SIGN LANGUAGE
    American Sign Language as a Foreign Language 19
    American Sign Language Browser 78
    SIGNhear 78
    Sign Language 79
SMOKING
    Health Fact Sheets 41
    Health Fact Sheets 42
    Smoking and Your Digestive System 43
    You Can Control Your Weight As You Quit Smoking 43
SNACKS AND SNACKING
    ABC's of Snacking, The 12

SOCIAL STUDIES
    Geographia 28
    Geo-Images Project 84
    Quiz Hub 24
    Spartacus Encyclopedia of British History, The: British History 47
    Teaching About Africa 31
    Using Primary Sources in the Primary Grades 91
    World Factbook 32
SOLAR ECLIPSE
    How to View an Eclipse 71
    Modeling Eclipses 72
SOLAR SYSTEM
    Journey Through the Galaxy 71
    Making a Comet in the Classroom 72
    Nine Planets, The: A Multimedia Tour of the Solar System 72
    StarChild 75
SOUTH AMERICA
    Achievements and Challenges of Peru, The 26
SPACE SCIENCE
    Astronomy Picture of the Day 66
    Auroras: Paintings in the Sky 67
    Eyes on the Sky, Feet on the Ground 69
    Journey Through the Galaxy 71
    Solar System Bowl 75
SPAIN
    Buen Viaje a Espana! 27
    European Voyages of Exploration 45
    Spanish Christmas, A 50
SPANISH
    Alien Language 19
    AllWords.com 10
    Assessing Young Children's Social Competence 80
    Communicable Disease Fact Sheets 40
    EspanOle! 19
    First-School 12
    Instructional Models for Early Childhood Education 85
    Jan's Illustrated Computer Literacy 101 8
    Language and Literacy Environments in Preschools 85
    Learn to Read Spanish 21
    Mathematics Standards for Pre-Kindergarten Through Grade 2 61
    Quiero Viajar a Espana! 31
    Recent Evidence on Preschool Programs 87
    Recent Research on All-Day Kindergarten 87
    Recess in Elementary School: What Does the Research Say? 87
    Student Mobility and Academic Achievement 89
    Teacher Preparation and Teacher-Child Interaction in Preschools 90
    UpToTen 25

SUBJECT INDEX

SPANISH (continued)
Your Voyage to Break the Language Barrier 22

SPECIAL EDUCATION
ADHD eBook 78
American Sign Language as a Foreign Language 19
Applications of Participatory Action Research with Students Who Have Disabilities 78
Chatback Trust, The 78
Creative Strategies for Teaching Language Arts to Gifted Students 52
Everything You Always Wanted to Know About Dyslexia 78
Issues in the Education of American Indian and Alaska Native Students with Disabilities 85
Students with Intellectual Disabilities: A Resource Guide for Teachers 79
Understanding Disabilities 79
Using Culturally and Linguistically Appropriate Assessments to Ensure that American Indian and Alaska Native Students Receive the Special Education Programs and Services They Need 91
What the Blind Can See 79

SPEECH
Oral Language Development Across the Curriculum, K-12 55

SPELLING
Funbrain.com 12

SPORTS
Baseball Hall of Fame and Museum 15
Building Leadership Skills in Middle School Girls Through Interscholastic Athletics 40
RunStat 3 42
Sports and Nutrition: The Winning Connection 43

STANTON, ELIZABETH CADY
Elizabeth Cady Stanton & Susan B. Anthony Papers Project Online, The 16

STATISTICS
Computer Almanac 6

STEREOTYPES AND STEREOTYPING
Determining the Existence of Gender Bias in Daily Tasks 82
Gender Equity in Fairy Tales 53
Gender Stereotypes and Advertisements 37
Language in Classroom Texts 37
Right to Equal Opportunity 38

STRESS
Test Anxiety 24

STUDY AIDS
Mrs. Glosser's Math Goodies 61
Prongo.com 24

SUPREME COURT
Interactive Constitution 33
Oyez Baseball 34

SWAHILI
Jambo Means Hello: An Introduction to Swahili 20

SWEDISH
Swedish Language Course, A 22

SWITZERLAND
Swiss Anthem 4

TEACHER REFERENCE
ABCteach 23
Action Research in Early Childhood Education 80
ADHD eBook 78
African Art and Culture 26
Alternatives to Behaviorism 78
America's Career InfoNet 36
Applications of Participatory Action Research with Students Who Have Disabilities 78
Are You With It? 80
Ask Dr. Math 58
Assessing Bilingual Students for Placement and Instruction 80
Assessing Young Children's Social Competence 80
Back to the Agora: Workable Solutions for Small Urban School Facilities 80
Boy/Girl Pieces 80
Building a School Web Site 6
Can Failing Schools Be Fixed? 81
Choosing Instructional Materials for Environmental Education 81
Classroom Learning 2.0 6
Collaborating on a Newspaper in the Elementary Classroom 51
Computer and Internet Use by Children and Adolescents in 2001: Statistical Analysis Report 6
Computer Assisted Writing Instruction 52
Creating a Blog: A Workshop for Teens 7
Creating an A+++ Classroom Library 82
Cultural Liberation: East-West Biculturalism for a New Century 82
Cultural Plunge, A 37
Developing a School District Web Presence 82
Developing Language Proficiency and Connecting School to Students's Lives: Two Standards for Effective Teaching 82
Digital Divide and Its Implications for the Language Arts, The 52
Diversity is About Change and Leadership 82
Diversity Within Unity: Essential Principles for Teaching and Learning in a Multicultural Society 82
Dr. Mac's Amazing Behavior Management Advice Site 82

SUBJECT INDEX

TEACHER REFERENCE (continued)
- Effective Use of Student Journal Writing 52
- EverythingESL.net 52
- Exploring Language: Definitions Activity 83
- Family Diversity in Urban Schools 83
- Family Finding: Exploring Multicultural Families Using Film 83
- Finding Funding for Environmental Education Efforts 69
- 4th Grade Treasure Trove 83
- Free Animated GIFs 7
- Free Education on the Internet 23
- Geo-Images Project 84
- GetNetWise 7
- Getting Started--Respect Activity 84
- Gifted Readers and Reading Instruction 53
- Global Issues and Environmental Education 70
- Hard of Hearing and Deaf Students: A Resource Guide to Support Classroom Teachers 78
- Help for They Won't Let Me Play with Them! 84
- Helping Children Overcome Reading Difficulties 53
- Helping Children Understand Literary Genres 53
- Helping the Underachiever in Reading 53
- Homeschooling 84
- Identification and Recruitment of Migrant Students: Strategies and Resources 84
- I Love That Teaching Idea 84
- Implementing the Multiage Classroom 85
- Integrated Curriculum in the Middle School 85
- Integrating Language and Content: Lessons from Immersion 20
- Integrating Literature into Middle School Reading Classrooms 53
- INTIME 85
- Involving Migrant Families in Education 85
- Irish Lessons 20
- Issues in the Education of American Indian and Alaska Native Students with Disabilities 85
- Jacques Lipetz 46
- Jefferson Lab--Science Education 71
- Kim's Korner for Teacher Talk 54
- Language and Literacy Environments in Preschools 85
- Language Development in the Early Years 54
- Language in Classroom Texts 37
- Latinos in School: Some Facts and Findings 86
- Lesson #29: Textured Pottery Using Self-Hardening Clay and Multicultural Designs 2
- Literature as Lessons on the Diversity of Culture 54
- Making Mathematical Connections in Middle School 60
- Mathematics and Reading Connection, The 54
- Mathematics Standards for Pre-Kindergarten Through Grade 2 61
- Middle Schools and Foreign Languages: A View for the Future 21
- Motivating Low Performing Adolescent Readers 54

TEACHER REFERENCE (continued)
- Multiage-Educators Home Page, The 23
- NCTM Illuminations 61
- New Look at Literature Instruction, A 54
- Nine Planets, The: A Multimedia Tour of the Solar System 72
- Oral Language Development Across the Curriculum, K-12 55
- OWL Handouts 55
- Peer Conflicts in the Classroom 86
- Phonemic Awareness: An Important Early Step in Learning to Read 55
- Physical Science Activity Manual 73
- Planning for Parent Participation in Schools for Young Children 86
- Planning for Success: Common Pitfalls in the Planning of Early Foreign Language Programs 21
- Poverty and Learning 86
- Practical Do-Ables for Unlearning Racism 38
- Preschool Coloring Book 14
- Primer on Digital Literacy, A 8
- Primer on Speaking and Writing Luganda, A 21
- Promoting Diversity in Elementary School Curricula 86
- Prospects for Education Vouchers After the Supreme Court Ruling, The 87
- Punctuation: Less Is More? 55
- Reading and Writing in a Kindergarten Classroom 56
- Recent Evidence on Preschool Programs 87
- Recent Research on All-Day Kindergarten 87
- Right to Equal Opportunity 38
- Role of Metacognition in Second Language Teaching and Learning, The 21
- School Productivity 88
- School Violence Prevention 88
- Sea Turtle Migration-Tracking Education Program 74
- 2nd Grade Treasure Trove 88
- September 11: What Our Children Need to Know 88
- Seventy-First Came, The...To Gunskirchen Lager 47
- Shared Decision-Making 88
- Should You Be the Boss? 88
- 6th Grade Treasure Trove 88
- Small Schools and Teacher Professional Development 88
- Songs for Teaching 3
- Spartacus Encyclopedia of British History, The: British History 47
- SSSH--Successful, Simple Simulation, Hassle-Free 89
- Starting Early: Environmental Education During the Early Childhood Years 89
- Strategies for Teaching the Value of Diversity 89
- Student Mobility and Academic Achievement 89
- Students with Intellectual Disabilities: A Resource Guide for Teachers 79
- Students with Visual Impairments 79

SUBJECT INDEX

TEACHER REFERENCE (continued)
- Substance Abuse Policy 89
- Substitute Teaching: An Insider's View 89
- Swedish Language Course, A 22
- Synthesis of Scholarship in Multicultural Education, A 90
- Teacher Files 90
- Teacher Preparation and Teacher-Child Interaction in Preschools 90
- Teacher's Guide for a Midsummer Night's Dream 56
- Teacher's Guide for Up From Slavery 56
- Teacher's Guide to As You Like It 56
- Teaching About Africa 31
- Teaching Creative Writing in the Elementary School 56
- Teaching Democracy 35
- Teaching History for Citizenship in the Elementary School 48
- Teaching History with Technology 48
- Teaching Ideas and Resources 14
- Teaching Poetry: Generating Genuine, Meaningful Responses 56
- Teaching Science in the Field 75
- Teaching Tips to Use with the Signet Classic Shakespeare Series 56
- Teaching Writing with Peer Response Groups Encouraging Revision 56
- Technology Tips for Classroom Teachers 8
- Ten C's for Evaluating Internet Sources 90
- Thinking Fountain 76
- Thirteen Ed Online 90
- This Is Mega-Mathematics! 62
- Understanding Hispanic/Latino Culture and History Through the Use of Children's Literature 57
- Using Culturally and Linguistically Appropriate Assessments to Ensure that American Indian and Alaska Native Students Receive the Special Education Programs and Services They Need 91
- Using Drama and Theatre to Promote Literacy Development: Some Basic Classroom Applications 4
- Using Film, Video, and TV in the Classroom 91
- Using Primary Sources in the Primary Grades 91
- Virtual Classroom, The 91
- Virtual Museum of Music Inventions, The 4
- What Federal Statistics Reveal About Migrant Farmworkers: A Summary for Education 91
- Who I Am Poems 91
- Whole-School Reform 91
- Working with Perfectionist Students 92
- Working with Shy or Withdrawn Students 92
- World-Class Standards and Local Pedagogies: Can We Do Both? 92

TEACHER REFERENCE (continued)
- Writing Instruction: Changing Views Over the Years 57
- YES I Can! Science 77
- Young Children's Emotional Development and School Readiness 92
- Your Voyage to Break the Language Barrier 22

TEACHER'S GUIDES
- Aeronautics Educator Guide 66
- Anne Frank in the World Teacher Workbook 15
- Atom's Family, The 66
- Birthday Moons 67
- Changing Faces: A Study of Solar and Planetary Rotation Rates 68
- Electrical Safety World 64
- Erwin E. Smith: Teaching Guide 45
- Out on a Limb--A Guide to Getting Along 38
- Random Acts of Kindness Activities 38
- Single-Use Foodservice Packaging--Facts and Fun Teacher's Kit 75
- Teacher's Guide for a Midsummer Night's Dream 56
- Teacher's Guide for Up From Slavery 56
- Teacher's Guide to As You Like It 56
- Teaching Tips to Use with the Signet Classic Shakespeare Series 56
- Wetland Ecosystems II--Interactions and Ecosystems 76

TECHNOLOGY
- Private See Dispute 34

TEENAGERS
- Teen Central.Net 39

TEETH
- What Causes Tooth Decay 43

TENNESSEE
- Endangered/Threatened Species 69

TERRORISM
- Face to Face--Stories from the Aftermath of Infamy 45
- September 11: What Our Children Need to Know 88

TESTS AND TESTING
- Can Performance-Based Assessments Improve Urban Schooling? 81
- French Online Grammar Quiz 20
- National Geographic GeoBee Challenge 30
- Test Anxiety 24
- Virtual Classroom, The 91

TEXAS
- Erwin E. Smith: Teaching Guide 45
- Handbook of Texas Online 29
- Mammals of Texas, The 72

THEATER
- Using Drama and Theatre to Promote Literacy Development: Some Basic Classroom Applications 4

SUBJECT INDEX

TRADITIONS
   Festivals Around the World 49
   Passion for Change: Investigating the Evolution of Cultural Traditions 31
   Where I Come From 48

TRUANCY
   Student Truancy 89
   Urban Policies and Programs to Reduce Truancy 90

TUTORIALS
   CGI Made Really Easy 6
   C-Language Course 6
   Classroom Learning 2.0 6
   How Do They Do That with HTML? 7
   Jan's Illustrated Computer Literacy 101 8
   MathDEN 60
   NewsDEN 24
   Programming in C 8
   SkillsDEN 8
   SkyDEN 75
   Teach Me HTML 8
   TestDEN 57
   Tutorial on Using Perl and CGI to Enhance a Homepage, A 9

UNITED STATES
   Across the USA 26
   Address to the Negroes in the State of New York, An 44
   Ben's Guide to U. S. Government for Kids 33
   Camp Silos 67
   Changing Attitudes in America 36
   Child's Daily Life in South Africa, A 27
   Civil War Through a Child's Eye, The 45
   Colonial Hall 15
   Constitution of the United States and the Declaration of Independence 33
   Declare the Causes: The Declaration of Independence 33
   Everyday Life in Africa 28
   Experience the Life 45
   First Person Narratives of the American South, 1860-1920 45
   History Happens 46
   How Our Laws Are Made 33
   Ideas for Exploring Our City and State 29
   Minnesota State Highway Map 30
   Music from Across America 3
   Our Flag 34
   Oyez Baseball 34
   Search Hawaii! Cultural and Educational Pages 31
   Thanksgiving on the Net 50
   ThisNation.com 35
   United States Climate Page 31
   U. S. States & Capitals Concentration Game 31

UNITED STATES (continued)
   Virginia State Transportation Map 31
   What They Left Behind--Early Multi-National Influences in the United States 48

URBAN EDUCATION
   Can Performance-Based Assessments Improve Urban Schooling? 81
   Changing Face of Racial Isolation and Desegregation in Urban Schools 81
   Education of Immigrant Children in New York City, The 83
   Gangs in the Schools 83
   Overcrowding in Urban Schools 86
   Retaining Good Teachers in Urban Schools 87
   School Programs for African American Male Students 88
   Southeast Asian Adolescents: Identity and Adjustment 89
   Urban Policies and Programs to Reduce Truancy 90
   Urban School Finance: The Quest for Equal Educational Opportunity 90
   Urban Youth in Community Service: Becoming Part of the Solution 91
   Year-Round Education: A Strategy for Overcrowded Schools 92

UTILITIES
   HJ-Install 2.9 7
   HTML Imager Version 1.2a 7

VAN GOGH, VINCENT
   Do You Know Van Gogh? 15

VIDEO GAMES
   Video Games and Children 91

VIDEOTAPES
   Single-Use Foodservice Packaging--Facts and Fun Teacher's Kit 75

VIETNAM
   Vietnam: A Children's Guide 31

VIOLENCE AND VIOLENCE PREVENTION
   Gangs in the Schools 83
   Out on a Limb--A Guide to Getting Along 38
   Resolving Conflicts and Making Peace: Basic Skills for Young Children 38
   School Violence Prevention 88
   Talking to Your Child About Bias and Prejudice 39

VIRGINIA
   Appomattox Court House Teacher's Packet 26
   Virginia State Transportation Map 31

VISION
   Make a Splash with Color 2
   Students with Visual Impairments 79

SUBJECT INDEX

VOCATIONAL GUIDANCE
  Career Development for All Students 36
  Career Guide for the Atmospheric Sciences, A 36
  Careers and Industries Overview 36
  Careers in Accounting 36
  Careers in Aging 36
  Careers in Psychology 36
  Careers in the Genetics Field 36
  Career WebQuest 36
  Challenges of Our Changing Atmosphere: Careers in Atmospheric Research and Applied Meteorology 36
  Communication Strategies for Employment Interviews 37
  Entertainment Careers 37
  50 Careers in Trees 37
  Job Genie 37
  LifeWorks 38
  Marinecareers 38
  Matching Yourself with the World of Work 38
  Military Careers 38
  Occupational Outlook Handbook 38
  Quick Facts 38
  Thinking of a Careers i Applied Mathematics 39
  Women in Oceanography 39

VOLCANOES
  Volcanoes of the United States 76

VOTING
  Voting Simulation 35

WARS
  American Civil War Webquest, The 44
  American Revolution at a Glance 44

WASHINGTON, BOOKER T.
  Teacher's Guide for Up From Slavery 56

WATER
  Educational Poster on Water Pollution 69
  Temperature and Water Density 76

WATER CONSERVATION
  Water Conservation Lesson Plan 76

WATER POLLUTION
  Educational Poster on Water Pollution 69

WATERSHEDS
  Studying Watersheds: A Confluence of Important Ideas 75

WATERWAYS
  Living Gulf, The: A Place to Treasure 29

WEATHER
  Dan's Wild, Wild Weather Page 68
  Hurricane Hunters, The 71
  Hurricanes and Tropical Storms 71
  Under the Weather 76
  United States Climate Page 31

WEATHER (continued)
  Weather Glossary 11

WEBQUESTS
  Across the USA 26
  Actions and Reactions 44
  American Civil War Webquest, The 44
  Bluebird Quest, A 67
  Buen Viaje a Espana! 27
  Career WebQuest 36
  Christmas Traditions 49
  Civil War Through a Child's Eye, The 45
  Comets 68
  Crool Zone? 64
  DNA for Dinner? 68
  Egyptian Mummies 45
  Famous Canadians 16
  Fire Safety WebQuest 64
  Hello Dolly: A WebQuest 70
  Homes Around the World 29
  How Fast Are You Going? 70
  Investigating Plants 71
  Light in the Forest, The 54
  Me? Live in a Rainforest? 72
  Mexican WebQuest 30
  Mousetrap Racer!!! 72
  My Day As an Insect 72
  Number the Stars: A WebQuest About the Holocaust 47
  Pizza Family Reunion, A 62
  Planets or Not, Here We Come! 73
  Plant Parts 73
  Questioning Techniques 24
  Quiero Viajar a Espana! 31
  Roll of Thunder: Hear My Cry Web Quest 39
  Shipwreck Island Adventure! 47
  Simply Sharks! 75
  Sworn to Serve 47
  Time Traveller 48
  Trial of Standing Bear, The 48
  Very Bad Horrible No Good Day, The 57
  What If? 39

WEB SITE DESIGN
  Developing a School District Web Presence 82

WEIGHTS AND MEASURES
  Metrics Matter 61

WHALES
  Whale Songs 76
  Whales on the Net 76

WILDER, LAURA INGALLS
  Laura Ingalls Wilder 17

WILDLIFE
  Animal Diversity Web 66
  Birds at the National Zoo 67

SUBJECT INDEX

WILDLIFE (continued)
  Bluebird Quest, A 67
  Endangered/Threatened Species 69
  Florida Panther Net 70
  Snakes of Massachusetts 75
  WildFinder 77

WOMEN
  Contemporary Art Experience, The 15
  EducatingJane.com 23
  Elizabeth Cady Stanton & Susan B. Anthony
      Papers Project Online, The 16
  Equal Mathematics Education for Female Students 59
  4000 Years of Women in Science 16
  Health Fact Sheets 41
  Health Fact Sheets 42
  National Women's Hall of Fame 17
  WASP on the Web 48

WORLD WAR I
  World War I: Trenches on the Web 48

WORLD WAR II
  History Textbook Controversies in Japan 46
  WASP on the Web 48

WORLD WIDE WEB
  Banner Generator, The 6
  Becoming Webwise 6
  Building a School Web Site 6
  CGI Made Really Easy 6
  CGI Resource Index, The 6
  Deutsch Plus 19
  Free Animated GIFs 7
  GetNetWise 7
  Glossary of Internet & Web Terms 10
  How Do They Do That with HTML? 7
  How the Internet Came to Be 7
  HTML Goodies 7
  HTML Imager Version 1.2a 7
  Internet Acronym Server 10

WORLD WIDE WEB (continued)
  Internet and Early Childhood Educators, The: Some
      Frequently Asked Questions 85
  Kids Farm 13
  KidsPsych 13
  Learn to Read Urdu 21
  Lissa Explains It All 8
  Making the Connection: How to Go Online 8
  Menuz 8
  Philip and Alex's Guide to Web Publishing 8
  Primer on Digital Literacy, A 8
  Prime Time Math 62
  Role of Online Communications in Schools,
      The: A National Study 87
  RunStat 3 42
  Ten C's for Evaluating Internet Sources 90
  Thirteen Ed Online 90
  Tutorial on Using Perl and CGI to Enhance a
      Homepage, A 9
  Web Pages for Absolute Beginners 9

WRITING
  Become a Logophile 51
  Busy as a Bee 51
  Effective Use of Student Journal Writing 52
  Funbrain.com 12
  Giggle Poetry 53
  Gunfighters of the Old West 46
  Horrid Homonyms 53
  OWL Handouts 55
  Photo Essay, A 55
  Poetry for Kids 55
  Punctuation: Less Is More? 55
  Reading and Writing in a Kindergarten Classroom 56
  Successful Paragraphs 56
  Teaching Creative Writing in the Elementary School 56
  Teaching Writing with Peer Response Groups
      Encouraging Revision 56
  Writing Instruction: Changing Views Over the Years 57

YOUTH PROGRAMS
  Urban Youth in Community Service: Becoming Part
      of the Solution 91

SOURCE INDEX

The SOURCE INDEX is an alphabetical list of the organizations from which the materials listed in the EDUCATORS GUIDE TO FREE INTERNET RESOURCES–ELEMENTARY/MIDDLE SCHOOL EDITION may be obtained. There are 806 sources listed in this Seventeenth Edition of the GUIDE, **769 of which are new**. The numbers following each listing are the page numbers on which the materials from each source are annotated in the body of the GUIDE.

Remember, computers are very literate machines. When typing the address (URL) of a web site, you must type it precisely. If you get an error message that the web site cannot be found, double check your typing.

Bold type indicates a source that is new in the 2016-2017 edition. Complete addresses for each source are found following the description in the body of the GUIDE.

A&E Television Networks 15

Aaron Rubin 22

Abilock Productions 24

Able Minds, Inc. 5

Abraham Lincoln Online 15

Abraham P. Hillman and Gerald L. Alexanderson 58

Academic Hallmarks 23

Academy of Achievement 16

A. Campitelli 20

Act360 Media Ltd. 8, 24, 57, 60, 75

Ada and Russ Gibbons 28

Adobe Systems 2

Adolescent and School Health 40

AfriCam 26

Alan Cooper 10

Alaska Department of Education 44

141

SOURCE INDEX

Alaska Department of Fish & Game 66

Alec M. Bodzin 68

Alfy.com 12

Alienlanguage.co.uk 19

Alison & Charlie 8

Alison Batt 27

AllWords.com 10

Aloha from Hawaii 49

Alphabet Soup 12

Amaki Ayikpa 57

American Academy of Physician Assistants 38

American Art Clay Co., Inc. 2

American Association of Physics Teachers 73

American Cetacean Society 68

American Coal Foundation 68

American Electric Power 69

American Foundation for the Blind 16

American Institute of Physics 68

American Meteorological Society 36

American Museum of Natural History 71

American Petroleum Institute 68

American Psychological Association 36

American Society for the Prevention of Cruelty to Animals 66

SOURCE INDEX

America's Career InfoNet   36

Amethyst Galleries, Inc.   72

Amon Carter Museum   45

Amye J. Cooley   39

Amy McMillan   30

Andrea K. Balas   54

Andrea W. Herrmann   57

Angie Bird   29

Animal Info   66

Anita M. Scanga   30

Anna Chan Rekate   18

Anne Lewis   91

Annenberg/CPB Math and Science Project, The   71

Annenberg Public Policy Center   33

Appomattox Court House National Historical Park   27

Archer   47

Arro & Wartoft AB   55

Asale Harris   58, 62

Associated Board of the Royal Schools of Music   4

Association for Gerontology in Higher Education, The   36

Astronomical Society of the Pacific   76

Australian Academy of Science   73

Autism National Committee   78

SOURCE INDEX

Baltimore Curriculum Project 23

Bancroft Library, The 46

Barbara Kent Lawrence 80

Barbara Pratt 12

Barbara S. Thomson and John R. Mascazine 80

Bassam Z. Shakhashiri 74

BBC Learning 6, 19

Bell Live! 67

Bernard Cesarone 91

Berwick Academy First Grade Students 17

Beth Nalker and Doug Casey 76

Beverly A. Qualheim 49

Bill Arnett 72

Bill Byles 72

Bill Metzker 87

B. J. Johnson 46

Blind Net, A 78

Bobbi Fisher 56

Bob Riddle 74

Bo Campbell 65

Bonnie Benard 90

Brad A. Myers 6

Brad Goorian 88

SOURCE INDEX

Brian Carusella 67

Bridge 69

British Columbia Ministry of Education 78, 79

British Museum, The 44

Bruce Robbins 52

Bry-Back Manor 14

Bunnie Brewer 49

Bureau of Labor Statistics 38

Caleb Rosado 38

California Energy Commission 41, 70

California Mall 50

California School Library Association 6

Candy Adams, Devon Fisher, and Amara Julian 47

Can Manufacturers Institute 66

Cara Bafile 33, 62

Careers-in-accounting.com 36

Caribbean Conservation Corporation 74

Carin Dewey 26

Carl B. Smith 53, 57

Carl B. Smith and Roger Sensenbaugh 53

Carl Rungius 1

Carl Tashian 7

Carmen E. Trisler 70

SOURCE INDEX

Carol Ascher 80, 81, 87, 88, 89, 91

Carol Goodrow 42

Carol Landis 75

Carol Moore 51

Carol Otis Hurst and Rebecca Otis 51

Carol Reitan 20

Carolyn Creger 55

Carolyn K. 23

Carolyn Kinder 36

Carolyn Pope Edwards and Kay Wright Springate 83

Carolyn Starmer 68

Carrie Flores 62

Caryl M. Stern-LaRosa 39

Carylon Weldon 62

Catharine A. Fisher 37

Catherine E. Snow, M. Susan Burns, and Peg Griffin 85

Catherine Fournier 3

C. Cybele Raver 92

Center for Applied Special Technology 87

Center for Auto Safety, The 64

Center for Research on Education, Diversity & Excellence 82

Center of Excellence for Science and Mathematics Education, The 73

Centers for Disease Control and Prevention 40

SOURCE INDEX

Central Hudson Gas & Electric Corporation 64

Central Intelligence Agency 32

Centro Studi Italiani 20

Chabad.org 50

Chandra Thomas Jones 49

Charlie Frankenbach 56

Charlotte Mecklenburg Library 14

Chas Spencer 62

Chatback Trust, The 78

Cheryl McCauley 46

Cheryl Nelson 1

Children's Partnership, The 7

Chris Hardakar 61

Chris Koletzky 44

Christine Elmore 89

Christine M. Brady 28

Christopher Colson 37

Christopher Essex 56

Christopher LaMorte and John Lilly 6

Christopher Mawata 60

Christopher Sawtell 6

Chubbie Cubbie's Preschool & Curriculum 12

Clive Belfield 87

SOURCE INDEX

CMPnet 11

Cobblestone Publishing Company 68

Colgate-Palmolive Company 42

Colin Kenney 47

Colleen Boyea 73

Colonial Williamsburg Foundation 45

Coloquio.com 16

Computer Knowledge 7

Computer Research and Applications Group 62

Consuela Llamas 72

Cornell University, Cooperative Extension 75

Counseling Center 24, 37

Craft & Hobby Association 1

Crews Middle School 6

Cynthia Lanius 30

Cynthia Warger and Jane Burnette 78

Dan Carrigan 42

Dan Satterfield 68

Dave Marshall 8

David A. Rojo 33

David L. Haury 75

David L. Haury and Linda A. Milbourne 59, 81

Dean Walker 88

SOURCE INDEX

Debbie Holm 24

Debbie Reese 90

Deb Gehrman 34

Deborah A. Werner 74

Deborah Bouley 89

Deb Wuest 80

Denis McCarthy 42

Dennis Schatz 72

Detroit Free Press 32

Diana Altenhoff 30

Diana Eades 19

Diana J. Quatroche 53

Diane E. McClellan and Lilian G. Katz 80

Dianne Rothenberg 83, 85

Dick Ainsworth 6

Dick Blick Art Materials 2

Dictionary.com 10

Digital by Design, Ltd. 14

Dr. James Banks 82

Dolores J. Hoyt 20

Dolores Carnahan 47

Donald G. Hackmann 89

Donna Lombardi 4

SOURCE INDEX

Dorota   70

Dorothy Morris   1

Doug Beeferman   11

Douglas Perry and Wendy Sauer   46

Ducks Unlimited   76

DuPage Children's Museum   58

Dyann Schmidel and Wanda Wojcik   24

DynoTech Software   2

Early Childhood Education Network   14

Earobics   12

Earth Force   69

ED Pubs   6

EDSITEment   3, 31, 33, 37, 48, 53

EducatingJane.com   23

Edyth J. Wheeler   86

Eileen T. Borgia and Dorothy Schuler   80

Eileen Urbanski   36

Elaine Seavey   48

Eleanor C. Macfarlane   51

Electron Farm Publications   46

Elinor H. Crecelius   58

Elizabeth Hertling   85, 87

Elizabeth Lawrence   56

SOURCE INDEX

Elizabeth Rexford   4

Elizabeth Roettger   76

Ellen M. Ilfeld   38

Elyse Fischer and Javaid Khan   31, 34

Empandiika y'Oluganda   21

Enchanted Learning Software   12

EntertainmentCareers.Net   37

Environment Canada   71

ePALS   28

ERIC Clearinghouse on Urban Education   84, 86, 90

Eric G. V. Fookes   7

Eric Lease Morgan   51

Ernestine Hightower   47

Eureka!Science   71

EuropeanServers SARL   15

Eva L. Abbamonte and Della Barr Brooks   45

Evelyn Birge Vitz, Nancy Freeman Regalado, and Marilyn Lawrence   3

Evelyn Holt Otten   91

Everything Preschool.com   12

Exploration in Education   69

FableVision Inc.   53

Farm Safety 4 Just Kids   64

FearOfPhysics.com   69

SOURCE INDEX

Federal Citizen Information Center   8, 9, 29, 33, 34, 38, 40, 41, 42, 43, 44, 64, 65, 68, 69, 80, 81

Federation of American Societies for Experimental Biology   36

First-School.ws   12

Florida Center for Instructional Technology   48

Florida Panther Net   70

Flying Turtle Company   70

Fonetiks.org   19

Foodservice Packaging Institute, Inc.   75

Forest Foundation, The   75

4Directions Project   83

4Kids2Play   12

Frances Rawnsley   1

Francisco L. Rivera-Batiz   83

Franco Cavazzi   46

Fred Genesee   19

Fred Lasswell, Inc.   1

Free-Ed, Ltd.   23

Funbrain.com   12

GardenWeb   10

Gary Burnett   81, 86

Gary Burnett and Garry Walz   84

Gary E. Meredith   28

SOURCE INDEX

Gary Fortune 37

Gary G. Huang 91

Gary Hopkins 41, 43

Gary Pierson 47

Gary R. Cobine 52

G. Donald Bain 84

General Libraries at the University of Texas at Austin and the Texas State Historical Association 29

Genetic Science Learning Center 70

Geneva Gay 90

Gerald Robillard and Bob Colvil 16

Gerald Robillard and Dee Charbonneau 71

Girlstart 23

GMB Services 74

GOALS, Inc. 28

GotFacts.com 23

Grethe Cobb 38

Hany N. Takla 19

Harmonica Lessons.com 2

Harrison Forman 26

Haythum R. Khalid 53

Heidi Qua 42

Helena Curtain 21

SOURCE INDEX

Helen Blank 91

Helen Smith and Will Dechent 22

Henk Hagedoorn 7, 82

HighBeam Research, Inc. 10

H-Net, Humanities & Social Sciences OnLine 29

Hollyce C. Giles 86

Hoover Dam 29

Hope Wenzel 74, 76

Houghton Mifflin Company 50

Howard Hughes Medical Institute 67, 68

Howard H. Wade 82

HowStuffWorks, Inc. 71

H. Stephen Straight 21

Hunger Site, The 84

HymnSite 2

Ida Hickerson 46

Idea Box 13

Illinois Department of Public Health 41

Ilona Lelli 27

I Love That Teaching Idea 84

Inner Learning On-line 71

Institute of Human Origins, The 67

interKnowledge 28

SOURCE INDEX

Internet Education Foundation   7

INTIME   85

IvyJoy.com   13

Jackie Johnson   17

Jack Mearl   2

Jacques Leon   19

Jacques Lipetz   46

James Barrett   13

James Beane   85

James Marshall   6

James Weldon Johnson   2

Jane Jurinak-Harris   20

Janet Weaver   74

Jane Whaling   75

Jan Smith   8

Jay DeKalb   89

J. Basden   58

Jean E. Sutherland   28, 57

Jeanette Vratil   73

Jean M. Beaird   52

Jeanne Marie   6

Jeanne Weiler   89

Jefferson Office of Science Education   71

155

SOURCE INDEX

Jeff Lowe 82

Jeff Mondack 54

Jennifer Wronkovich 39

Jenny Rasmussen 1

Jere Brophy 92

Jerry Citron 40

Jerry Goldman and Paul Manna 34

Jerry Lipka 88

Jerry L. Johns and Susan J. Davis 54

Jerry Smith 53

Jessica O'Connell and Stuart C. Smith 81

Jill Britton 60

Jim Conrad 67

Jim McChesney 91

Jimmy Lazenby 3

Joan Franklin Smutny 52

Joan Gaustad 85

Joanne Groff and Bev Crouch 64

Jodi Cochran 9

Joe Burns 7

Joe E. Heimlich and Dawn D. Puglisi 70

Johanna Wilson 86

John Agresto, et al 88

SOURCE INDEX

John Dawkins 55

John D. Hoge 48

John Guyton, Dave Burrage and Rick Kastner 73

John H. Lounsbury 85

John J. O'Connor and Edmund F. Robertson 17

John J. Patrick 35

John Mooney 47

John Rickey 14

John R. Long 51

John Simkin 47

John S. Pitonyak 61

John Vinci 15

John V. Sullivan 33

John Weidner 24

John W. Tippeconnic and Susan C. Faircloth 91

Jonathan Mazurczak 43

Jonathan Mott 35

Jon Cohrs 46

Joseph Sanacore 89

Jose Soto 82

Joy C. Blanton 89

Joyce Dejoie and Elizabeth Truelove 75

Judie Haynes 52

SOURCE INDEX

Judith E. Stroud, James C. Stroud, and Lynn M. Staley   80

Judith Langer   54

Judy Ezell   57

Julia Gordon   70

Julia Meritt   44

Julie Van Osdol   14

Jupiter Hammon   44

Kaboose Network, The   12

Kahon:wes   20

Kamusi Project   20

Karen E. Diamond, Linda L. Hestenes, and Caryn O'Connor   78

Karen Fung   26

Karen Harness   48

Karen Martin   45

Karen Walkowiak   83, 88

Kari Giles   50

Kathleen Beveridge   14

Kathleen C. Rende   83

Kathleen E. van Noort   53, 82

Kathleen Woods Masalski   46

Kathy L. Peck   35

Kathy Richardson   61

Kaye Miller   58

SOURCE INDEX

Keith Nuthall   70

Kelly Garthwaite   72

Kelly J. Glodt   23

Kelly Markham   89

Kenn Nesbitt   55

Ken Rohrer   1

Kerri Byrd   31

Kevin J. Swick, Gloria Boutte, and Irma van Scoy   83

KGM Group, Inc., The   74

Kids Farm   13, 69

KidsKonnect.com   23

KidsPeace   39

KidsPsych   13

KidsReads.com   54

Kimberly Baker-Brownfield and Jacques Marquette Branch   71

Kim-Scott Miller   65

Kim Steele   54

Kim Whittaker   30

Kim Winters   40

KinderArt   5, 13, 49, 50

Kristen Carvell   62

Kristina Davenport   37

KU Medical Center   49

SOURCE INDEX

Lance Leonhardt   76

Lanette Westerland   25

Larry Hoefling   11

Larry Sessions   73

Laurent Lecerf   66

Laurie Hinman   43

Lawrence Goetz   7, 13

Lawrence Hart et al.   40

Lawrence J. Schweinhart   81, 85, 87

Lemeil Norman   42

Leslie Blakeburn   48

Library of Congress   17, 44

Library of Congress, American Memory   45

Lilian G. Katz   88

Linda Bray   55

Linda C. Joseph and Linda D. Resch   77

Linda Good   54

Linda Starr   26

Lisa Hrubey   47

Lisa Marchant   19

Lisa Nash   60

Lisa Price, Walda Brooks, and Ann Abbuhl   72

Lisa R. Bartle   52

SOURCE INDEX

Lissa 8

Liz Cannon 52

Logos Group 11

Lois Cullipher 58

Loreen McDonald 26

Loretta Greenough 59

Lorna Hockett 39

Lorraine Tanaka 51

Lorrie Jackson 7

Lorri Mon 22

Lucien Ellington 29

Luis Fernandes 58

Lula M. White 3

Lynn Balster Liontos 88

MAD Scientist Network, The 69

Major Val Salva 71

Mandy Wallace 28

Manjari Singh and Mei-Yu Lu 53

Maori.org.nz 21

Marcia Rosenbusch 20

Margaret Hadderman 87, 88

Margaret R. Dittemore 66

Marge Simic 52, 55

SOURCE INDEX

Marguerite Wills   70

Marie Ponterio   19

Marilyn J. Brackney   2

Marilyn Western   8

Mariner's Museum, The   15

Mark Gregory   1

Mark Overmars   12

Mark Whitener   59

Mark Woodard   61

Martha Adams   56, 60

Martindale's   58

Martin L. Kutscher, M.D.   78

Mat Brandy   20

Math Forum, The   58

Math League Multimedia   61

Matt's Script Archive, Inc.   6

McIntyre Library, UW-Eau Claire   90

Meadowbrook Press   53

MediaSmarts   8

Megan Simon and Asha Bandal   31

Mei-Yu Lu   52, 54

Melanie McCool   34

Melinda Swain   29

SOURCE INDEX

Melissa Armstrong 45

Melodie Hill 43

Merriam-Webster, Incorporated 11

Mexico Online 50

Miami Museum of Science/Science Learning Network 67

Michael Burgoyne 51

Michael Furstner 2

Michael Karbo 8

Michael Klonsky 89

Michele Delattre 2

Michelle C. Massion 23

Michelle K. Reed 60

Michelle Sale and Bridget Anderson 35

Michigan State University, Communication Technology Laboratory 78

Mick Coleman 86

Micki M. Caskey and Paul Gregorio 45

Mike Iavarone 48

Mike Wales 59

Mila Stoicheva 52

MindTravellers Inc. 31

Minnesota Department of Agriculture 26

Minnesota Department of Transportation 30

Miriam Furst 14, 39

SOURCE INDEX

Mish Denlinger   67

Mississippi Soil and Water Conservation Commission   74

Missy J. Kasbaum   47

MIT   17

MoA   46

MoMi.org   3

Monica R. Greene   51

Morgan Cottle   62

Morton Inger   82, 92

Morton Subotnick   1

Mountain Data Systems   10

Mr. Dowling   30

Mrs. Glosser's Math Goodies, Inc.   61

Mrs. Taverna   16, 31

Ms. L. MacDonald   36

Musicians United for Songs in the Classroom, Inc.   4

Myriam Met   21

Myrna Caron   39

Nancy Bocian, Christi Guptill, and Barbara Grollimund   67

Nancy Parrish   48

NASA Johnson Space Center   15, 74

NASA/MSU-Bozeman CERES Project   67, 68

NASA Quest   66

SOURCE INDEX

NASA Spacelink 66

National Alliance for Hispanic Health 42

National Association of Comics Art Educators 4

National Baseball Hall of Fame and Museum, The 15

National Campaign for Public School Improvement, The 86

National Center for Research on Cultural Diversity and Second Language Learning 20

National Constitution Center 33

National Council of Teachers of Mathematics 61

National Digestive Diseases Information Clearinghouse 43

National Education Association Health Information Network 6

National Film Board 24

National Fire Protection Association 65

National Geographic Society 30

National Institute on Alcohol Abuse and Alcoholism 40

National Institutes of Health, Office of Science Education 38

National Oceanic and Atmospheric Administration 31

National Park Service 48

National Women's Hall of Fame 17

Neil Grieve 11

Neil J. Anderson 21

Nemours Foundation, The 43

New York Department of Health 41

SOURCE INDEX

New York Life   47

New York University Scientific Visualization Laboratory   61

Nick Jurman   40

Nola Kortner Aiex   37, 52, 54, 55, 91

Norma Decker Collins   54

Norma Decker Collins and Nola Kortner Aiex   53

North Carolina Department of Agriculture and Consumer Services   42

Odyssey, The   26

Office of Naval Research   74

Offshore Operators Committee   30

O'Flynn Consulting   3

Olga S. Jarrett   87

Oriental Institute at the University of Chicago   44

Origami-Fun   3

Owen Leonard   21

Owl & Mouse Educational Software   13, 30, 45, 47

Pablo Stafforini   16

Pam Harper   62

Papers of Elizabeth Cady Stanton and Susan B. Anthony Project, The   16

Patrice Flynn   54

Patricia Clark   87

Patricia Kuntz   19

Patricia M. Lines   84

SOURCE INDEX

Patrick Farley 55

Patti Emley 65

Paul Gilster 8

Paul Gorski 81, 83, 84, 91

Paul T. Williams 24, 60

Peace Corps 27, 28, 48, 80, 83, 84, 86

Peanut Software 63

Pearson Education 10

Peg Stout 34

Penguin-Putnam Inc. 56

Peter Flynn 10

Peter Marston Sullivan 1

Peter Weingartner 7

Philip Greenspun 8

Ping-Yun Sun 4

Pinsoft Software 8

Planet Pals 73

Polishworld.com 49

Power of Culture 86

Powersource Art & Education Center 29

Preschool Education/Preschool Coloring Book 14

Prescient Code Solutions 6

Priscilla Chan and Andrea Perelman 76

SOURCE INDEX

Priscilla Mestas   12

Project Bartleby   10

Prongo.com   24

Public Library of Charlotte & Mecklenburg County   51

Purdue University Writing Lab, The   55

Rainbow Raccoons   14

Randi Jones   67

Random Acts of Kindness Foundation   38

Random House, Inc.   54, 56

Randy Bartholomew   23

Ray McCarter   27

Ray Melecio and Thomas J. Hanley   84

R. De Vall   27

Rebecca Caldwell   27

Rebecca Sexson   55

Richard Canalori and Joyce Listro   4

Richard Dibon-Smith   68

Rita Irene Esparza   35

RJ Networks   8

RM   14

R. Mark Herzog   69

Roberta Bernstein   88

Robert Beard   20

SOURCE INDEX

Robert Nemiroff and Jerry Bonnell 66

Robert Valadez 72

Robin Ann Henry 70

Rob Mikuriya 45

Roger Sensenbaugh 55

Roland Williamson 45

Ronald C. Brady 81

Ron Hipschman 71

Ron Renchler 86

Roseann Fox 44

Roxane J. Johnson 72

Roxie Carroll 13

R. Soleste Hilberg and Roland G. Tharp 90

Russell Cates 24

Russell Schuh 20

Russell W. Rumberger 89

Ruth Ann Bingham 28

Ruth A. Wilson 89

Ruth Livingstone 9

Sam Smith 4

Samuel Stoddard 23

Sandy Kemsley 23

Sandy Meadors 2

SOURCE INDEX

Sandy Montgomery   51

San Francisco Symphony   3

Sara Gant   4

Sara J. Archambault   27

Save the Rainforest.org   74

Scholastic--Teaching with Technology   10

School Express   31, 58

Science Fairs   74

Science Museum of Minnesota   76

Scott Diamond & Cats   42

Scott Wallace   34

Scripps Institution of Oceanography   39

Search Hawaii   31

Sharin Manes   66

Shawna Brynildssen   51

Shayni Tokarczyk   90

Shelby Madden, et al   75

Sheppard Software   31, 58, 61, 62

Sherman Wilcox   19

Shirley Kapitzke   39

Shirley Lomax   32

Sierra Prasada Millman and Andrea Perelman   49

Silos & Smokestacks National Heritage Area   67

SOURCE INDEX

Smithsonian Institution   69

Smithsonian National Museum of American History   46

Smithsonian National Museum of Natural History   72

Smithsonian National Zoological Park   67

S9.com   10

Social Studies School Service   26

Society for Industrial and Applied Mathematics   39

Sodaplay   75

Soil Science Society of America   11

Sonja de Groot Kim   87

SOON Ministries   49

Southwest Educational Development Laboratory   70

Space Telescope Science Institute   66

Spencer Kagan   22

S. Ruth Harris   3

State of Queensland, The   37

Stephanie Ashley   29

Stephanie Bennett   61

Stephanie Sirvent   73

Stephen Fournier   37

Steve McCarty   82

Steve McFarland   76

Steve Silcox   16

SOURCE INDEX

Stuart Robbins and David McDonald 71

StudentNewsNet 24

Studio Melizo 49, 50

Study Technologies 11

Sue Bouchard and Claire Gerin Buell 64

Sue Worthen 24

Susan Boone 59

Susan Cowles 73

Susan E. Hume 31

Susan Faircloth and John W. Tippeconnic 85

Susan Kontos and Amanda Wilcox-Herzog 90

Susan L. Golbeck 85

Susan Schoket 36

Susan Seraphine-Kimel 19

Susie A. Scott 34

Syque 24

Syts and Ade Van der Mal 27

Tad Perry 21

Tana Carney Preciado 33

Tara Berge 28

Tara Prindle 3

TeachersFirst 1

TeAch-nology.com 82

SOURCE INDEX

Tech4Learning 3

Tennessee Department of Health 42

Tennessee Wildlife Resources Agency 69

ThinkQuest 1, 3, 4, 9, 10, 13, 15, 16, 17, 18, 34, 49, 59, 61, 62, 64, 65, 78, 79, 80, 84, 90, 91

Thirteen Ed Online 90

Thomas J. Gibbs and Aimee Howley 92

Thomas McIntyre 83

Thomas S. Vontz and William A. Nixon 33

Three Dads Courseware 29

Tim Olson 59

Timothy Collins 81

Tim Reichard 4

Today's Military 38

Tod Schneider 87

Tom Daccord 48

Tom March 64

Tour Egypt 30

Tracey Roudez 29

TRAMsoft GmbH 4

Trecia Olson 27

Tree Foundation of Kern 37

Tricia McGregor 27

SOURCE INDEX

Tubehead.com   75

tuSPAIN   50

UK India   21

U. S. Department of Health & Human Services   42

U. S. Department of Housing and Urban Development   34

U. S. Department of Justice   34, 20

U. S. Department of State   27

United States Fire Administration   64

U. S. Government Printing Office   33

U. S. National Library of Medicine   76

USS Constitution Museum   44

University of Alabama   16

University of Arizona   59, 60

University of Calgary   45

University of Illinois Extension Disaster Resources   81

University of Illinois Extension Urban Programs Resource Network   38, 42, 70

University of Kentucky Entomology   72

University of Manitoba Counseling Service   37

University of Massachusetts Extension   75

University of Michigan Poison Prevention Project   14

University of Michigan Museum of Zoology   66

University of Pennsylvania, African Studies Center   26

SOURCE INDEX

University of Toronto Mathematics Network 60

University of Wisconsin--Madison 91

UpToTen 25

USGS Information Services 28, 31, 76

Utah State Office of Education 15

Val-Jean Belton 2

Verbix 22

Veronica Paget 62

Vicki Pierson and Renee Cloe 41

Vinton Cerf 7

Virginia Department of Transportation 31

Walter Sanford 67

Waterford Press Ltd. 76

Wayne Fulton 7

Weather Channel, The 11

Webseed.com 45

Weekend Gardener, The 73

Wendi Petti 60

Wendy Schwartz 53, 59, 83

WetFeet, Inc. 36

WGBH Educational Foundation 75

Whales on the Net 77

WHOI Sea Grant Program 38

SOURCE INDEX

William B. Davis and David J. Schmidly   72

William Chavez   70

William E. Peace   68

William Kreidler   84

Willie Jefferson   33

Wisconsin Historical Society and National History Day   44

Wisconsin Public Service   64, 65

Woodlands Junior School   29

World Wildlife Fund   77

Yi-Ching Chen   26

Yolanda G. Martinez and Jose A. Velazquez   85

York University   77

Zhang Hong and Nola Kortner Aiex   55